THE 10 DUMBEST MISTAKES SMART PEOPLE MAKE AND HOW TO AVOID THEM

By Dr. Arthur Freeman and Rose DeWolf

Woulda, Coulda, Shoulda

Other Books by Dr. Arthur Freeman

The Practice of Cognitive Therapy

Cognitive Therapy of Personality Disorders
(with A. T. Beck)

Clinical Applications of Cognitive Therapy
(with J. Pretzer, B. Fleming,
and K. M. Simon)

Cognitive Therapy with the Suicidal Patient
(with M. Reinecke)

Other Books by Rose DeWolf

The Bonds of Acrimony

The Best Defense (with J. Moldovsky)

How to Raise Your Man

THE 10 DUMBEST
MISTAKES
SMART PEOPLE MAKE
AND HOW TO AVOID THEM

Simple and Sure Techniques for
Gaining Greater Control of Your Life

DR. ARTHUR FREEMAN
ROSE DeWOLF

HarperCollins*Publishers*

HarperCollins books may be purchased for educational, business, or sales
promotional use. For information, please call or write: Special Markets Department,
HarperCollins Publishers, Inc., 10 East 53rd Street, New York, NY 10022.
Telephone: (212) 207-7528; Fax: (212) 207-7222.

FIRST EDITION

Designed by Joan Greenfield

Library of Congress Cataloging-in-Publication Data

Freeman, Arthur M.
The 10 dumbest mistakes smart people make and how to avoid them :
simple and sure techniques for gaining greater control of your life /
Arthur Freeman, Rose DeWolf.—1st ed.
p.   cm.
Includes index.
ISBN 0-06-016685-1
1. Decision-making.   2. Errors—Psychological aspects.
3. Cognitive therapy—Popular works.   4. Conduct of life.
I. DeWolf, Rose.   II. Title.
BF448.F74   1992   91-50440
158'.1—dc20

92 93 94 95 96 CC/HC 10 9 8 7 6 5 4 3 2 1

For B.I. and K.M.S.

CONTENTS

PREFACE

More than 30 years ago, one of my patients provided the clue that led me to develop the therapeutic approach that has come to be called cognitive therapy. This is the approach you will learn about as you read *The 10 Dumbest Mistakes Smart People Make.*

At the time, I was conducting research into Freudian theories and practicing traditional psychoanalytic psychiatry—listening to patients recount their memories and doing free associations in hopes of plumbing their unconscious. My patient felt frustrated at the slowness of the process and told me so. He was angry at me. He said that just thinking about me made him feel upset and guilty. And he went on to recount his upsetting thoughts in detail. The crucial thoughts—which he had not previously revealed to me—were to the effect that he was a very bad person for feeling angry at me.

He gave me much to think about. I began to ask other patients about the thoughts that ran through their minds as feelings of unhappiness or anger descended on them. I found that the thoughts they repeated fell into very specific, definable patterns. These patterns describe ways in which people—no matter how bright and accomplished—misread situations they face, misinterpret the actions of others, and exaggerate the importance of specific events.

It took many years of research to make these observations and to determine the most effective therapy. But the data I developed led inescapably to the conclusion that how we think determines to a large extent whether we will succeed and enjoy life or even survive—and that it is possible to use a higher level of thinking to correct troublesome thinking patterns.

Through research, I was able to find techniques that not only have had significant success in relieving emotional pain, in improving effectiveness, and in avoiding a host of self-defeating behavior, but also bring about these results relatively quickly and easily.

Decades of further research, that of others as well as my own, have led to the use of cognitive therapy in a wide range of emotional problems. I naturally take great satisfaction in seeing what has been called "the cognitive revolution" take hold not only in the United States but in other countries around the world.

And, I take satisfaction too from the efforts of others to further this revolution. One such effort is this book, which explains the way common distortions in thinking affect you, and what you can do to avoid or correct them.

Dr. Arthur Freeman, in the past one of my students and later a colleague at the Center for Cognitive Therapy at the University of Pennsylvania, has become one of the major teachers of cognitive therapy in the world today. Rose DeWolf is a writer skilled in presenting the complexities of cognitive therapy in an easy-to-read and easy-to-use manner. The helpfulness of this team of authors will already be apparent to anyone who has read their earlier collaboration, *Woulda, Coulda, Shoulda: Overcoming Regrets, Mistakes, and Missed Opportunities.*

If you would like to rid your life of the negative thinking patterns that bring mountains of misery to millions of people, this book will show you the way.

Aaron T. Beck, M.D.
Director of the Center for Cognitive Therapy and
University Professor of Psychiatry,
University of Pennsylvania

INTRODUCTION

HOW DO WE KNOW
WHICH ARE THE
TEN DUMBEST MISTAKES?

Everybody makes mistakes. It goes with the human condition. We catalog them as minor (you realize that—oops—you've put your sweater on backward) or major (you realize—sigh—that the person in whom you have invested your love or your trust is not worthy of it). We describe them as dumb if, afterward, we think *we should have known better at the time*. And, alas, that is all too often the case.

You might wonder how it is possible, given the hundreds— even thousands—of dumb mistakes we humans are prone to, to select the ten dumbest of all.

The answer lies in selecting a particular category of mistake. These are the ten dumbest because they are the mistakes that *lead us to make countless other mistakes*. They are the mistakes that inflict all manner of needless emotional suffering. These are mistakes that deal not with the specific decisions we make but with *the way we make our decisions*. In short: They are mistakes we make in *the way we think about the circumstances of our lives*.

We are not talking here of any such Pollyanna prescriptions as: "Just think positive thoughts and all your problems will go away." Or: "Cheer up. It's not so bad" (whatever "it" is). We are talking of very *specific* mistakes in thinking that create problems for us, worsen our existing problems, or make it more difficult to find problem solutions. These are mistakes in think-ing that cause us to *misinterpret* experience, *misjudge others*, and *misjudge ourselves*.

These misinterpretations and misjudgments have a way of stirring up painful emotions—and those emotions then lead us to take actions we later regret or, what may be worse, stop us from taking actions that have life-enhancing potential. People often say: "I was feeling so miserable (or anxious or guilty or angry or stressed) that I couldn't think straight." But, in fact, as this book will make very clear, it is precisely when you are *not* thinking straight that you *develop and deepen* feelings of anxiety, misery, guilt, anger, and stress. By learning how to avoid the ten dumb thinking mistakes described in this book, you will find you can lessen anxiety, alleviate misery, and diminish stress.

The Gateway to Your Emotions

Cognitive therapists differ with other schools of therapy in the emphasis placed on the role that "thinking straight" plays in relieving emotional suffering. Within the therapeutic commu-nity there is a variety of conflicting opinions on the best way to get at the root causes of—and alleviate—such pain. The debate centers on what matters *most*: feelings, actions or thoughts.

Some therapists believe that we are totally governed by our feelings. That is, they claim that feelings determine both thoughts and actions. Those therapists believe that if you simply "get in touch with your feelings," "stop repressing your emo-tions," and "let it all hang out"—you will be better able to cope with the problems life invariably hands out. These therapists contend that if you dig deep inside yourself, you will find a well of buried emotion—filled to the brim by the actions of your parents, your mate, your life circumstances. They believe that if you dig down and clean out this buried emotion, much as a dentist digs out tooth decay, you can achieve a feeling of well-being.

Other therapists believe you must not only dig out that buried well of emotion but also learn to act in more positive ways. Put another way, that insight about your inner emotions must be accompanied by changes in your behavior.

Still others hold that behavior alone holds the key to changing your life for the better. They contend that if you make deliberate efforts to act in a more positive way, you will achieve more in life, even though your inner turmoil may continue.

Cognitive therapy—the therapeutic view propounded in this book—holds that each of these theories contains a piece of the answer. But each also leaves many questions unanswered.

Undoubtedly, the way you feel is important. Emotions are central to our very being. Yet experience has shown that it is possible to get in touch with your feelings, to understand exactly *why* you feel as you do—and *still hurt*. You can understand *why* you feel as you do and still *behave* in a self-destructive way. Certainly, catharsis—the releasing of emotion—can make you feel better. After you cry, you feel a sense of relief. If you put down a heavy burden, you are immediately more comfortable. However, if the problem that made you cry remains, you will soon cry again. And if you resume carrying that burden, you will again feel its weight.

That would seem to reinforce the view that *doing something* to solve your problems is, indeed, a vital component in improving your life. Yet experience has also shown that it is possible to learn how to behave in more productive ways—and *still feel miserable*.

What would be most helpful, then, is to find a life formula that leads both to taming inner turmoil and to acting in more positive, productive ways. That is where cognitive therapy comes in. What sets cognitive therapy apart is that it *combines* all the pieces in a different way—a way that people find brings them relief *faster, more easily,* and *in a more long-lasting manner*.

Cognitive therapy does not require you to dig out your emotional past as a prelude to taking action to improve your present and future. No matter what others have done to you in the past, you don't have to punish or forgive them to *allow yourself to move on*. No matter what your past circumstances—despite very real cause for anguish or uncertainty—you will discover that you have the ability *within yourself now* to improve your own life if you are willing to take responsibility for yourself.

Taking responsibility for yourself means taking charge of your own emotions. It's always tempting to blame others—or unfortunate circumstances—for feelings of anger or guilt or depression or anxiety or shame or insecurity. You may very well think: "I would not feel this way if it weren't for him (or her or them or what happened)." But look at that word *blame*. It's just a coincidence that the last two letters spell the word *me*. But that coincidence is worth thinking about. Other people or unfortunate circumstances may have caused you to feel pain, but only *you* control whether you *allow that pain to go on*. If you want those feelings to go away, you have to say: "It's up to *me*."

Taking Charge of Your Emotions

"But what can I do?" you ask. You can change the way you *think* about the events of your life.

The word *cognitive* means thinking. The cognitive approach *begins* by using the amazingly powerful reasoning abilities of the human brain. This is important because our emotions and our actions are not separate from our thoughts. They are all interrelated. Thinking is the *gateway* to our emotions—and our emotions are the gateway to our actions.

You will discover, as you read this book, how changing the way you think can enable you to take charge of your emotions instead of allowing your emotions to rule you. You will discover that those emotions that bother you are *not* stored somewhere deep inside you, always churning away. Emotions are, in fact, manufactured on the spot as we feel a need for them. We do it in the way we *think*.

If you find that hard to believe, consider these examples:

The Inconsiderate Driver

A snowstorm has dumped six inches of snow on the ground. You have to get a prescription filled at the pharmacy, so you drive there and discover that a single car is blocking the only two completely shoveled-out spots in the parking lot. That means you have to park in the snow and hope you don't get stuck. It means you have to wade through a drift to get to the door. What emotion do you think you would feel? Dismay? Probably some. Anger? Probably a lot.

Your thoughts might run something like: "I'm furious. I can't believe anybody would hog both spaces. It's so inconsiderate. What a nerve. I hope the jerk gets a flat tire on the way home."

As you enter the pharmacy, a man runs past you to the offending car, too fast for you to say anything to him. You are about to make a comment to the pharmacist when she says: "Poor guy. His baby is dying. His doctor gave him a prescription to get filled, but there's really nothing that will help."

What happens to all that anger? Even if you still feel a little annoyed, do you continue to hope the man gets a flat tire on the way home? More likely you now think about him differently. You feel sorrow or pity rather than anger. The next time you stop at the pharmacy, you'll probably ask about the baby.

The Lost Friend

You need some help, so you telephone a friend. She is not home, so you leave a message on her answering machine. "I have a big problem," you say. "This is important and I need your help desperately. Please call me the minute you get in."

But your friend doesn't call—not that night, or the next, or the next. You think she is ignoring you; a call to you is obviously not a priority. How do you feel? Disappointed? Hurt? You might think: "I have always been there for her. All I asked for was a telephone call. A real friend would have phoned."

A week later, your friend calls. She has been out of town. A family emergency. Didn't have a chance to call you before leaving. Just got your message. Called immediately. Wants to help. Hopes it's not too late. Feels just terrible to have missed your call.

How do you feel now?

The Abusive Parents

Your childhood was rough—there is no denying it. Your mother was an alcoholic; your father was rigid and unfeeling. You grew up envying the love and material comforts other children seemed to have and you lacked. You believe your parents have blighted your life in many ways. It's hardly surprising that every time you think of them, you feel angry and miserable. You think: "Everything in my life is harder because of them. I'm a mess because of them. I feel as if there is a big empty hole inside me."

These thoughts are running through your mind when, suddenly, the door opens and in walk Michael Jackson and Madonna. As part of a TV special, they have picked one person at random—you—to entertain. They are dressed—well—like only Michael Jackson and Madonna dress. They have brought along an orchestra. They have brought along a dozen other celebrities they want to introduce to you. They are determined to make sure you have a good time.

How do you feel? Surprised? Amazed? Disbelieving? Stunned? The more pertinent question, were such an outlandish scenario possible, is whether you would still be thinking about how *angry* and *overwhelmed* you are. Can you imagine yourself meeting Michael Jackson and Madonna for the first time and saying something like: "Let me tell you about my rotten parents"? More likely, you would—at least temporarily—forget your anger, forget your misery. You are too busy thinking: "Wow! Michael and Madonna together!" Or: "Why couldn't Sinatra have shown up instead?" Or: "I don't have room in here for an orchestra." Or: "I must be dreaming and this is a very strange dream."

The Determinant of Your Actions

The situations may vary, but the point is the same: Different thoughts produce different emotions. It doesn't make any difference whether what you face is something that affects your work, your personal relationships, your sense of security, your appraisal of self-worth, or your appearance—the way you *think* about your situation determines how you feel about it, and how you feel about it largely determines whether you will do any-thing about it and what you will do. It doesn't matter whether the event or conversation that triggers your thoughts of anger, shame, bitterness, or sadness happened one minute ago or al-most a lifetime ago—your immediate thoughts will determine what you are feeling, and what you are feeling then shapes your behavior.

If you believe a situation is hopeless, you behave differently than if you think that, maybe, there is one more thing that might work. If you believe someone has deliberately hurt you, you behave differently toward that person than if you think what happened was just an accident.

If you believe other people are totally responsible for your life—and therefore you can do nothing about your own situa-tion—you will not be motivated to make an effort. But if, on the other hand, you think that you can get ahead despite them and everything that has gone before, you will be able to move on to start thinking about *what kind* of effort to make.

Smart People, Too, Are Only Human

To be human is to be fallible.

If each of us possessed, at every step of our lives, all the information and knowledge needed to make absolutely correct judgments 100 percent of the time . . .

If each of us was able to be at all times calm, cool, rational, and totally in command of all the information and knowledge at our disposal . . .

If we never did things we regretted or messed up something we thought would be easy or ended up in a relationship that didn't work out . . .

If no one ever felt overcommitted, overworked, and over-whelmed . . .

If we never, ever felt like a bundle of nerves or a pile of manure . . .

If no one ever ended up saying: "How did this happen?" Or: "Why did I do that? What could I have been thinking of?"

If no one ever made dumb thinking mistakes . . .

Then . . .

Well, then there would be no need for this book.

But unless you are very different from all others, you will probably find that you sometimes think in ways that hurt you. Perhaps you thought something was true and later found it was not. Perhaps you made a decision or choice when you were feeling rushed, angry, or upset, and later had to admit you were wrong. No matter how smart you are—even if others acknowledge you as a genius—you have probably committed more than one of the dumb thinking mistakes described in this book. Indeed, you have probably committed several of them at the same time because it is the nature of these mistakes to occur in combination.

Admittedly, a list of dumb thinking mistakes cannot be as precise as the identification of blood types under a microscope or the ranking of the ten largest cities in the United States, but the list this book will present has behind it thousands of years of human observation. These ten thought patterns are those that seem to get us into the most trouble. There is nothing complicated about any of them. And yet they cause endless complications, distress, and discomfort for us.

What all the mistakes described in the chapters of this book have in common is:

1. They occur in our thought processes.
2. They cause us great difficulty.
3. They make us feel terrible.
4. They are relatively easy to avoid.
5. They are reactions we *would avoid* if we thought about them *in a clear and reasonable way.*

The Role of Cognitive Therapy

Cognitive therapy is a powerful psychotherapy that was specifically developed to confront and combat these thinking mistakes. Cognitive therapy is based on a number of clinical developments that share the assumption that most of us possess sufficient common sense to deal with life's crises and challenges—but all too often that common sense deserts us when we most need it. Our so-called better judgment is swamped by a tidal wave of emotion—be it love or excitement or anger or unhappiness or fear or whatever. The emotion takes control and the brain takes a sabbatical. We rationalize rather than logically analyze. This happens so often to so many people that expressions like "blinded by love," "intoxicated by happiness," "paralyzed by anxiety," and "scared out of one's wits" are clichés of our language.

To avoid making these common thinking mistakes we need a set of smart thinking tools that enable us to push back on that emotion and return our common sense. Cognitive therapy provides just such tools. The twenty-five techniques that will be described in this book rely heavily on a therapeutic model developed by Dr. Aaron T. Beck, a psychiatrist at the University of Pennsylvania, who is recognized as one of the foremost psychiatric theoreticians in the world today.

Will learning these techniques that improve your decision-making capabilities enable you to avoid *all* mistakes in the future? Alas, no. After all, it is quite possible that even the most carefully considered decision can turn out to be a mistake. Many actions we take seem like a good idea at the time. Given the information you had at the time you made the decision, you'd probably do the same again. You can't claim you weren't thinking clearly.

Sometimes you might do something dumb that you know full well is dumb, but you quite deliberately choose to do it anyway. Most often, this is a case of opting for immediate pleasure rather than for some longer-term goal. Like watching TV rather than getting that income tax information together—even though the deadline for filing your tax return is drawing near. Or playing golf instead of tackling the weeds in the yard—even though you know that putting off weeding only makes the job tougher later.

Not so long ago, a researcher asked a group of people who had been treated for skin cancer if they would now avoid sitting outside in the sun. Many replied: "What? And lose my tan?" Would they use a sun-blocking lotion? they were asked. No, these same people said, because they liked having a tan. It made them feel good. You might argue that they are refusing to face grim reality. And perhaps some are. But it is equally possible that they are simply *choosing between two unpleasant alternatives.* Unfortunately, that is often the choice we get. In this case, the choice was between increasing their medical risk or doing without their beloved tan. Thinking it over, the suntan lovers decided on the alternative they found *least* unpleasant—even if others felt they were making a mistake.

You are hardly unusual if you sometimes coolly, calmly, and *knowingly* decide to do something you know perfectly well you would be better off not doing, like eating a second helping of chocolate cake or continuing a two-pack-a-day smoking habit. You decide you want to enjoy the cake, even though it will add pounds you don't want. You choose to avoid the pangs of giving up cigarettes, even though you know your lungs would appreciate it.

Thus, the information in this book won't prevent you from making so-called honest mistakes—the kind you make because you can't foretell the future or the kind you make because you want to. And it probably also won't prevent you from making "dishonest" mistakes either, if you are so inclined. The chapters that follow do not discuss negative character traits like dishonesty or greed or immorality because, for one thing, not everyone agrees on how those terms should be defined. And for another, it is rarely the case that a career burglar could plead: "I just wasn't thinking clearly, your honor," and be believed.

What these techniques *can do* is combat those misjudgments and missteps you make only because you are not thinking clearly at the time. And that is a very significant contribution. Learning how to use these techniques can mean avoiding or, at the least, doing a better job of dealing with mistakes that have *major impact on your life.*

Mobilizing Your Thinking Power

To reiterate: This book concentrates very specifically on the kinds of mistakes people make when they fail to take full advantage of their thinking capacity. These are the kinds of mistakes that can cloud your vision and distort your decision-making abilities. These are the ways in which smart people simply ignore their own common sense. These are the ways in which smart people quite literally *think* themselves into hassles, disappointments, fear, anxiety, depression, and a lifetime of misery. They are dumb not because scientists have labeled them with that admittedly unscientific term, but because *that is how most people who make such mistakes describe them to themselves.*

These are the kinds of mistakes you make when you can't quite put a finger on exactly what you did wrong—but you know that something that should have gone right has gone awry. This book will enable you to become aware of your own patterns of thinking. It will enable you to diagnose dumb thinking mistakes if and when they occur—and to *do something about them.*

When you change your patterns of thinking, you change the way you feel about yourself, about others, and about the world. And changing the way you feel enables you to deal more productively with your problems and burdens and to take actions necessary to improve your life. Once you learn how to deal with these dumb thinking mistakes, you will find that things that used to go awry now go right.

A Mistake-Maker's Quiz

No matter how smart you are, you have probably made most of the mistakes described in this book at one time or another. But it's also very likely that you will find some mistakes cause you more trouble than others. The following quiz can help you zero in on those chapters that will be of most interest to you.

Rate your reaction to the following fifty statements on a scale of 0 to 4, with 0 representing the least relevance to your life and 4 representing the most relevance to your life. Put an X in one block after each statement. Scoring directions will be found at the end of the quiz.

Think of the numbers in this way:

0 means: There is no time in my life when this statement would apply to me.
1 means: There have been rare instances when I have felt this way.
2 means: I sometimes feel like this.
3 means: I frequently feel like this.
4 means: I feel this statement applies to me most of the time.

	0	1	2	3	4
1. I overreact to minor problems.	☐	☐	☐	☐	☐
2. Others accuse me of making mountains out of molehills.	☐	☐	☐	☐	☐
3. I am pretty excitable.	☐	☐	☐	☐	☐
4. There's no point in trying because I know that nothing will work.	☐	☐	☐	☐	☐
5. I know in advance that things will go wrong.	☐	☐	☐	☐	☐
6. I can tell what others are thinking.	☐	☐	☐	☐	☐
7. People who are close to you should know what you want.	☐	☐	☐	☐	☐
8. You can always tell what people are thinking from their body language.	☐	☐	☐	☐	☐

	0	1	2	3	4
9. When people spend time together, they become attuned to each other's thoughts.	□	□	□	□	□
10. I've been upset about what I thought someone was thinking—then found I was wrong.	□	□	□	□	□
11. It's my responsibility to keep my loved ones happy.	□	□	□	□	□
12. When things go wrong, I always feel it's my fault.	□	□	□	□	□
13. I find I am criticized more than other people.	□	□	□	□	□
14. You can tell when people are attacking you—they don't have to be specific or mention your name.	□	□	□	□	□
15. I feel I've been unfairly blamed for things that are beyond my control.	□	□	□	□	□
16. I get into trouble because of overconfidence.	□	□	□	□	□
17. My confidence in myself seems to put people off.	□	□	□	□	□
18. I feel that if you are successful in one thing, you can be equally successful in anything.	□	□	□	□	□
19. Other people have been responsible for my failures.	□	□	□	□	□
20. Once you achieve success, you can relax because momentum keeps you at the same level.	□	□	□	□	□
21. People have a way of honing in on the areas where I am most sensitive to criticism.	□	□	□	□	□
22. I have a sixth sense about criticism. I can always tell when people mean me.	□	□	□	□	□

	0	1	2	3	4
23. Negative comments from others can really hurt me, even make me feel depressed.	□	□	□	□	□
24. I hear negative comments and dismiss compliments.	□	□	□	□	□
25. I think all comments have about equal weight.	□	□	□	□	□
26. I get upset if I leave something unfinished.	□	□	□	□	□
27. Being considered "just average" or "one of the crowd" is an insult.	□	□	□	□	□
28. I'd rather turn in no work at all rather than turn in work that is below the standard I have set for myself.	□	□	□	□	□
29. It's important to me that others see me as someone who never deviates from impeccable standards.	□	□	□	□	□
30. Even a small mistake is enough to ruin my day—or my life.	□	□	□	□	□
31. Compared to others, I'm a loser.	□	□	□	□	□
32. I'm very competitive.	□	□	□	□	□
33. Hearing about the success of others upsets me.	□	□	□	□	□
34. Not being where I ought to be now gets me down.	□	□	□	□	□
35. I think you have to make comparisons with others if you want to be successful.	□	□	□	□	□
36. The world is a very dangerous place.	□	□	□	□	□
37. You have to be very careful about what you do and say if you don't want to get into trouble.	□	□	□	□	□
38. I don't like to take chances.	□	□	□	□	□

		0	1	2	3	4

39. I've lost some opportunities because I wasn't willing to take a risk. ☐ ☐ ☐ ☐ ☐

40. I avoid doing things if I think I could get hurt or be rejected. ☐ ☐ ☐ ☐ ☐

41. I feel guilty about something I should have done in the past. ☐ ☐ ☐ ☐ ☐

42. I believe it's important to live by the rules. ☐ ☐ ☐ ☐ ☐

43. When I look at the past I see more failure than success. ☐ ☐ ☐ ☐ ☐

44. I feel under pressure to do the right thing. ☐ ☐ ☐ ☐ ☐

45. I find myself overwhelmed by all the things I need to do. ☐ ☐ ☐ ☐ ☐

46. The opinions of others don't matter to me. ☐ ☐ ☐ ☐ ☐

47. People accuse me of not listening to them. ☐ ☐ ☐ ☐ ☐

48. I feel defensive when people ask—or tell—me to do something. ☐ ☐ ☐ ☐ ☐

49. I think things should be done my way or no way. ☐ ☐ ☐ ☐ ☐

50. I tend to procrastinate. I even put off doing important things. ☐ ☐ ☐ ☐ ☐

How to Score Your Answers

Look at the pattern of X's you have drawn. If you find that, next to every statement, you have marked only those boxes numbered 0 or 1, then you have very little difficulty with these mistakes—and probably very little difficulty in dealing with the challenges of your life.

However, most people will find that they have marked a 2 or above to at least some of the questions. Where that is the case, you may very well find a cluster of X's in the higher numbers. Those clusters provide a clue to the particular mistakes of thinking that are most troublesome to you.

If you find a cluster of X's in the 2 to 4 range:

- In questions 1–5, focus particular attention on Chapter Two.
- In questions 6–10, focus particular attention on Chapter Three.
- In questions 11–15, focus particular attention on Chapter Four.
- In questions 16–20, focus particular attention on Chapter Five.
- In questions 21–25, focus particular attention on Chapter Six.
- In questions 26–30, focus particular attention on Chapter Seven.
- In questions 31–35, focus particular attention on Chapter Eight.
- In questions 36–40, focus particular attention on Chapter Nine.
- In questions 41–45, focus particular attention on Chapter Ten.
- In questions 46–50, focus particular attention on Chapter Eleven.

CHAPTER ONE

KNOWING BETTER

A series of scenes from the popular movie *Indiana Jones and the Last Crusade* illustrate that all-too-human tendency to "know better"—and yet ignore that which we know.

Intrepid explorer Indy and the beautiful-but-evil Elsa Schneider have at last found the Holy Grail—a vaselike object they have gone through all sorts of difficulty to find. But no sooner does Elsa hold the Grail in her hand than an earthquake causes the ground beneath her to tremble and split apart. Suddenly she finds herself dangling dangerously above a deep chasm. All that saves her is Indiana Jones desperately holding on to one of her arms.

The Grail has slipped out of her hand and landed on an outcropping just out of her reach. Elsa stretches her free arm in an effort to retrieve it. Indy warns her that his grip is weakening. "I can't hold you," he says frantically. "Give me your other hand!" Elsa ignores him. Only the Grail has her attention. "I can reach it," she insists. But as she reaches out one more time, she slips from Indy's grasp and falls to her death.

Indiana Jones now knows—how could he not?—how dangerous it is to try to reach for the Grail, and yet when, only seconds later, he too finds himself dangling above the abyss, he *forgets everything he knows* and takes a turn at trying to grab it. This time, it is Indy's father hanging desperately on to one arm while Indy reaches with the other. "I can't hold you," says the elder Jones. *"Give me your other hand!"*

"I can reach it," says Indy. He is thinking only of how badly he wants that Grail, even though *just minutes before* he was pleading with the foolish Elsa just as his father now pleads with him. Luckily for Indiana Jones—and for his fans in the theater—he comes to his senses before he, too, drops into the deep.

And that is what all of us would like to do—come to our senses before we have done something disastrous, defeating, depressing, or just plain dumb. Alas, all too often, we drop into some chasm of our own making before we do.

When Your Smarts Desert You

Hasn't this happened to you? After the fact—after you have said or done something you regret, or failed to take what now seems to have been an obvious, sensible step, you groan: "How could I have been so dumb?" Or you smack your forehead with your palm in frustration and moan: "I could have done it so easily. Why didn't I?" Or, perhaps, someone close to you says: "I can't understand it. You know better than that."

You hear about famous people who, given their position in life, must be pretty smart, doing incredibly dumb things that ruin a valued relationship, sink a business, cost a bundle, wipe out a chance for an important government office, cancel a lifetime of effort, or simply embarrass that famous someone all over the front page and the evening news. And you wonder: What were they thinking about? What happened to their vaunted brain power?

What happened is unlikely to have a physical explanation. They were not suddenly struck by a lightning bolt or a radio-wave from Mars. Psychologists know that some very specific reasons cause smart people to do things they surely would not have done *had they made better use of their thinking abilities.*

If you review the reasons your smarts deserted you when you needed them, you are likely to say something like: "I wasn't thinking." Or: "I was so discouraged by that time, my brains had turned to mush." Or: "I was so nervous about it, so keyed up, I just blanked out." When we say, after the fact: "I knew better, but . . ." it usually is because we really *do* know better. What happened was that we based our action on *emotional thinking* rather than on *logical reasoning*—and got into trouble.

The Power of Thought

The way we think about a situation can literally either make it easier to handle or make it almost impossible to deal with. The way we think about a situation can calm us down or stir us up. It's even true that simply thinking about an experience from a different point of view can affect the way we experience pain. Psychologists have discovered, for example, that soldiers wounded on the battlefield report feeling less pain than civilians who, in the objective view of physicians, have suffered equal wounds.

Why should this be so? In theory, one might assume equal wounds would cause equal pain. The difference lies in the way the two groups *think* about the wound. To the soldier, the wound might mean: "I'm leaving the battlefield and I'm still alive. Hooray!" From this point of view, the wound is a relief. Not a great thing to have happen, of course—but certainly not the worst possibility a battlefield offers. That feeling of relief diminishes pain. From a civilian point of view, however, being wounded raises the *possibility* of death, rather than an *escape* from it. The civilian expects continued health, not a sudden need for hospitalization. Therefore, the civilian feels anxiety rather than relief, and anxiety increases pain.

An old story about a man who wants to borrow his neighbor's lawn mower also illustrates just how the way we think can affect our moods. In this story, when Bert, the would-be borrower, leaves his own house, he's confident that his good friend and neighbor, Ed, will be happy to lend him his lawn mower. He is thinking: "Good old Ed. He's such a nice guy." But as he walks down the road, he has second thoughts. "What if he says no?"

He starts to argue with himself. "He won't say no. He's a good friend. And, after all, I've done lots of favors for him." But the thought occurs: "Yes, but what if he doesn't appreciate those favors? Maybe he's the selfish sort who is willing to take but never gives anything back." He then conjures up mental images of being turned down by this neighbor. He imagines the neighbor claiming not to own a lawn mower. ("Does he expect me to believe that?") He imagines the neighbor claiming to be using the lawn mower himself. ("I know that's not true. It's obvious his lawn has already been cut.") He imagines the neighbor just saying no. ("The creep!")

By the time he reaches Ed's house, he is so sure his request to borrow the lawn mower will be turned down that he believes it would be a waste of time even to ask. He is now angry that he came all this way for nothing. Thus, when Ed, who is working outside, calls out to him: "Mornin', Bert," Bert is in no mood for friendly banter. He grunts a quick greeting to his neighbor and continues on his way, pretending he has some other errand in mind.

Would Ed have loaned Bert the lawn mower? Who knows? Certainly not Bert, who never gave his neighbor the opportunity to say either yes or no. He turned Ed from a generous neighbor to a selfish one entirely in his own head.

There is just no doubt that what goes on in your head affects your frame of mind, and your frame of mind affects your actions. After his divorce, Jerry sadly told himself: "I guess I'm just not cut out for marriage." As a result, he shied away from any relationship that might turn serious. He yearned to have a happy marriage, but because he believed it was impossible, he denied himself the opportunity of achieving it. Linda had a different point of view. After her divorce, Linda vowed: "I've learned my lesson. I won't make the same mistake again. I'll make a wiser choice next time." She thereby left herself open to the possibility of a new and better relationship. In each case, it was not the event (divorce) that was determinative, but rather the way the individual involved saw that event.

Crossing Your Stress Threshold

Does an individual always see the same event in the same way? No. And that is a crucial point to make. The way you see and think about something—that is, your frame of mind—can change, quite literally, from one moment to the next. Many popular expressions drive this point home. We talk about "losing control" or "losing your head" or just "losing it." We talk of "freezing" or, alternatively, of "going off half-cocked." We say: "I just wasn't thinking." All of these are ways of acknowledging, after the fact, that something we either did or said really doesn't make sense: Indiana Jones forgetting the chasm under his feet in his frustration at not being able to grab the Grail. What is often the case in such situations is that you have unknowingly crossed your stress threshold.

Each of us has a stress threshold below which we operate quite well and beyond which our circuits begin to misfire. Science has no explanation for where individual stress thresholds come from. It's possible that people are born with an inherited ability to handle stress. But it's equally possible that our individual thresholds arise as a product of early childhood experience. Or perhaps the explanation lies in some combination of heredity and environment.

All we know now is that people differ greatly in their ability to absorb stressful situations without harm. The ability to absorb stress is not an either you can or you can't proposition. If there were such a thing as a stress meter to measure this ability on a scale of 1 to 100, you would find people of varied backgrounds at every degree of the scale. People with stress thresholds at the low end of the scale tend to be quite anxious. They may be almost constantly oppressed by a feeling that something bad is about to happen. People with stress thresholds at the high end are known as Rock of Gibraltar types: able to take just about any calamity in stride.

Indeed, a new term, *transcender*, is being used now to describe people who as children faced stresses far in excess of what would be considered usual. They were able to transcend being horribly abused or neglected or afflicted in some terrible way. They were able to shed the stress somehow and grow up to be perfectly stable, emotionally healthy, and successful adults. At the other extreme are people who seem to have had all the advantages throughout their lives and who, on a day to day basis, face far less stress than most others—and yet these people easily fall prey to anxiety, anger, and depression.

Most people are somewhere in the middle of the stress scale. You don't have to pinpoint exactly where your own threshold might fall on this imaginary measure to know when the stress you are receiving at any given time is exceeding your own particular limit. You know because you feel it. When you cross your stress threshold, your nerves and muscles seem to rise in protest. Your entire nervous system is switching into one of three automatic modes that, so the theory goes, nature has given us as protective devices. These automatic modes are known as fight, flight, and freeze, and it's easy to understand how these may well have protected humankind in prehistoric times.

Suppose, for example, an ancient caveman is threatened by a saber-toothed tiger. This caveman might be able to save his life if, charged by an automatic flow of adrenaline, he attacks the tiger before it can attack him, or if he screams, rants, and raves so convincingly that he scares the tiger away. Or he might be able to save his life by running away. Or he might become so numb with terror that he can't move a muscle—but remaining motionless might also save his life if the tiger then fails to notice him and goes off to find other prey. When you cross your stress threshold, your system is protectively reacting to a saber-toothed tiger, which means that, one way or the other, your brain is no longer under your *voluntary* control.

The problem, however, is that today the dangers we face are unlikely to be saber-toothed tigers, and those involuntary responses that nature designed to protect us are more likely to hurt than help. If you fear making a fool of yourself when giving a speech, going numb is not helpful. If because you fear rejection, you run away from opportunities to meet others, the unhappy result may be loneliness. If the threat you face is an unsympathetic boss, ranting, raving, and picking fights may only scare the boss into firing you.

Changing Your Threshold

Obviously then, if you can decrease the occasions when you cross your stress threshold, you will increase your control over the events of your life. Fortunately, this is not hard to do.

Your individual stress threshold is not an unchanging characteristic like the color of your eyes. Various conditions and situations you face act to *lower* your usual stress threshold—that is, they lower that point at which your autonomic responses to stress (fight, flight, freeze) take over.

It works something like this: Say your normal stress threshold would rate a 50. Your job, although difficult and challenging, is nothing you can't handle because on a day to day basis it offers a stress level of about 30—well below your threshold. There are times when the stress of your job rises to 40 or 45—but you remain relatively cool, calm, and collected. It's still below your stress threshold, so you can handle it.

But now something happens that *lowers* your usual stress threshold to 35. You have a grinding headache or you didn't get any sleep the previous night or you have recently suffered a death in the family. Now those stressful complications in the 40 to 45 range that you customarily handled with ease seem overwhelming. You make mistakes. Your brain feels like cotton. You lose your temper. Others notice that you are not your normal self.

For example, Amy drives to work each day over the same route. There's always a lot of traffic, but ordinarily Amy isn't bothered about it. It's just part of the commuting routine. But last night, Amy was up till the wee hours finishing a report and left the house late—and without breakfast. So now she's tired, she's late, and she's hungry—and her stress threshold is down by at least 20 points. The result? Today every pothole seems like the Grand Canyon. She curses the state highway department. A car cuts her off. She barely suppresses the urge to follow the car and force it off the side of the road. ("If that driver wants a fight, I'll give him a fight.") In other words, ordinary stresses that Amy normally takes in stride now seem like personal insults.

Vulnerability Factors

Factors that result in lowering your stress threshold are known as vulnerability factors: situations that make you more vulnerable to stress. A vulnerability factor serves to decrease your threshold so that events that you coped with quite successfully in the past now overwhelm you. A tenet of Alcoholics Anonymous is to make members aware of the acronym HALT. The letters stand for Hungry, Angry, Lonely, and Tired. AA emphasizes that these are conditions under which an individual is most likely to lose control and resume drinking. But these four are not the only vulnerability factors. Others include pain, illness, lack of sleep, substance abuse, a major loss, and a major change of any kind—even one for the better.

Sometimes people recognize the ways in which they are particularly vulnerable. Someone will say: "I can't talk to anybody until I've had my first cup of coffee." Or: "If I don't get my eight hours of sleep, I'm not good for anything the next day." Sometimes people recognize a vulnerability factor only after it has become the proverbial straw that breaks the camel's back. Someone will say: "I'm sorry. I really didn't mean to say that. I'm upset today because I had a fight with my fiancé last night." Or: "My patience was short that day. I wasn't feeling well." Others are unaware that they are affected in this way. A severely depressed person may tell a therapist: "I had some bad moments this week. There were four times I felt like killing myself was the only way out. But then later I felt better." Some vulnerability factor had disappeared and stress was easier to handle.

A Vulnerability Checklist

You will probably find that certain of these factors affect you more than they do other people—just as some affect others more than they do you. Here's a quick quiz that will help you zero in on those factors that have the greatest influence in your life. Rate each factor on a scale of 1 to 5. One represents "doesn't affect me at all." Five represents "bothers me greatly." And 2, 3, and 4 represent positions in between.

Rate these separately for how they affect your feelings (Do you sense an emotional change?), your thoughts (Do thoughts about this factor tend to occupy your mind?), and your behavior (Do you act differently when this factor is present?). The higher your score on an individual factor, the more important that factor is to you.

	Feelings 1 2 3 4 5	Thoughts 1 2 3 4 5	Behavior 1 2 3 4 5
1. Hunger			
2. Anger			
3. Substance abuse			
4. Loneliness			
5. Fatigue			
6. Pain			
7. Illness			
8. Major loss (job, loved one, etc.)			
9. Lack of sleep			
10. Major life change			

Stress Increases Mistakes

Being aware of how these vulnerability factors act to lower your individual stress threshold is very important. Even though you might not be affected by the ten thinking mistakes described in this book under ordinary, everyday circumstances, you could become victimized by them when events conspire to push you *past your stress threshold.*

You may fall victim to mistakes in thinking—which you

would not make when you are feeling fine—when you feel lonely or when you have a headache or when you are rushed or when you have had too much to drink. Even if you normally have a relatively high stress threshold, you may fall victim to dumb thinking mistakes if several vulnerability factors accumulate—if, for example, you have a headache *and* you are rushed *and* you have had too much to drink.

Clearly then, you are most likely to remain in control of your thoughts, feelings, and actions if you can minimize those vulnerability factors. If, for example, you know that you operate better after eight hours of sleep, it makes sense to try to arrange your schedule to ensure that you get those eight hours of sleep—especially if you are facing a major challenge the next day.

But, obviously, it is not always possible to control vulnerability factors. Sometimes they just happen. Sometimes they are an unavoidable part of everyday life. Your stress threshold is lowered; your nervous system goes on alert. And your brain is likely to go on automatic. Does that mean you have to resign yourself to losing control? Do you have to behave like a caveman? Does it mean you are helpless? Do you have to give up and give in?

No way. Not if you understand what happens when your thinking process goes on automatic. Not if you understand the most common thinking patterns that occur in such situations—and how to break through those patterns and *regain control*.

Recognizing Your Own Thought Patterns

The ten thinking patterns described in this book are so common that you probably have been affected negatively by some of them at some time, although at this moment you may not realize it. Therapists sometimes talk of the "aha reaction." That is, people who learn about these thinking mistakes for the first time will say of one or the other: "Aha, that's me. I do that." Or, "Uh-oh, I can see that I have done that on occasion." Recognition is the first step to getting these troublesome reactions under control.

Each chapter in this book takes up a different dumb mistake

that smart people make and explains how it affects your decision making, your behavior, and your feelings about yourself and others. You will quickly recognize which of these bothers you the most. But recognition is only the first step. You will also learn how to deal with each of these mistakes and how to free yourself from their inhibiting effects.

A brief summary of the ten dumbest list follows. But, before you read it, a few words of warning: You may feel inclined to argue that we are wrong to include this or that on the list. For example, topic number seven is perfectionism, that is, the demand for perfection. You might say that it is anything but dumb to adhere to high standards. Indeed, you might point out that it is usually a compliment to be called a perfectionist. You may well argue that an insistence on perfection is a virtue.

It is—sometimes. But sometimes an insistence on perfection can become a vice, a trap. If, for instance, you resolve that you will not turn in an assignment at work until it is perfect—but you *never* think it is perfect—you may delay turning it in. That is likely to infuriate the person who made the assignment. To that person, your failure to produce is not perfection. As you read the chapter on perfectionism (as well as the other chapters in this book), it will become very clear that the difference between a helpful mode of thinking and a thinking mistake is very often simply a matter of degree. Therapists use two words to describe this: dysfunction and discomfort. Something only becomes a mistake if it *gets in the way* of what you want to do instead of helping you, or if it causes emotional pain. Thus, if your devotion to perfection in all things leads to success and happiness for you, then, clearly, it's not a dumb mistake. But if you have found that your pursuit of perfection has led more often to failure than to success, more often to misery than to happiness, it's time to reevaluate your position. It's time to give that particular thinking pattern more thought.

The Ten Dumbest

That said, here is the summary list:

1. The Chicken Little Syndrome. In the children's story, Chicken Little is bopped on the head by a nut falling from the tree, and immediately thinks the sky is falling. In the same way, people jump to all sorts of catastrophic conclusions without a second thought. And this can be paralyzing.

2. Mind Reading. One of the most dearly held illusions is that we know what others are thinking—and that others should know what we are thinking. "I don't have to tell him—he knows," is an all-too-common remark, and one that has a way of leading to disappointment when it turns out that he not only doesn't know, he doesn't even know you think he should know.

3. Personalizing. Some people seem to take everything personally. They assume responsibility for others' bad moods, even for bad weather—and as a result tend to feel either angry or guilty much of the time.

4. Believing Your Press Agent. This is a common failing of the famous, but quite ordinary folks who don't have press agents to glorify them in the media fall victim to it too. It involves, among other things, believing that success in one area automatically translates to success in every area without a need for the same effort that led to the first success.

5. Believing (or Inventing) Your Critics. This mistake is the direct opposite of believing your press agent. It can be just as troublesome, if in a different way, to accept without debate anyone who criticizes you about anything—or to assume that others are criticizing you—without bothering to determine how qualified those critics are to judge you or whether those critics even exist.

6. Perfectionism. This is the desire to be perfect in all things. It sounds quite admirable—and no one would deny that it's smart to set high standards for yourself. However, perfectionism becomes dumb when the standards you set are so high

you can never meet them—nor can anyone else. It's dumb when the desire to be 100 percent perfect leads to zero accomplishment.

7. Comparisonitis. To compare and contrast is a respectable way of analyzing differences, but people often get into trouble by focusing only on negative comparisons of themselves to others—or by accepting negative comparisons of themselves made by others. This is very discouraging and usually inaccurate.

8. What-If Thinking. Worry. Worry. Worry. That's what what-if thinking is all about. It's worrying about things that don't exist or are highly improbable in addition to worrying about those threats to health and happiness that are of real concern. And it is worrying about those real threats to a degree that diminishes your power to deal with them instead of increasing your coping power.

9. The Imperative *Should*. *Should* is an ordinary, everyday word—except when it is used to indicate an order that may not be refused. Then *should* becomes a finger waving under the nose. This imperative says: "Don't you dare deviate by as much as a millionth of a millimeter or you'll be sorry. You'll feel guilty; you'll feel ashamed." *Should* users build prison cells for themselves. They are so focused on what they should do—or should have done in the past—that they cannot think about what they can do, what they might do in the future.

10. Yes-Butism. The yes-but person always manages to find a negative that outweighs any positives. Or dreams up improbable rationalizations to excuse an obvious negative. Yes-but people get in their own—and others'—way.

Using Cognitive Therapy to Combat Mistakes

Every one of these mistakes in thinking can be combated by using the techniques of cognitive therapy. These techniques have had proven success in dealing with emotional extremes—with people who are so severely depressed that they don't want to get up in the morning, with people who are so anxious that they suffer panic attacks that literally take their breath away. And these techniques have had equal success in helping people avoid the kind of *common, everyday emotional mistakes* that ensnare and befuddle the best of us. Once you are able—helped by these techniques—to review the thoughts that rush through your brain, you will find you can literally unleash your brain to come to your rescue in times of stress. You can stop yourself from making those dumb thinking mistakes that lead to so many other mistakes. Your common sense will recognize when you are letting emotion get the better of you and will help you to gain a firmer grip on the events of your life.

Is this, as some unknowing critics have claimed, merely a matter of rationalizing our behavior—the psychological equivalent of applying cosmetics to make things look better than they really are? Not at all. This is a matter of logical analysis, which is a totally different thing. This is a matter of making better use of our ability to reason, not of improving our ability to make excuses (something that most of us do only too well now).

Is this an attack on acting by instinct? After all, you might argue, sometimes the gut reaction is the best reaction. Sometimes all your previous experience tells you this is the way to go. Sometimes that's true, but at other times gut reaction is just another name for emotional thinking that leads to one mistake after the other. Or, to put it another way: There are times when your instincts need some help from your brain.

Imagine yourself at a railroad crossing. A sign there says: "Stop, look, and listen." Ninety-nine times out of a hundred, you could probably ignore the sign and zip across the tracks in perfect safety. You could assume that if a train was coming, a safety gate would descend to bar your way. But if you realize that the safety gate at this crossing does not always work perfectly, your common sense would tell you that if you don't stop, look, and listen, you may very well be run over by a locomotive. If a little extra thought can keep those locomotive wheels away, why not?

Making Unspoken Thoughts Spoken

Cognitive therapy teaches us to make unspoken thoughts spoken. These unspoken thoughts lie just below the level of your awareness, and you can easily make yourself aware of them. Many people believe that thoughts are divided sharply between conscious and unconscious—the latter being so deeply buried that a great effort is required to bring them to the conscious level. But unspoken thoughts are not like that. True, they may not be immediately in your mind, but it doesn't take much effort to bring them to the fore—just as you can bring in a clearer radio signal by fine-tuning the radio dial.

If you are not aware of every thought zipping through your mind, it's probably because these thoughts are habitual. Most people think of habits only in terms of actions. There are good habits like brushing your teeth and bad habits like biting your nails. But, in fact, we have good and bad habits in the way we think as well. Habits of action and of thought are alike in that both occur *automatically*. You ordinarily don't have to concentrate and plan how you will get your key into your front door to unlock it. You just do it—automatically—by habit. Your brain is involved, but it's in the background.

The habits we develop in the way we think are heavily influenced by what psychologists call our individual "schema." Schema are basic ways you organize the information you receive. You acquire your own particular schema by incorporating some or all of the rules to live by that you are taught at home or at school, that you learn through your religion or from your friends.

An individual schema is like a pair of glasses through which you view the world. If your glasses have purple lenses, you will see the world as shaded in purple. In the same way, a person who sees the world through lenses marked "dependent and helpless" is likely to believe that it's dangerous to disagree with anybody, that it's dangerous to complain, that it's important to be liked by everybody.

Your own individual schema—the way you view the world—explains why you will find that you are more affected by some of the ten dumbest thinking mistakes than by others. If your schema says that the world is a very dangerous place in which survival depends on being very, very cautious, you probably tend to think automatically—by habit—in a Chicken Little or what-if way. If your schema says that being seen by others as outstanding is all-important in life, your thinking habits may include comparisonitis, believing your critics, or believing your press agent.

Because we grow up believing that our particular schema is simply "the way things are," we tend not to question it. But just because you believe something—and everybody you know believes it too—doesn't necessarily mean it's true. If you wore glasses with blue lenses, the things you looked at would seem shaded by blue. If you looked at a lemon through those blue glasses, what color would it be? Many people promptly answer "Green"—because when you mix blue and yellow, that's what you get. But the answer is that the lemon is still yellow. Just because you and everybody else wearing glasses with blue lenses see green, the lemon does not turn into a lime. As you analyze your own particular habits of thought, you may well decide to switch lenses—to look at the world in a new way.

New Thinking Habits

This is the bottom line: Harmful habits can be broken. You can break a bad habit of thought, just as you can break a bad habit of action. And you can develop new habits that are more helpful and healthful for you.

Learning how to break a bad habit of thought is the easy part. Installing new, helpful habits is the hard part. Isn't that true of physical habits, too? It's easy for someone to learn the proper way to hold a tennis racquet. A tennis pro places your hand just so, and you have no difficulty holding that position when you think about it. The trick is to change your old grip to this new one *every time* you hold the racquet—even (maybe that should be especially) in the middle of a hotly contested match. Doing that requires some effort. Doing that requires practice.

It's easy for a two-finger typist to learn the mechanics of touch-typing. But gaining speed takes some practice. The two-finger typist says: "I know I could double or even triple my speed if I am willing to spend a little time practicing using all ten of my fingers instead of two. But is it worth it to me to spend that time?" The answer may be no if typing slowly isn't causing the two-fingered typist any problems. But the decision will probably be yes if the typist believes the long-run payoff will be greater success as well as greater ease.

The same question must be asked when it comes to developing new habits of thinking: Is it worth the effort? If an occasional lapse, such as we all make, isn't causing you any problems or pain, you may not be willing to practice the techniques described in this book. On the other hand, if you feel uncomfortable, if things are not turning out as you wish, then you will find it extremely worthwhile to learn how to stop, look, and listen, and change the way you cross the tracks.

Can the techniques contained here guarantee that you will never, ever again make a wrong choice, lose your temper, lose money, be rejected or dejected? Sorry, no such guarantees are possible. What this book can promise is that it will show you how to gain greater control of your own brain power and minimize these very common errors.

These techniques won't enable you to make floodwaters recede—but they will enable you to cope more calmly with the resulting emergency. Raising your level of determination and self-confidence will not automatically bring career success—but it certainly makes that success more likely. Becoming more open to love will not guarantee that Prince Charming will appear at your door—but it removes the lock that would otherwise prevent him from coming in.

A User-Friendly Therapy

In the chapters that follow, each dumb thinking mistake is discussed separately. That is not because they necessarily occur
separately. In fact, as often as not, several factors will intertwine,
just as the problems we face in life do not necessarily occur
precisely one at a time but overlap or crop up in batches. However, fully describing each mistake by itself will lead to a *more
complete understanding* of how these mistakes affect you both
separately and in combination. That understanding is necessary
to learning the techniques that enable you to deal with these
mistakes. It is not the purpose of this book to deny the complex-
ity of either the human condition or human beings but rather to
make a powerful therapeutic process easily accessible. The intent
of this book, to use an expression from the world of computers,
is to be user-friendly.

The twenty-five specific techniques in this book will help
you to mobilize your thoughts, cut through emotional barriers,
and take greater control of the events of your life, rather than
allowing those events to take control of you. You will find
some of these techniques useful in dealing with every thinking
mistake, whereas some apply to certain mistakes but not to
others. Many of these techniques are best when used in combination. But here again, these techniques are introduced separately—and slowly—so that you will gain mastery of them on a
step by step basis. In some chapters, you will learn how to
apply a previously described technique in different circumstances.

At the conclusion of the book, you will find a grid chart that
matches the therapeutic techniques most applicable to each specific thinking mistake. Undoubtedly, that chart will mean more
to you after you have read through the book, but you can refer
to it at any time.

Further, in Chapters Twelve and Thirteen, every technique
described in the previous chapters is restated and more fully
described. You can, at any time, refer to those chapters to find

and learn more about those mental tools you feel would be most useful to you. All these techniques together form a kind of brain owner's user's manual—a troubleshooting guide for occasional malfunction. When you use the information this book provides, you will not only know better, you'll be able to live better, too.

CHAPTER TWO

THE CHICKEN LITTLE SYNDROME

When Chicken Little of children's storybook fame was hit on the head by an acorn that fell from a tree, he immediately jumped to the conclusion that the sky was falling. And he went forth to spread the alarm.

This is the sort of behavior known as catastrophizing. The mind leaps to believe the worst. Disaster appears to lie just around the corner. Psychologist Albert Ellis calls it "awfulizing," because the individuals involved imagine a consequence so awful that they will not be able to stand it. But by any name, this is easy enough to do.

We all know that on some occasions the mind seems to leap automatically toward pessimism rather than optimism. Suppose, for example, you get a letter from the Internal Revenue Service. Would this be your first thought? "Great! I just can't wait to open this envelope. I'll bet it contains a notice that I am entitled to a big refund." If that's what you would think, you are amazingly optimistic, because most people would think something closer to: "Uh-oh, I hope this isn't a notice that I owe more money." Or: "Oh no, I'll bet this is a notice of an audit." Similarly, if Junior unexpectedly brings home a note from the principal's office, Mom is more likely to ask Junior: "What did you do wrong?" than to assume the envelope contains an invitation to a Parent-Teacher Association tea.

The expression "sinking feeling" perfectly describes Ann's reaction to a message that the boss wants to see her in his office in twenty minutes. Her heart seems to have fallen into her stomach and her stomach into her knees. Her feet feel like lead weights. She is sure it will be criticism—or worse. As she mentally reviews every mistake she made in her five years with the firm to determine which is the cause of the disaster she is sure is in store for her, the twenty minutes pass like twenty years. It turns out the boss wants to know if she's willing to head the office charity drive. All the physical and mental pain she had endured was for nothing.

A few years ago, there was a report about an increasing number of people in their early twenties panicking because they believed they had Alzheimer's disease. These individuals had all read stories about how victims of Alzheimer's lose their memory. And then *they forgot something* and jumped to the conclusion that they must have been stricken by this incurable disease. This thought was so terrifying that their bodies responded with a feeling of numbness, or palpitations, or chills. Those physical reactions to fear only served to further convince the young people that they were dying. But physicians found no symptoms at all. Their suffering was needless.

But needless pain may well be the least of the problems caused by the Chicken Little syndrome.

Losing Your Cool and Other Symptoms

Chicken Little isn't merely worried, he is *terrified*—because he is convinced not only that he is faced with imminent disaster but also that *there is nothing he can do about it*. This brings about the condition that is sometimes called losing your cool. Chicken Little can't manage to do much more about this supposed catastrophe he faces than run around screaming.

There are all sorts of situations in which it is easy enough to lose your cool:

• The kids are not home on time. Mom says to herself: "They've been killed." "They've been kidnapped." Her heart starts pumping wildly. She is so panicky, she can't even use the phone.

• Ralph is driving to an important job interview and takes a wrong turn. He realizes he will be late and thinks: "I've blown it. Now I'll never get that job." He is so upset about losing the job that he isn't concentrating fully on driving. As a result he misses a turn that would have gotten him back on the right road.

Sometimes the end result of the Chicken Little syndrome is not just missing a turn but failing to look for one. A common tendency of those who believe that disaster is unavoidable is to simply give up—to make no effort to resolve the problem. After all, if you have concluded that there is nothing you can do, then it follows you will probably do nothing:

• Emily has mislaid a report she knows would be very helpful in a meeting that is scheduled for today. "I must have thrown it away," she thinks. "It's just like me to throw away something important. No use looking for it. I'll never find it."

• Joe is laid off from his job and "knows" that he'll never find another. He sends out a few resumés and hears nothing. That proves his point. "It's hopeless," he says. A friend hears of an opening and tells him about it. "They'd never want me," says Joe, who doesn't bother to call.

• Marcia turns down a friend's invitation to a party because she is positive she will be ignored, rejected, and humiliated. So instead she stays home and cries.

Bringing About What You Fear

Unfortunately, this tendency to think the worst has a way of actually making the worst—or something just as bad—happen. This is the infamous self-fulfilling prophecy. Obviously, if Emily does not look for the report, she won't find it, even if it's there. If Joe does not continue to look for a job, he is not likely to find one. Therefore, he will make his own prediction come true. If Marcia does not go to the party, she will avoid the humiliation of being rejected—but she will also eliminate the possibility of having a good time. And she certainly isn't having a good time at home if she fills her hours with weeping.

Thinking the worst can bring about the disaster you fear in very subtle ways. Here again, Chicken Little is a perfect example because he is so unnerved by his belief that he can't manage to do anything more functional than run around in a panic. This behavior scares his barnyard friends, Ducky Lucky and Turkey Lurky, into running around in panic too. At that point, along comes the clever Foxy Loxy, who offers them the "safety" of his den. Now really. Surely no chicken, duck, or turkey who is thinking clearly would willingly accompany a fox to his den. They would say to themselves: "Safety, my feathers! That fox just wants to eat us for his dinner." But, alas, all Chicken Little and his friends have on their minds is escaping a falling sky. So they don't question the fox's offer of refuge but unthinkingly go with him. And so, although they are not crushed by the sky as they feared, they are fatally crunched by the fox. Their catastrophic thinking made it possible for a real catastrophe to happen.

This sort of thing happens all the time. Take Mark, for example. He is ordinarily self-confident about his abilities as a sales representative. But the thought of giving a speech to a large audience turns him into walking Jell-O. He has never given a speech before, and he is sure he will flub it. As he walks up to the podium, a series of horrible scenes fly through his mind:

"The microphone won't work.

    ↘

  I'll get upset and lose my place.

      ↘

    Which will cause me to stutter.

        ↘

      Then I'll get it all messed up.

          ↘

And everyone will laugh at me.

That will make my boss furious.

I can forget any hopes I have of getting a promotion.

I'll be lucky if I keep my job.

I'll be destroyed."

In a matter of seconds, Mark has both written a script for disaster and convinced himself it is inevitable. No wonder, then, by the time he opens his mouth to speak, his tongue is stuck to the roof of his mouth, his palms are sweaty, his knees are knocking, and his voice is wobbly. He does stutter. He does lose his place. "I knew it," he says to himself miserably. More accurately, he *caused* it by falling victim to the Chicken Little syndrome.

Thinking Realistically

All this is *not* a call for what is generally known as positive thinking. Far from it. This entire book is a call for realistic thinking. And there is a big difference. You may have heard the story of the little boy who is overjoyed to be given a roomful of smelly manure as a gift. A friend asks: "How can you be so happy to get this?" And the little boy, cheerfully digging through dung, replies: "With all this manure, there must be a pony in here somewhere." This is a case of a positive thinker who is out of touch with reality.

Indeed, there are times when negative thinking has the most positive results. For example, a recent study of the sexual practices of college students showed that many engaged in intercourse without the protection of a condom. Were they aware of the terrible threat of AIDS or the possibility of contracting some other sexually transmitted disease such as herpes? Yes. They said they knew about the dangers—but preferred not to think about them or simply to assume: "It won't happen to me." If they are lucky, nothing will happen to them, but statistics indicate that not all will be lucky. In this instance, a more pessimistic attitude ("If I don't protect myself, I'll probably get a fatal disease") could actually save a life.

The entire insurance industry is based on the actuarial tables that predict that a certain percentage of people will suffer losses (auto accident, bad health, fire damage, premature death) while most people will remain unscathed and continue to pay premiums. To buy insurance you don't have to believe you are *guaranteed* to be among those who will suffer but rather that you accept the *possibility* and prepare financially for it.

In other words, thinking *realistically* does not mean cheerfully assuming: "Everything will turn out right" or "It can't happen to me." But it also does *not* mean dolefully assuming: "Nothing will turn out right and therefore I am doomed."

We all know that bad things happen. One day's scanning of the headlines and possibly your own past experience tells you that. Yet, more often than not, a hasty conclusion that the sky has fallen, or that it is about to, turns out to be *wrong*. And that can create a problem that might not otherwise exist. It can bring about pain that might have been avoided.

If you had a nickel for every time you ever thought the worst had happened when either nothing happened or it wasn't as bad as you'd thought, you might be very comfortably fixed right now. Unfortunately, what we generally collect instead of nickels is a lot of needless suffering.

Realistic thinkers recognize that there can be a middle ground, that there can be other explanations. Realistic thinkers do not deny that the worst is *possible*, but they also don't assume the worst is *guaranteed* without investigating first.

Chicken Little does not say: "I wonder what hit me on the head?" He does not say: "I think a portion of the sky may have fallen and I'd better ask an expert to come check." He goes nonstop into a state of panic. Chicken Little takes a single piece of evidence (something hit him on the head) and magnifies the negative consequences of it (this must mean the sky is caving in). This is what we commonly refer to as making a mountain out of a molehill.

Realistic thinkers can recognize danger and suffer disappointment, but they don't exaggerate the greatness of that danger or disappointment, and they don't automatically assume there is nothing they can do to improve things.

Listening to Yourself

If you recognize that, in the past, you have fallen victim to the Chicken Little syndrome, it's likely that you start out with a heightened awareness of the fact that terrible things *do* happen. That may simply be part of the way you view the world. Chicken Little may have been convinced by a source he found credible that under certain circumstances the sky really could fall. That thought is tucked away in his brain. Then something happens (the acorn) to release that thought. This release doesn't happen all at once. As psychiatrist Dr. Aaron T. Beck discovered in his groundbreaking research, what happens is that you quite literally talk yourself into that worst conclusion.

Take Mark, the speaker, for example. Somewhere in the back of Mark's mind is the view that it is *possible* for him to be fired from his job. That is not what he is thinking about, however, when he first approaches the podium. He starts out merely being concerned about whether the microphone will work. But that thought, like the acorn, is enough to trigger the next thought (that he'll get upset and lose his place), which leads to the next thought and the next and the next, until Mark can actually visualize himself getting fired from his job for failure at the podium.

Mark is not aware that he is quite literally persuading himself that a disaster is about to befall him. His internal conversation takes place not in minutes but in seconds, maybe even milliseconds. His thoughts fly through his mind so quickly that each individual thought is barely noticed. Dr. Beck calls these quick-flying thoughts "automatic thoughts."

Here's another example: Valerie is packing for a business trip. She can't find a file she needs to take with her. Her first thought is: "I can't find the file." She is naturally a little bit upset about that. And she realizes that she does not have an unlimited amount of time to search for the file because she has a train to catch. A thought about the train pops into her mind: "If I don't find that file soon, I'm going to miss my train." That launches an entire series of automatic thoughts:

"If I miss that train, I'll miss the meeting.

↘

If I miss the meeting, I won't make the sale.

↘

If I don't make the sale, it will affect my standing at work.

↘

If I lose respect at work, I might even lose my job."

Valerie may not even realize that she has been constructing a scenario for disaster. She senses only a rising tide of panic that churns in her stomach and seems to be swamping her brain. She is so busy thinking of how terrible will be the outcome of not finding the file, she can't think clearly about where it might be. She can't concentrate on where she last saw it. Her automatic thoughts are working against her.

Automatic thoughts are perfectly normal. Most people have a constant stream of thoughts running through their minds. They might merely be quick little daydreams that have nothing to do with the task at hand. "Sorry, my mind was drifting," you might say. Or those thoughts might be critical to accomplishing the task at hand. Running quickly through a catalog of thoughts is necessary in any decision-making process. "Should I do this . . . or that?" you ask yourself. You mull over the reasons for one choice or another before deciding what to do.

But because your thoughts—whether positive or negative—

have a profound effect on what you do, there are times when it is vital to make yourself *consciously aware* of precisely what you are thinking. You can easily replay the tape of your thoughts if you concentrate on doing so. When you review the thoughts that led to your conclusion, you give yourself a chance to evaluate their accuracy. You can even challenge your own thoughts just as you might challenge someone who tells you that the world will end in twenty minutes. ("Are you sure? How do you know that? Why should I believe you?")

Learning how to challenge a conclusion to which your brain has leaped will help you to recognize when that conclusion is unjustified by facts. Learning how to argue with your automatic thoughts will help you avoid those self-fulfilling prophecies of disaster and enable you to cope—realistically—with upsetting situations. Obviously, you can't always keep bad things from happening, but you can make sure that you do not read more into them than they actually mean. Or to put it in Chicken Little terms, you may not be able to prevent an acorn from falling on your head, but you can prevent the pain, panic, and self-fulfilling prophecies than might result if you simply jump to the conclusion that the bump on your head means the sky is caving in. This does *not* mean you have to constantly monitor *every* thought you have. It doesn't mean analyzing everything you do. It is a technique to be called on when you are facing a stressful situation and thus are most likely to rush into a mistaken reaction.

If you were a munitions expert called on to defuse a bomb, you would want to concentrate all your attention on that delicate task while engaged in it. But you wouldn't have to be equally intense later while having lunch or shopping in the supermarket. The point here is to develop your skill so that you can call on that skill *when you need it*. Life has a way of producing lots of emotional bombs that need defusing.

Challenging Your Thoughts

The time to challenge your thoughts is when you feel yourself getting upset—and you know when that is happening. You first become aware of your conclusion: "All is lost." "I'm going to mess up." "It will never happen." "I'll be destroyed."

The first—and most important—technique you can use to combat this self-defeating thought is *checking for meaning* This is simply a matter of asking yourself: "What exactly do I mean by this thought that is churning my stomach, straining my nerve ends, and numbing my brain?"

Suppose, for example, you have concluded: "I'll be destroyed." What do you mean by "I"? Do you mean your person—do you fear a physical attack? Do you mean your money or property? Do you mean your self-esteem? What do you mean by "destroyed"? Is your life threatened? How exactly will you be destroyed?

This simple technique is amazingly helpful. Why? Because it forces you to confront your worst scenario. Mark tells himself: "I'll be destroyed." But he doesn't really mean his body will be destroyed—he isn't going to die if he messes up the speech. What he means is that he'll be embarrassed. What he means is that his boss may be displeased with him. Those are not pleasant prospects—but do they equal total destruction? Are they survivable? Once Mark realizes what he *really* means, he may well change his panicky all-is-lost point of view.

We like to think that we always say what we mean and mean what we say. But, if you think about it, you'll have to admit this isn't true. We do a lot of talking—and thinking—in shorthand: "This is the pits." "This is great." We engage in a great deal of hyperbole—popularly known as hype: "I was so embarrassed, I almost died." (Do you know anybody who actually died from embarrassment?) "I didn't eat until 8 P.M. and I was starving." (Hungry, yes. Starving, doubtful. Starving means to perish from lack of food or to suffer extreme hunger.) We attribute meaning out of habit. There is a joke about a ten-year-old boy who asks his father: "Where did I come from?" The father thinks: "I've dreaded this moment, but I guess I'll have to answer his question." He then launches into an explanation of human reproduction in terms he hopes his ten-year-old can understand. "Any more questions?" the father asks his son. "Yeah, Dad," the boy replies. "All that was very interesting, but I still want to know where I come from. Jimmy says he is from Cleveland and . . ."

Often you don't really mean what you are thinking. You will recognize that if you stop long enough to review your thoughts and ask: "What exactly do I mean by those words that are in the forefront of my mind?"

De-Catastrophizing

If Mark had stopped to analyze the thoughts that raced through his mind as he approached the podium, he could also have easily refuted each and every point using another technique called de-catastrophizing. It involves analyzing your thoughts, starting with your worst conclusion and working your way back.

Suppose Mark had ended with the conclusion that his job was threatened. That alone was enough to make him feel sick. He might not even be immediately aware that he has concluded this. He is aware, however, that he is becoming more and more nervous. Now, let us assume that Mark is aware of the Chicken Little syndrome. He knows that people, when stressed, very commonly start to catastrophize. So he stops and asks himself: "Have I been doing that?" Mark reviews his thoughts—bringing them one by one to the forefront of his mind. As he does this, he gives each a reality check.

"I can forget any hopes I have of promotion here. I'll be lucky if I keep my job."

"Is that really true? Is it really possible or even probable that a single speech, even if badly delivered, will cancel out every other positive contribution I have made? Has anyone else at the office ever been fired for stuttering in a speech? For the first speech ever delivered?"

"I'll lose my place. I'll stutter. I'll get it all messed up. Everyone will laugh at me."

"Is that really true? The speech is ten pages long. Am I going to mess up on every page? Probably not. Am I really expected to deliver a speech like Winston Churchill or Jesse Jackson? No."

Even if the joke Mark makes falls flat, even if he does stutter, will *everyone* laugh? There must be some in the audience who have suffered through speeches themselves. And made mistakes themselves. They are likely to be sympathetic. Some are likely not even to notice. Mark can remind himself of this.

"The microphone won't work."

"If the mike doesn't work, I'll have to talk louder."

Thinking realistically does not mean that Mark now has a guarantee of wowing his audience. Naturally he wants to do a good job. Naturally he will be disappointed if he does not do as well as he'd hoped. But by simply making himself aware of his Chicken Little thoughts and analyzing them, Mark calms himself down. He can now focus on the speech rather than dreaming up one disaster after the other. He may still be nervous, but he won't be a nervous wreck. And by being able to focus on that speech, he is less likely to bring about the disaster he fears.

The students who jumped to the conclusion that they had Alzheimer's did not, of course, bring on the disease they feared simply by thinking they had it. But they did bring themselves unnecessary physical and emotional suffering. That is a common result of catastrophizing. That is why it is so helpful to realize that catastrophizing can occur. By questioning the meaning of their conclusion, the students might realize that what they meant when the thought "fatal disease" flashed through their brains was that they had forgotten something. That, at least, opens the way to thinking further about forgetting—and whether forgetting is always a symptom of a fatal disease.

Questioning the Evidence

That brings us to still another technique: *questioning the evidence.* When you leap to a conclusion, you tend to jump over evidence that, had you considered it, might have led you to a different conclusion. When your emotions take control of your thinking process, you are likely to make a decision based on no evidence at all, or even on evidence absolutely contrary to that which supports your Chicken Little conclusion.

Suppose Chicken Little stopped for just a second to say: "What makes me think the sky is falling?" He knows he got a bump on the head. He could look up at the sky. "Looks okay." He might ask himself how many times the sky had fallen in the past. He might even look around and find the acorn. He might, that is, if he stopped long enough to ask any questions at all.

Suppose those students had stopped to question their deadly disease conclusion. It might go something like this:

"I have a deadly disease."

"How do I know that?"

"Because I just forgot the name of my state senator and I know I should know it."

"Is Alzheimer's the only reason that names or other facts sometimes slip from people's minds?"

"No."

"Does everybody who forgets something have Alzheimer's?"

"No."

"Have I ever forgotten anything before?"

"Yes."

"Was that forgetfulness due to disease?"

"No."

"Do I know for sure that I have this disease?"

"Not really."

"Is it possible I am getting all worked up about something that may not be true at all?"

Recording the Argument

The Chicken Little syndrome isn't a mistake people make only when under some special pressure—such as rushing for a train or making a speech. It can occur at any time. You might be mulling over a social or business situation at home at night and end up feeling just terrible. Your heart feels like a lump of lead. You recognize that as the it's-no-use feeling. The conclusion might be: "There is no way I can get through to my children." Or: "There is no way I can succeed on this project." Or: "I'll never find a job." Or: "He has no interest in me." Or: "Women don't like me." No way. No how. Never. Awful. Disaster. Catastrophe.

At times like this, it can be very helpful not only to make yourself aware of those automatic thoughts that led you to this conclusion but also to write those thoughts down. Yes, you can argue with yourself in your mind, but you will find that seeing those thoughts in black and white can help in that arguing process. Writing down your thoughts helps you to reach them.

Try this: Write down your conclusion. Now think about—and write down—the thoughts that led you to that conclusion. What meaning do you ascribe to those words? Why do you think the worst has happened or is inevitable? What evidence are you using to sustain and nurture this belief?

Ask yourself: "Why do I think this? Do I know it for sure? What's really the worst that can happen? Can I survive it? Have others survived it?" You will find you know the answers. You just have to remember to ask yourself the questions. Sometimes merely listing those thoughts of disaster and reading them over is enough to lift a black mood because what seems to be a dire event seems less so when you see it in writing. But even if that is not the case, once you have listed your thoughts, you are in a good position to begin questioning them.

Coming to Your Own Defense

It may help you to imagine yourself trying to convince *somebody else* that things are not as bad as you claim. If you were a defense attorney in a criminal case, your job would be to raise questions and bring to light any facts that might raise a reasonable doubt in the jury's mind: "How can you be sure my client shot him? Did she confess? No. Did anyone see her shoot him? No."

Even when there isn't any doubt that the defendant has committed the deed, the defense attorney will attempt to bring before the jury every mitigating factor that might lessen the seriousness of the charge:

"Yes, she shot him, but he shot at her first."

"Yes, she shot him, but she was aiming at a target and he walked in front of it."

"Yes, she shot him but she didn't know the gun was loaded."

"Yes, she shot him, but it happened in the middle of a heated argument so it was not premeditated, therefore my client deserves prison but not the electric chair."

When you feel yourself about to render the verdict that catastrophe is inevitable and unavoidable, you need to review the evidence. Is what you fear as sure as you claim? Are there any mitigating factors?

Let us take the example of the mother who, when the children fail to come home on time or telephone, races through a series of negative thoughts to a conclusion that the kids have been either kidnapped or murdered. As she feels the tide of panic sweep over her, she must stop and question her thoughts.

"Do I know for sure that the catastrophe I fear has actually happened?"

"Since I have not gotten a ransom note or a phone call from the police, the answer is no."

Many, many times, when you believe, in one form or another, that the sky is falling, and you ask yourself this key question, you will similarly find the answer is no. That is, what you believe *may* be true, but you do not have *conclusive evidence* of it.

"Have the children ever failed to come home on time in the past? And, if so, was that because they had been murdered or kidnapped?"

"Yes, they have been late before. And it was not because they were victims of a crime."

If your conclusion has not happened in the past, why assume the situation is different this time?

If they have never been late before, go on to the next question:

"Are there any other possible explanations for the children not being home now?"

"The car has had a flat tire and the kids are not near a telephone."

"The kids are sitting in a restaurant talking to other kids, having a great time, not noticing the lateness of the hour."

"The kids have disobeyed my order to come home right after the game and have succumbed to the temptation to go out with the other kids for a snack. They are disobedient but not dead."

You might point out that this mother doesn't have conclusive proof that any of those explanations are true either. Can she be sure? No. But since she does not know which, if any, of the explanations is so, why believe—and get hysterical about—the worst one?

Here's another example: Arlene was going to invite Jason to Thanksgiving dinner, but doesn't make the call. Why not? She has concluded that Jason doesn't want to see her again—and therefore it is pointless to set herself up for rejection. How does she know how Jason feels? Her thoughts run like this: "He yelled at me. He was angry, and I don't think I did anything to deserve it. It just means he's not happy. And that means he's not happy with me. And if he's not happy, it means we're through. So why would I want to invite him to anything?"

Maybe Jason does want out. But if Arlene stops to question how her reasoning got from situation A to conclusion B, she might take a chance and issue the invitation. After all, does she really know for sure that Jason doesn't want to see her again? He hasn't actually said that, so the answer is no. Could there be an alternative explanation for his behavior? Maybe. He could have been angry about a specific issue—and that issue can be resolved. Possibly he was frustrated about something else that had happened that day and just exploded in the wrong direction. If Arlene cares about Jason, she may well finally conclude that perhaps she should discuss the matter with Jason before assuming he is out of her life.

What Is Wrong With This Picture?

You may have seen those puzzles that ask you to pick an element in a picture that is not logical, not reasonable. That illogical element might be an upside-down tree, a faucet dripping upward, a dog strolling with a person on a leash instead of vice versa. Sometimes you have to ask yourself: "What is wrong with this picture?" when examining a catastrophic scene that you have drawn in your mind.

Here is an example: Mary Ellen's car has broken down on the expressway, far from an exit, far from a service station. Her first thought is: "I'm going to be stuck here for hours." But her last thought is: "I'll run out of air and suffocate."

Mary Ellen has jumped to the conclusion that she is locked in the car and *can do nothing about it*. Mary Ellen can see herself suffocating inside the car.

Is anything wrong with that picture? Picture the car. Is there anything about that car that might help Mary Ellen in this situation?

Does the car have windows? Can those windows be opened before the air runs out?

Does the car have a door? Could the door be opened before the air runs out? Is it possible to step outside the door?

Mary Ellen might very well realize that she can open the car's windows or doors, but she is afraid that will make her vulnerable to would-be robbers or attackers who could very well be in a car going past her. She can then consider the advantages and disadvantages of alternate courses of action: Is there a greater danger to opening a window than to staying inside the car? Is there some middle position? Would the advantage of opening the window an inch, for example, outweigh any presumed disadvantage?

The object is always to question that first disastrous conclusion, to rethink that no-win premise, to reconsider that panicky or defeated capitulation. The object is to resist the temptation to rush right down the mental shortcut that takes you from a single negative thought to a conclusion that disaster is imminent and unavoidable—*when you have no evidence that this is, in fact, the case.*

The Many Paths to Disaster-ville

There is no shortage of paths to travel when you allow yourself to take that shortcut to disaster. When you analyze your thoughts, check to see whether you are heading down one of these troublesome paths.

The Path of Global Effect

You say to yourself: "I didn't do that well, which means I can do *nothing* well." You take a single failure in one segment of your life and draw conclusions from it for your whole life.

Kate had hoped to be a nurse but did not do well in her science courses and finally had to drop out of nursing school. A friend points out that other caring professions do not require a science background. But Kate scoffs: "I'd just flunk that, too," she says. "I'm just stupid." Kate has no way of knowing—without investigating—whether some other field would be a good match for her talent and interests.

The Path of Generalization

You say to yourself: "That didn't work well this time," which means it will never work.

You might say: "I asked two young women out on dates, and both turned me down. That means women don't like me. I will never have a date, no matter what I do." How can you be sure? Psychologist Albert Ellis likes to tell the story about how he improved his sex life when he was a young man. Up to the age of nineteen, he was exceptionally shy, because he catastrophized about possible rejection. So he never actually talked to any of the scores of young women he flirted with in the Bronx Botanical Gardens, even though many of them actively flirted back. By thinking about his shyness, he figured out that nothing "awful" *would* happen if they actually rejected him and he gave himself the cognitive-behavioral homework assignment of sitting on the same bench with a hundred different women and within one minute—yes, one single minute—talking to them, no matter how uncomfortable he felt while doing so. Carrying out this "shame-attacking" exercise (which he many years later incorporated into rational-emotive therapy), he opened conversations with a hundred women within one month. Out of the hundred he spoke to, he made only one date—and she never showed up! But, by seeing that nothing catastrophic had happened, he thereafter was completely comfortable and uninhibited about picking up strange women. And, going on to his second and third hundred pickups, he soon had more success—and more sexual encounters—than almost any other young man in New York.

There's a line in Shakespeare's *Julius Caesar* about assuming that every future experience will be the same as your last one. "A coward dies many times before his death," Shakespeare wrote. "The brave man tastes of death but once." The generalizer needs to fail only once to imagine a million failures thereafter. And those imagined failures are as painful as real ones.

The Path of Imitation

Imitation might well be called the Turkey Lurky effect because it involves adopting—without any examination or questioning—the catastrophic conclusions of others. When Chicken Little ran around screaming that the sky was falling, his barnyard friends just took his word for it. And the tension spread.

Catastrophizers seem to have the ability to transmit their tension to others. We talk about walking into a room in which "you could cut the tension with a knife." The very air seems filled with anxiety. That anxiety is usually brought on by somebody's belief that catastrophe is just around the corner. If you wear a sign that says: "The World Will End Tomorrow," you are bound to convince some people you are right. Yet even if it really were true that some part of the world was about to collapse, that might not be the catastrophe *you* would fear the most. What we view as the worst that could happen is a highly individual matter. For some, catastrophe looms only in matters of love. For others, it involves career. For still others, it has a straight money—or lack of money—definition.

You might think that every resident of San Francisco prone to catastrophize would have moved out of the Bay Area following the last major earthquake, since experts have said that such a quake may well happen again. But no. Not every catastrophizer—even in San Francisco—thinks about the seismic movements of the earth. They may be too busy drawing dire conclusions in the realm of love or career or money or social status or something else quite personal and specific.

The Path of Magnification

You make a mountain out of a molehill. You make a small mistake or have a minor negative experience and assume that it will have major consequences. This is a favorite path of hypochondriacs. The slightest sniffle is viewed as a threat of imminent death. There's a joke told about a hypochondriac who dies at the age of ninety-eight and has inscribed on his tombstone: "See, I told you I was sick."

An old morality tale is told to children to impress upon them the importance of paying attention to details. It begins: "For the want of a nail a shoe was lost." The shoe in question is a horseshoe. The story goes on to relate that as a result of losing its shoe, the horse is lost. Then because the horse is lost, the rider can't get a crucial message through. Because the message is lost, the battle is lost. And because the battle is lost, the kingdom is lost. And all for the want of a nail.

Thinking in Terms of Intermediate Steps

Suppose it was your job to rally troops to battle. One of the soldiers says to you: "We might as well surrender now because a nail fell out of the shoe of the horse the messenger was riding." Could you think of anything to say that might convince him that your side still has a chance? Look at it this way: Do any intermediate steps have to take place between the nail falling out and the kingdom being lost? If so, might the situation be changed at any of these steps?

This is what we know for sure: The nail has fallen out. True, but the shoe may not fall off. There is more than one nail in a horseshoe.

But suppose the shoe does fall off. The horse may be able to get along without it. Not every horse wears horseshoes.

But suppose the horse goes lame and throws the rider. Maybe the rider can pass the message to someone else or find another horse or walk the entire distance in time.

But suppose the message doesn't get through. The soldiers may find a way to win the battle anyway.

But suppose the battle is lost. There might still be a possibility of a counterattack that will save the kingdom.

All this is not to argue that details don't count. Indeed, a single component of a plan may be crucial to that plan. But the critical word here is *may*. It may be crucial. It may not. Realistic thinking means that you don't magnify the results of a single negative event without investigating, challenging, or even giving it a second thought.

Suppose you realize, a day after putting an important set of papers into the mail, that you left out one vital page. You might leap to the conclusion: "It's too late to do anything now. I'm finished." Or you might think: "Oh no. Now I'll have to drive over there with the missing page to make sure the document is complete by the deadline. And I don't have the time to do that." Someone might suggest: "Why not call a messenger service?" If you are still in catastrophe mode, you are likely to answer: "They'll probably charge too much." And that might be true.

But all it would take to determine the charge is a single phone call. Making it a point to check out intermediate steps can help prevent catastrophic thinking from *bringing on catastrophe*.

Protection, Not Destruction

It's reasonable to be self-protective. If you simply assume that nothing can ever happen to you no matter what you do, you may well stroll in front of a moving truck and be run over. If you never go for a medical check-up, you might be allowing a major problem to develop. The issue—as it is for all mistakes in thinking—is whether your thoughts are in proper proportion to the event.

Believing that you can do nothing to help yourself may indeed be realistic in some situations, but as a way of life it leads only to emptiness. It does not allow for building relationships ("There is no point in showing I care because I'll only be rejected"). It doesn't allow for carefully developing solutions ("All my energy is spent crying"). It doesn't allow for finding those steps that might improve your performance and thereby lead you away from disaster the next time.

Believing the worst has happened or is about to happen makes you less functional, less motivated to take action, less able to protect yourself and your loved ones. Conversely, simply giving yourself—and events—the benefit of the doubt will open your mind to possible solutions and opportunities that you would not otherwise see. Taking a small risk can be seen as simply the admission ticket one must buy to bring about success, gratification, and satisfaction.

True protection lies in realistically assessing your situation. True protection lies in being willing to test alternative conclusions. Just a moment's reflection, just pausing long enough to ask yourself a few questions, just taking a brief look before you leap to a negative conclusion can bring about the kind of positive change that lasts a lifetime.

CHAPTER THREE

MIND READING

There, throughout the ages, audiences have paid admission to watch shows in which some "Gonzo the Great" or "Merlin the Magnificent" displays an amazing ability to read minds.

"Concentrate on the playing card you hold in your hand, sir. It's a four of clubs, is it not?"

"Think of an item you have in your purse. You were thinking of your lipstick, madam, isn't that so?"

"Incredible," we say. "Amazing. Unbelievable." If someone asked you to get up on the stage and attempt to describe what a member of the audience was thinking, you'd probably say: "I'm no mind reader. I can't do that."

Deep down, all of us know that mind reading is either impossible or, giving the various Gonzos and Merlins the benefit of the doubt, at least extraordinarily rare—and yet, even while admitting this, it's quite common for people to go through life *acting as if* mind reading were just another physical human ability like breathing or swallowing! Nothing special at all.

It's an illusion that can occur in two ways: (1) *assuming* that we can tell what other people are thinking ("There's no point in my asking for the job, I *know* he would never hire a woman, or someone my age, or me") or (2) *assuming* that other people not only can, but should, know exactly what we are thinking without having to be told ("If she really loved me, she'd have cooked my favorite meal on my birthday. She *knows* that's what I want").

Someone once said that the word *assume* is short for "making an *ass* out of *u* (you) and *me*." A language expert would certainly dispute that. However, the coiner of that whimsical explanation obviously recognized just how common it is to stir up a problem by assuming you can tell what someone else is thinking or by assuming that someone else can and should respond to your unspoken thought.

The Closer the Relationship, the Greater the Illusion

You may say: "I don't claim I know what *everybody* thinks, however I *know* I'm right about what Joe thinks because I know him so well. I know him well enough to know how he will respond."

Or: "I don't claim that everybody knows what I want, but Josephine and I have worked together for years. So, come on, she *knows*."

This is where the illusion that it's possible to read minds wreaks the most havoc, because it's true that you can often anticipate the wishes or actions of someone you know well—and vice versa. But trouble lies in wait if you assume that you can know how someone will react *every time.*

Ellen knows that Jody hates French fries, has hated them all her life. So Ellen would never serve French fries if Jody was coming to dinner. But then one day Ellen and Jody are having lunch together, and Jody orders French fries. "But you hate French fries," exclaims a surprised Ellen. "I always have," replies Jody, "but the fries this place makes are really special. A friend convinced me to give them a try, and I've been eating them here ever since."

This sort of thing happens with great frequency. When you know someone well, it's possible to make informed guesses that will be right much of the time—maybe even most of the time. But even with someone you know very well you cannot count on being right all the time. People have a way of being unpredictable. It's always possible that people you think you know very well will decide to change their minds—even if only on one occasion for one particular reason. It's also possible that you don't know those other people as well you think you do. People also have a way of keeping little pieces of themselves secret—even from their nearest and dearest.

Here's an example of how the two forms of mind reading can work *together* to cause trouble between two people who know each other very well indeed.

Rachel returns home from work before her husband, Tom, arrives. She leaves Tom a note, telling him that she is going to the supermarket and will be back within an hour. When she returns, laden down with packages, she sees Tom's car in the driveway, so she assumes he is home. As Rachel carries the groceries into the kitchen, she enters an anger spiral and becomes increasingly upset.

"Why isn't he here helping me?" she says to herself. "He knows I went to the supermarket. He knows I've worked all day just as he has. But what does he care? He's sitting in the living room now, relaxing and reading the paper, while I struggle. He doesn't care about anybody but himself."

Rachel says all this to *herself*. She isn't saying this to Tom. She does not, for example, call out to him: "Honey, could you give me a hand with these packages, please?" She expects Tom to read her mind. She expects that he will know, intuitively, without being asked, that she would like his help. And she is angry because Tom has failed to fulfill her unspoken wishes and expectations. She would like Tom to be clairvoyant.

Further, she believes she has correctly read *his* mind. She assumes Tom is saying to himself: "She'd like me to come help her, but I don't feel like it, so I'm going to pretend I don't hear her."

Rachel would argue that mind reading is not involved here at all. She would say: "I left him a note saying I was going to the supermarket, and that means coming home with packages to unload. He doesn't have to be a mind reader to realize that I would need and want help. Of course he is ignoring me."

However, it could be that Tom, absorbed in the news, really hasn't heard Rachel come in and so is *unaware* that his help is needed right now. Or it could be that, in the past, Tom offered to help lug bundles but Rachel said then: "Never mind, I can handle it. You just relax and enjoy your paper." So he reads *her* mind on this occasion and gets that same response.

It could also be that despite the evidence of the car in the driveway, Tom is not at home sitting on the couch, reading the paper. Maybe their next-door neighbor asked Tom to help with something, and Tom is there.

If Rachel had called out: "Tom, I'm home. Would you give me a hand with these packages?" and he had replied: "No, I prefer to sit here with my paper while you do all the work," *then* Rachel's anger would be reasonable.

The bottom line is that Rachel cannot *know* what Tom is thinking unless she asks him. He cannot *know* what she is thinking unless she tells him. When you merely assume, you take a chance that your assumptions are wrong.

Why We Make Assumptions

Everyone makes assumptions about the thoughts, wishes, and needs of others to some extent. And just as well, too. Making assumptions is a form of mental shorthand—and it's extremely helpful in keeping life moving along. If you investigated the implications of every smile, wink, and wave sent in your direction; cross-examined the writer of every note, memo, and form letter sent your way; or challenged the meaning of every casual expression you hear, you would be weary indeed at the end of the day—and the people you dealt with would be weary of you.

Maybe you've heard the joke about the psychiatrist who meets a friend on the street. The friend says hello and the psychiatrist immediately ponders: "Now what did he *really* mean by that?" In fact, as a self-protective device, psychologists and psychiatrists learn how to turn off their professional ear in purely social situations so that they are not constantly pondering: "What did he really mean by that?" If they did not do this, they would be overwhelmed by the problems of the human condition. So one psychiatrist meeting another on the street would likely assume that hello just means hello, knowing that such an assumption is probably correct. Just as most of the time when you make assumptions about what others expect from you or they make assumptions about what you expect from them, those assumptions are probably correct.

Or, if not correct, at least they are harmless—not worth making any kind of fuss about. A doting aunt watches a newborn baby in his crib and says: "Oh, look, he's smiling at me." She's wrong. Smiling is a learned social response. It's not a response that babies are born with. What the baby is doing is grimacing because he has gas and hasn't burped it up—quite a normal situation for babies. But the doting aunt prefers to mind read pleasure instead of pain.

Doting pet owners are inclined to endow their birds and animals with human attributes and read their minds accordingly. "Poor Fido is sad because he didn't get to run in the park today." Some people even attribute human intellect to furniture. You know the kind of thing. You bump into a chair and jokingly say: "Excuse me" to it—or you bump into the chair twice and complain: "That chair is out to get me." Now you are "mind reading" the chair.

All this is part and parcel of life. It's normal. But it's *not* mind reading—not even when you are correct in your conclusions about what another human is thinking. It's more a matter of good detective work—of noting cues and clues and drawing conclusions from them. Most of us can read cues and clues pretty well and, most of the time, they are available to be read.

Cues and Clues

We draw from all sorts of cues and clues in our detecting efforts. We attribute meaning to what we see and hear—as well as to

what we *don't* see and hear—and to what has and hasn't happened. We draw conclusions from body language (facial expressions, gestures, and postures) as well as from verbal statements.

When you were a child and your mother greeted you at the
door with her arms folded across her chest, her foot tapping, her
brow furrowed, and her lips in a straight line, you probably said
to yourself: "Mom's angry." She didn't have to say a word.

If you came upon a friend whose chin seemed to be dragging
on the floor, whose shoulders were slumped, whose eyes were
puffy and cheeks tearstained, how difficult would it be to conclude she is upset? Unless, of course, she is an actress playing a
part. We sense when someone seems glum, or nervous, or
happy, or any other mood because—well—that's how they look.

But looks can be deceiving. Just as a small baby's grimace may
be mistaken for a smile, the same is true with adults. A nervous
laugh is not a sign of amusement. Tears may flow from disappointment or happiness. Some people are more open about what
they are thinking than others. They wear their hearts on their
sleeves, their thoughts on their faces. But others are not as
obvious—or not obvious all the time.

When we draw conclusions from spoken language, we not
only evaluate the words but also the tone of voice, the emphasis,
the volume (loud or soft), and the context of the situation. The
simple word *oh* might convey awe or surprise or disappointment
or simply a temporary inability to think of something else to say.

A speaker breaks the ice at a seminar by claiming he will read
the mind of someone in the audience. He appears to concentrate
and then says: "Same to you, fella" or "Sorry, I'm a married
man." That gets a laugh because the audience is able to fill in
what he hasn't said: He is implying that someone in the audience
has had a negative thought about him, or someone in the audience has had a positive sexual thought about him.

We draw conclusions from familiar situations. Take, for example, a woman walking down the sidewalk, lugging bundles.
One of them starts slipping from her grasp. She would need
three hands to hold everything. So you reach out and help her.
She didn't ask for your help. But you know—or are pretty

sure—she wants it. When she thanks you—the response you expected—it confirms the accuracy of your conclusion. That doesn't mean you read her mind.

We draw conclusions based on the background of the person we are attempting to mind read. This isn't a terrain crossed only by bigots who jump to negative conclusions about others based on race, creed, sex, or national background. It is often just another clue. You might interpret a situation differently if, for example, the person involved is a grandmother rather than a teenager, or if the person looks rich rather than poor.

Possibly the best illustration of group "mind reading" comes from Madison Avenue. There is, in the world of advertising, a well-known theory that divides all Americans into different groups based on their supposed lifestyles. For example, two of these groups are called the belongers and the achievers. Belongers are defined as middle-class Americans who want more than anything else to do the accepted thing. Therefore, an advertiser who wants to sell a product to people in this group would be well-advised to stress that the product is the most popular. That same pitch would not work with a group of achievers, defined as financially successful people who want to buy the top of the line. Achievers, so the theory goes, would not want to buy the most popular product because they know *most* people can't afford to buy the top of the line. For them, popular isn't good enough.

An example of how this particular theory is put into practice can be seen in advertising campaigns for the financial firm of Merrill Lynch, whose slogan is: "We're bullish on America." (In Wall Street jargon, to be bullish is to be optimistic.)

At one time, Merrill Lynch had a TV ad that showed a herd of bulls running. Arnold Mitchell, the researcher who developed the theory that differentiates between belongers and achievers (among others), argued that this herd image was all wrong for an ad designed to attract wealthy investors. "A herd is a belonger symbol," he said. "Rich people with money to invest don't want to think of themselves as one of a herd. They want to think of themselves as achievers." If you have seen recent Merrill Lynch ads on TV, you know that the company has heeded Mitchell's advice. One 1991 ad showed a lone bull (an achiever) pushing its way through a herd of sheep (an achiever's view of belongers).

Mitchell never claimed he had the ability to read the minds of all rich people, or that all persons who fall into his category of achiever think exactly the same way. He said only that given the research he has done into the habits of various groups of people, he is more likely to be right than wrong about them most of the time.

The Closure Phenomenon

And maybe that is true for you, too. But it's important to remember that no matter how we go about assembling the evidence from which we draw conclusions, one thing about them is almost always true—they provide only a *partial* picture. Our brain then plays Sherlock Holmes and fills in the missing pieces for us. This is a phenomenon of perception called closure.

Consider the following drawing. It's a partial picture of a simple shape. What is that shape?

Would you say a circle? That's definitely a possibility. A circle would contain those parts. On the other hand, it might also be a half moon, or a drawing of an ice cream cone lying on its side:

Obviously, the more clues you see, the more accurate your guess
is likely to be.

The popular TV show "Wheel of Fortune," based on the old
paper and pencil game Hangman, puts its contestants' closure
abilities to the test. The challenge is to guess a phrase that is first
revealed only as a series of blanks, indicating how many words
are in the phrase and how many letters are in each word. The
contestants get chances to guess the letters, and the first to guess
the entire phrase wins.

For example:

What's this word?   B E A _ S

Is it Beans? Bears? Beats? Beads? Beaks? Beams?

Does this help?

_ _ _ _ _ _ _ _ _ S A _ _ _ _ E _ _ R E E B E A _ S?

Or this?

_ _ _ _ _ _ _ _ _ S A _ _ T H E T H _ E E B E A _ S?

Or this?

G _ _ D I _ _ C K S A _ _ T H E T H _ E E B E A _ S?

Got it yet?

G O L D I L O C K S A _ _ T H E T H _ E E B E A _ S?

Obviously, the more clues you have, the easier it becomes to make a guess—if "Goldilocks and the Three Bears" was a tale you grew up with as a child. (And also presuming that in the version of the tale you grew up with, the heroine was called Goldilocks. Familiar tales change titles as they make their way from culture to culture. The story that Americans call "Hansel and Gretel," for example, is known as "Hans og Greta" in Norway.)

Misreading the Evidence

The better you know someone, the more aware you are likely to be of that person's special messages. Does he slam the door when he's had a tough day? Does she lick her lips when she's in the mood for Chinese food? Possibly you know that when your favorite uncle makes a certain kind of face he is suffering from indigestion—because that's how he always looks when he has indigestion. You detect a clue and say: "Aha!"

Given the multitude of clues available—and how frequently it is possible to fill in the blanks and come up with the right answer, to make informed guesses that seem to reach a lot of people where they live—it's not surprising that so many people take it for granted that they know what another thinks, and feel certain that someone else knows what they are thinking.

And that can mean trouble.

Remember: Mind reading gets us into trouble when we believe it is something we can do

- with everybody
- perfectly
- all the time

What you actually can do is to guess the thoughts of

- some people
- with some accuracy
- some of the time

When You Get the Wrong Message

Let's list some of the most common ways people who assume they know what is in another's mind can go wrong.

You draw a conclusion about what someone else is thinking based on what you would think in that same position.

A large city newspaper has an opening in its Washington bureau, and members of the staff are buzzing with guesses about which of their number will be picked for that plum assignment. There is general agreement that it will be one of the three stars of the staff: the state capital correspondent, the city hall bureau chief, or the top investigative reporter. And so it comes as a surprise when the managing editor names Rick, a relative newcomer to the staff. When the managing editor is asked how he arrived at his decision, he replies: "Rick was the only one who applied for the job." The reporters who had been sure they knew the boss was thinking: "I'll pick one of my top people" came to that conclusion because that's how *they* thought the choice should be made. In fact, the boss was thinking: "I'll make my choice from among those who indicate they want the job."

You draw a conclusion based on past behavior.

When she opens the door to meet her child, a mother has crossed arms, a furrowed brown, tightened lips and a tapping foot. The child reaches the conclusion that Mom is angry with her because, in the past, whenever Mom has looked like that she *has* been angry. Past experience is certainly an excellent source of good information. But it is important to remember that no source is infallible. Perhaps, on this occasion, Mom is angry—but not with the child. Or Mom is anxious about something that has nothing to do with the child.

You reach your conclusion based on what you expect—having written the end of the story first.

Hal is hesitant to ask Steve for help with a project at work. Steve has the experience that Hal lacks, but Hal doesn't know Steve well. Hal feels insecure about his position. He knows he has nothing to offer Steve in return except gratitude. He says to himself: "He'll never do it. I know he doesn't want to help me." But he steels himself and makes the request. Steve replies: "I'd like to help you, but I can't do it right now. I have to finish up a project I'm working on."

"Well," thinks Hal. "I know what *that* means. I knew he didn't want to help me. I'm sorry I asked, and I'll never bother him again."

Hal may be right in concluding that Steve has merely offered a more polite version of no. On the other hand, it could be that Hal is only hearing what he concluded *in advance* he would hear. Possibly Steve is simply telling the truth: He hasn't time *right now* but will have time later. Or possibly, for some reason, Steve doesn't want to become involved with this particular project—but, if asked, he would be more than willing to help on another.

Here is another example:

Lisa has been coaxed to a party by a close friend. "There is no point in my going," Lisa thinks. "I never meet anybody at these things. I'll be sitting by myself feeling foolish while everybody else is having a great time. I hate these parties. I always come home feeling worse than before."

Having thus already concluded that the evening will prove a disaster, Lisa interprets all cues and clues accordingly. A young man smiles in her direction. "He must be looking at somebody over my shoulder," thinks Lisa, carefully keeping her eyes averted. And, of course, it might be true that Brooke Shields is standing behind Lisa and drawing the young man's smile. On the other hand, it might also be true that, despite Lisa's low expectations, *this time* the young man is smiling at *her.*

You may draw a conclusion based on what you want the answer to be.

Tom receives a phone call from his former girlfriend Annette. She says a mutual friend told her that his father had died
and she is calling to offer her condolences. "She still loves me,"
thinks Tom. "Calling me proves that. She is only marrying that
other guy to hurt me."

Maybe, but maybe not. Before Tom rushes off to buy an
engagement ring, he'd be well advised to check Annette's feelings further.

You draw a conclusion based on insufficient data.

Just as two curves do not necessarily make a circle, the negative reaction of one or two people does not necessarily indicate
the opinion of an entire group.

"Women don't like me" mourns Max. How does he know?
He had two unsuccessful dates. Little did those two women
know that they were representing every woman in the world.

Betty was nervous about speaking to a professional group—
she'd never done anything that ambitious before. And no sooner
had she begun than she saw two members of the group nod off.
One's head literally dropped onto his chest. "I bored them
silly," she thought afterward. "They think I'm a dolt."

But everyone hadn't fallen asleep. Maybe those two had been
up late the night before. Maybe they wouldn't have been interested in the topic no matter who the speaker was. And if, indeed,
her speech was less than a rousing success—did that prove the
audience thought her a dolt? They might also have been sympathetic, remembering some less successful speaking efforts of
their own.

*Your conclusion ignores the existence of cultural or personality
differences.*

Movie maker Woody Allen based his movie *Annie Hall* on
the existence of such differences. In one split-screen scene, Annie
and boyfriend Alvy are having dinner with their respective parents. Annie's family is proper and quiet. Alvy's family (who live
under a roller coaster at Coney Island) are emotional personali-
ties who have to scream at one another to be heard. It's easy to

conclude that Annie's family would consider Alvy's family unstable, while Alvy's family would consider Annie's family aloof and dull. No wonder this couple has problems communicating their feelings to each other.

They have other problems, too. In another split-screen scene, Annie and Alvy are talking to their respective psychiatrists. His therapist asks him: "Do you often sleep together?" Alvy replies: "Hardly ever. Maybe three times a week. Annie's therapist asks her, "Do you have sex often?" And she replies: "Constantly. Three times a week."

You are misreading visual or verbal clues.

As mentioned before, many emotional reactions look alike. Tom thinks Rachel is angry at him. Her lips are clamped in a thin line. Her body is visibly tense. Absent is her usual cheery hello.

Tom's first reaction is guilt. "She's still mad because I didn't help her with the groceries yesterday." His second reaction is anger: "How was I supposed to know she wanted my help? She's making too big a deal of this."

If this time, instead of mind reading, Tom asks Rachel: "Is something wrong?" she might just say: "Yes. I've had a terrible day. I'm exhausted, and I have a splitting headache."

In other words, just because you may correctly read the mood does not mean you have correctly guessed the cause. Even if you have correctly guessed the cause in the past, that does not mean you are right *this time*.

The object of your mind reading is sending false messages.

Just as detectives in murder mysteries are sometimes misled by red herrings—false clues left to mislead them—would-be mind readers can also be led astray. Haven't we all experienced the politician or salesperson who exudes concern only about our welfare—when actually pursuing a more self-serving goal?

People sometimes lie with the best of intentions. Richard dresses to the nines to impress his date, Jill—only later will she learn that he rarely changes out of his favorite jeans and flannel shirt. Jill pretends to love baseball because she wants to impress

Richard—only later will he discover that she'd much rather go to the ballet.

When They Get the Wrong Message

Since mind reading is a two-way illusion, there are also ample ways that others can fail to grasp what you think.

You have not made yourself clear, verbally or any other way.

All of the reasons that mind reading doesn't always work for you apply equally to your expectations that it works for others—at least where you are concerned:

- They may have a different idea of what you want to do, based on what they would want to do in your place.
- They may not realize you have changed your mind, that you want something now that you didn't request before.
- They may have written the end of the story first, and need some encouragement from you to rewrite it.
- They may simply assume the answer they want to hear.
- They may be filling in clues you haven't provided or misreading clues you have provided. Or maybe they simply aren't very good at detecting.
- Maybe, for the most noble of reasons, you have been misleading.

You are sending your message in a code the other person cannot understand.

A *Wall Street Journal* report on a service called Chef's Hotline told of a woman who asked its cooking experts for help in preparing a meal. Her husband's friends were coming to town, she said, and she wanted to prepare correctly a meal they would dislike. She didn't like these friends, and she wanted to send them a coded message that would discourage a repeat visit—without directly insulting them.

Therapists call this passive-aggressive behavior. The message sender is afraid to confront an issue directly and so conveys feelings in some kind of code.

The problem with this is that the recipient of such a message may not understand it. Such was the case with a couple who ate Shake 'n Bake coated chicken every night for ten years. The wife told a marriage counselor that she cooked just once a week—the same dish—and simply warmed up a portion each night. Why? the counselor asked. The wife said she was angry because her husband insisted that it was her duty to cook every single night. "He wants me to cook—let him eat the same thing," she said. She wanted to hurt him (even at the cost of hurting herself at the same time, since she would have preferred a more varied diet). She wanted him to ask her why she was doing this. But he never did. Finally, the counselor asked the husband: "Why did you never complain?" And the man replied simply: "I like Shake 'n Bake chicken. It comes in so many different, wonderful flavors."

Although a hostile action is a common means of sending in code, it is far from the only way. Here's another very common example: Jill is feeling depressed and in need of a diversion to take her mind off her troubles. She'd like to go to the movies. She asks Rich: "Do you want to go to the movies?" Rich takes the question at face value and gives a straight answer: "No, I'd rather stay home." Jill, assuming that Rich understood that her question *really* meant: *"Please* take me to the movies," concludes that Rich doesn't care about her feelings. When she then shows her anger, Rich gets angry in turn. "How am I supposed to know?" he asks. And it's not a silly question.

When you send a message in code, you can't be sure the other person can decipher it. If, when asked what you would like for your birthday, you coyly reply: "Something warm and furry"— thinking of a mink coat—you may find that the same words also accurately describe a pet kitten.

In this matter of expecting others to know what we are thinking, movies and literature have a lot to answer for. So many of them fuel this expectation—particularly where it concerns those closest to us:

- "One touch and I knew."
- "I could see it in his eyes."
- "Ned, you darling. I love being surprised and it is just what I wanted."
- "He didn't answer the telephone and he knew I was going to call. There is no other explanation for it, sergeant . . . he's dead."
- "A mother always knows."

In real life, it may take a few words in addition to a touch, it may take action as well as a look, the surprise may be that he didn't know what you wanted, the explanation may be that he went out to buy a newspaper, and a mother knows quite often—but not always.

Why It's Difficult to Give Up the Mind Reading Mistake

The first step in improving your ability to communicate without relying on mind reading is the most difficult: You must surrender your belief in mind reading.

It's difficult because, as explained earlier, you probably do size up others—and find that others are able to read you—with a fair degree of efficiency some of the time. It's difficult to give up because it means taking more risk—becoming more vulnerable. *Mind reading avoids the need to speak up, to go on the record, to put yourself on the line, and maybe even to find out that the bad news you suspect is true, really is true.*

You may find it more comfortable to think: "He's insensitive to my needs" than to expose your needs and be rejected.

You may find it more comfortable to think the boss is a jerk for not realizing you want that job than to ask the boss for the job and risk being turned down.

You may find it more comfortable to think: "He knew that I didn't want that assignment and would have trouble with it" than to confront the issue head-on and maybe face a discussion on other aspects of your job as well.

You may find it more romantic to expect another person to know what you want. Maybe you enjoy thinking that love is never having to put anything into words. You feel sure that if the person you love simply loved you *enough*, this ability would come.

You may not want to face the fact that some people really *are* stupid or selfish or uncaring.

You may feel it is less embarrassing to read the critical thoughts in other people's minds rather than to have to actually listen to them.

In short, you may feel that mind reading is self-protective behavior—you absorb a measure of hurt to avoid even greater pain.

The problem with this is that you may very well be protecting yourself out of your heart's desire. That is, by not checking, not analyzing, not speaking up, you, in effect, turn yourself down before anyone else actually gets the chance to do it. You may find it more romantic to send out erotic signals—dinner by candlelight—than to put your feelings into words. But if your partner fails to read those signals correctly, you may well translate that response into the very unromantic message: She doesn't care for me. If your mind reading is incorrect—or your "vibes" are not sending as strong a signal as you think—you may be denying yourself all kinds of positive reactions.

Unless you are willing to admit that you may be reading a given situation wrong, you do not give yourself a chance to (1) get an answer much more to your liking, or (2) at least get an accurate reading of your situation so that, if necessary, you can do something to change it.

Once you are willing to accept the fact that mind reading does not always work, you are well on the way to knowing better *when it matters*—as opposed to realizing only when it's too late that you misread obvious clues, or that you leaped too quickly to fill in the blanks, or that you failed to offer a cue that another needed.

Naming the Problem

In coping with the mistake of mind reading, as with all other mistakes cited in this book, a first line of defense is simply to identify the mistake. This is a technique known as labeling. It is the goal of this book not only to describe the ten dumbest thinking mistakes so that you can determine if and when you make them, but also to enable you to give each mistake a name. It is often possible to stop your automatic thoughts from running away with you by the simple act of labeling your thinking pattern.

When you find yourself becoming angry at someone for something you believe he is thinking, before you confront him, you might ask yourself: "Am I mind reading? Do I really know what he is thinking?"

Questioning Your Assumptions

Labeling helps you to question your assumptions. If you catch yourself mind reading, you can go on to check out whether what you think another thinks is true.

Here again, as with every thinking mistake, it helps to write down your assumptions if you can. Writing your thoughts makes it easier to analyze them. When you write something down, you often find that simply seeing it in black and white causes you to change your conclusion.

Here's an example:

Bonnie is upset because she believes her boss thinks she is incompetent. She finds herself unable to concentrate on her work because that thought keeps running through her mind. She is getting angrier and angrier because she feels the boss is being unjust.

Bonnie is fortunate because she has just finished reading this chapter and so she asks herself: "Am I mind reading?" She stops, gets out a pencil and paper, and writes down exactly what she thinks her boss thinks: "He thinks I am incompetent."

Next, she writes down the meaning she ascribes to this. That is, what it is about that thought that upsets her so: "If he thinks I'm incompetent, it means I'm not succeeding in my job. There is no point in making an effort because I won't get anywhere."

Finally, she asks herself: "How do I know what he thinks? And she writes her answer to that question: "After all the work I did on that report, he never said one word to me. He walked past my desk as if I weren't there."

Bonnie is now ready to do some analysis. Particularly useful here is a trio of techniques known as *developing alternatives in thought, developing alternatives in feeling,* and *developing alternatives in action.*

Developing alternatives in thought means asking the question: "Can you think of any alternative explanations for the behavior?"

It's true that one explanation for Bonnie's boss's behavior is that he doesn't value her work. But she realizes she does not know that for sure. He did not compliment her, but he did not comment negatively either. Could there be any other alternative explanation for his actions—or lack of them? Bonnie might ask herself: "Am I the only person in the office to whom he does not give feedback on a report? Does he say hello to everyone else as he passes their desks?"

If the answers are no, an alternative explanation may be that this boss has a mind reading management style. He expects his subordinates to know he likes their work without actually telling them so. Another possibility might be that he is under pressure because of some other project and simply is not thinking of Bonnie's project now.

Developing alternatives in feeling means asking the question: "Is it possible for me to react to the lack of comment in a different way?"

Bonnie can reason with herself thusly: "As long as I assume that his failure to mention my report is deliberate, I'm going to stay angry and upset. Since I don't know that for sure, I might well assume that he has troubles of his own that are weighing on his mind. That makes me feel curious and concerned more than hurt." Or she might say to herself: "The man is a complete jerk. His opinion is not worth getting upset about."

As Bonnie considers these alternatives in thought and feeling, she also mentally changes the meaning she has ascribed to her original conclusion. If he has other problems that are diverting him or if he is a jerk, then his lack of comment does not mean she is failing at her job.

Developing alternatives in action means asking: "Is there something I can do (other than sit and stew) to get a better fix on this situation?"

Bonnie may decide to ask for a conference with the boss. She might check just to make sure the report was received. Or she might simply admit to herself that since there is no way of knowing what the boss thinks, she might as well dismiss the matter from her mind until she gets better information.

Admittedly, many people find this last action difficult. They will ask: "How do you *know* that he is *not* thinking I'm incompetent? How can you be *sure* that his lack of comment doesn't mean exactly what I *think* it means?

It's true that no one but the boss can be *sure* of what he is thinking since he has not said anything either way. Bonnie's initial negative conclusions about his opinion of her may be correct. But the point is that since the boss has not *said* what he thinks, alternative conclusions are *equally valid*. Bonnie gains nothing by making herself miserable *before* she has any real evidence that she has something to be miserable about.

Testing a Perception

It would be helpful indeed if it were always possible to check out a mind reading conclusion by simply asking the person. But sometimes that particular alternative is simply not available. However, it may be possible to test your perception in small ways.

For example, Robert is attracted to a young woman he sees

at a party, but he thinks that she thinks he won't be good enough for her. Fearful of rejection, he can't bring himself to go over to her and ask her to dance. Yet, he doesn't *know* for sure that he will be rejected. What can he do?

- He might try smiling at her to see if she smiles back.
- He might try asking a friend to introduce him to her.
- He might try starting a casual conversation, using an introductory remark he has practiced for just such occasions. (For example: "I have difficulty finding the right thing to say at parties like this." She is likely to say "Me too," since feeling awkward at parties is such a widespread phenomenon.)

Developing a Replacement Image

Robert might also try a technique known as *developing a replacement image*. Because Robert feels awkward at parties, he expects the women he meets there to reject him. That's his image of himself and his image of them. Thus, he tends to read the expression on the faces of the women he meets as indicating rejection. He is sure he knows what they think—so he doesn't have to ask. And consciously or not, he is probably projecting signals that hint to others that he expects rejection and is resigned to it. This can become a self-fulfilling prophecy if that's how they read his mind.

In such situations, it can be helpful to imagine a different image for yourself and others. Picture yourself having a good time. Picture yourself meeting others. Picture others meeting you and enjoying the experience. Practice projecting this image. Perhaps a friend will let you know how you are coming across. Or you can study yourself in a mirror. Practice enhances performance. So the more you practice looking as if you are enjoying yourself, the more likely it is that when you get an opportunity, you do enjoy yourself. More than that, if others are going to read your mind, give them something positive to read. Self-fulfilling prophecies can work two ways.

Speaking Your Mind

On occasion, however, giving up the mind reading mistake means speaking up in a direct way. If you would like information, you must request it. If you want something, you must say so. No hints, no codes, no body language, but clear, spoken language.

Marie says: "I find smoking offensive. Doesn't that man at the next table realize how annoying his smoke is to people?" What she means is: "Doesn't he realize how annoying his smoke is to me?" The answer may be: No, he doesn't.

Marie might say: "Excuse me, sir, but I am very bothered by smoke. Would you mind not smoking until you get outside?" At which point the man will either graciously extinguish his cigarette or not so graciously tell her that he'll smoke if he darn well wants to and if she doesn't like it, she can leave. Obviously, then, it can't be said that speaking up will *guarantee* that Marie will get the result she desires. But only by speaking up does Marie make it possible for that result to occur. This is a situation in which not speaking up guarantees that she will continue to breathe smoke.

It's possible that you have to deal with someone who does not like being approached directly—it makes them feel pressured. You might say: "Where I work, if I specifically asked for a particular job, I'd guarantee that I wouldn't get it." But are you *sure* about that? Or are you mind reading? You could take steps to check this perception, such as:

- Ask the person in charge whether she would like staff members to let her know if they are interested in a particular job opening.
- Ask colleagues about past experience in this regard.
- Ask for the job, having decided to take the risk of being turned down. (After all, there is no guarantee that you will get the job if you *don't* ask, is there?)

Most people would much prefer to win a contest without having to go through the bother of entering it, but that's not the way things generally work. Yes, there are times when we are recognized or rewarded without having to ask—but you can't always count on it. Speaking your mind doesn't mean you have to be blunt, nasty, demanding, unromantic, or unwilling to negotiate. It doesn't mean accusing another person of wronging you. It means just saying something like:

- "I'd like it if you bought me flowers."
- "Honey, can you give me a hand with these packages?"
- "Mr. Smith, I want you to know that, if it's possible, I'd be interested in working on that project."
- "Ms. Jones, I heard there was a position open in your firm. I'd like to come talk to you about it."
- "Dear, could we do some advance dinner planning so I'll know not to eat for lunch what we'll be eating for dinner?"
- "I've had a terrible day. I could use some sympathy."

Reading Your Own Mind

In this, as with just about every decision you make in life, you have to consider the advantages and disadvantages of alternative ways of reacting. If you feel more comfortable going with your gut feelings than speaking up or making an effort to find out what others are thinking, you must accept the consequences of sometimes being wrong. If you would rather be surprised with a gift than tell the gift giver exactly what you'd like, that's fine. But if you get angry or hurt when the surprise is not the one you had mentally ordered, then perhaps surprise is not as important to you as you thought. The most important mind to read is your own.

CHAPTER FOUR

PERSONALIZING

Someone once said that if you ask a man: "Where did you get that steak?" he'll reply: "At the supermarket." If you ask a woman, she'll reply: "Why? Is there something the matter with it?" Supposedly a woman would interpret that perfectly inno-cent question as a personal attack on either her shopping or cooking abilities because, traditionally, food purchasing and preparation were strictly female responsibilities.

The further implication of that story is that only women make the personalizing mistake. Not so. Like all the other mis-takes cited in this book, personalizing is an equal opportunity error. The man who can be totally objective when discussing steak may not feel equally objective when the subject under discussion is his favorite football team. After all, the stereotype of men is that they are all crazy about sports. ("You insult the Cowboys, you insult me. How would you like to step outside and repeat that remark?")

Personalizing simply means interpreting the comments, ques-tions, and behavior of others as attacks on your worth as a human being, or on your looks, ability or domain. It can be said of personalizing, as with other thinking mistakes, that when used in a balanced and realistic way, it is both normal and helpful, but when it goes awry, it causes difficulty and emotional pain.

If you pass two strangers in the street and hear one of them laugh, there are two possible interpretations: (1) You can take that laugh personally. That is, you can *assume* that, for some reason, one stranger has made some crack about you that makes his partner laugh. (2) You can hear that laugh as a neutral comment. Probably one of the strangers has made an amusing remark to the other that has nothing to do with you.

One Remark—Varied Reactions

Here is an example of how personalizing works:

The teacher stands in front of the class and says: "Some of you have not been working very hard to learn this material."

"She means me," thinks Ellen.

The teacher has not mentioned Ellen by name. She is speaking generally to everyone and anyone in the class who has not been working very hard. If the shoe fits Ellen, then she has good reason to believe she is among those to whom the message is directed. And if that message convinces her to devote more time to studying, she may well benefit from it.

But consider this scenario: Ellen has been working very hard in this class. But because she assumes that the teacher is speaking about her, the comment makes her feel resentful.

"She means me. How unfair! I've actually worked harder than anybody else. What's the point of knocking yourself out if your efforts not only aren't noticed, but you get criticized as well? I'm discouraged. I might as well quit trying."

Here the harm in Ellen's personalizing is evident. By failing to screen out criticism when it does not apply to her, Ellen has suffered a wound from a shot that was never aimed her way. She's hurt. She's angry. She's disgusted. And she's wrong.

Maybe not, you might argue. What if the teacher really did mean to include Ellen in her criticism? What if she doesn't realize how hard Ellen has been working? What if she really *is* being unfair?

Ellen is still better off if she does not take the criticism personally. She knows the teacher is saying something that is not true even if the teacher does not. Recognizing the situation for what it is will help Ellen choose the proper strategy for dealing with it. And that could range from simply ignoring the comment since it does not apply to her to finding a way to be sure the teacher knows of her efforts.

Finally, there is still one more possible reaction here.

This teacher's comment is not the only one Ellen has taken personally, and as a result she feels she has gotten more than her share of unfair insults and criticism. That has led her to become prickly, defensive, quick to protect herself from more of the same. She has become so self-protective, in fact, that she not only rejects criticism that doesn't apply to her, she also rejects criticism that *does* apply to her.

Let us say that Ellen has *not* been working hard and that, to pass this course, she must make a greater effort. However, instead of thinking: "She's right, I'd better stop fooling around and hit those books," Ellen thinks: "Here we go again. Teachers are always dumping on me. I don't have to put up with that kind of treatment. I don't care what she says."

In sum, depending on how Ellen *interprets* the teacher's remark, she may

- decide to work harder—and possibly to do even better.
- ignore the remark because it doesn't apply to her,
- become so resentful and discouraged by it that she gives up trying, or
- reject the timely warning and flunk the course.

Me-Scanning

When out meeting and greeting the voters, former New York mayor Edward Koch liked to shout out: "How am I doing?" His enthusiastic supporters would yell back: "Great," while his critics, of course, yelled something else.

Not everybody asks the question out loud as Mayor Koch

did, but all of us ask it. We monitor our acceptance, our approval rating, our reception as keenly as any politician among us does. We tend to be on the alert for rivals and enemies, the better to defend ourselves against them. We tend to be watchful of the responses of our loved ones, the better to respond to them. In a myriad of ways we constantly ask: "How am I doing?"

If this trait were a machine it could be called the Me-Scanner —its function to scan constantly for negative opinions about "me." The Me-Scanner is a sensitive mechanism. It has to be adjusted just right.

If set too low, it will miss vital information. You wouldn't want to know someone who has zero ability to recognize or be affected by criticism. The name for such a person is psychopath. No guilt. No feeling. No sense of responsibility. The world would be a terrible place if we took nothing personally.

If set too high, the Me-Scanner antennas will quiver all the time. They will detect insults and personal rejection everywhere. You may have heard of spy satellites that can reveal the brand of vodka a Russian leader is drinking a hundred miles away. That is nothing. Some personalizers have Me-Scanners that can spot the exact nature of an intended insult a thousand miles away.

But, most important to remember, this internal sensing device is so sensitive that just increasing your level of personalizing a little bit can cause all kinds of distress.

The Results of Taking It Personally

What kind of distress?

Personalizing leads to unnecessary hurt feelings.

When you perceive an insult where none was meant, the pain you feel is self-inflicted.

For example: Your friend asks you to join her for a lunch at a new vegetarian restaurant, and you think: "This is her way of saying I'm too fat and ought to go on a diet."

Is it possible that your friend is, in fact, sending you a coded message? Yes. But it is also possible that your friend simply wants to try out a new restaurant and would like your company. Unless and until you know which is the case, assuming the former rather than the latter results only in pain, in weakening a friendship, and in reducing the pleasure of having lunch with a friend. This is a case of combining two thinking errors: mind reading and personalizing. You read your friend's mind in a way that makes her remark a personal insult.

Marian's mother-in-law tells a story about her neighbor, Mary. Marian hears the story and thinks: "She really means me. She says Mary, but she means Marian." Why does Marian think this? Because she is insecure about how her mother-in-law feels about her and so she is scanning for negatives. Sooner or later she is going to find one. It causes a rift between Marian and her mother-in-law that the mother-in-law does not understand.

Personalizing keeps anger alive.

Hurt leads to anger. And thus by reviewing your perceived hurt—and constantly replenishing it with other personalizing "evidence"—you nourish your anger and keep it alive and active. You may reveal this by a tendency to bring up past incidents in arguments.

At Marian's wedding, her mother-in-law asked her son, Marian's new husband, to round up members of the family for a photo. "Get your brother, get Uncle Dan, find Aunt Theresa . . ." Marian felt slighted because her mother-in-law did not specifically list her among members of the family.

Her mother-in-law later explained that she simply took it for granted that the bride and groom would be in every picture. But to Marian, that incident was evidence that her husband's mother did not accept her. "I know how your mother feels about me," Marian tells her protesting husband. "She didn't want me in the family picture at my own wedding."

Personalizing wastes energy.

If you tend to take things personally, you probably spend a vast amount of energy scanning for potential problems and agonizing over wounds that either are really not there or are not serious.

When you feel you have been insulted, you may well do more than just seethe and feel resentful. You may devote time and energy to deciding what to do about it. Can you rebuff it? Can you counterattack? Should you counterattack? If no insult was meant, obviously all these internal dialogues are wasted.

And such dialogues are upsetting. Personalizers tend to record every conversation in their brains and then replay them, hearing the perceived negative message over and over. "He said he was tired. But he wasn't tired. He really meant he didn't want to be with me."

When you marshal your forces to deal not only with attacks that exist but also with those that are not meant or are not important, you may find yourself always at the barricades. And that's exhausting. It leaves little time or energy for more productive pursuits. And it puts distance between you and others who may not wish to spend their energy fighting.

Personalizing can reduce your opportunities.

Nobody likes to be hurt. Nobody likes to be rejected. You are hardly unusual if you don't like putting yourself in a situation that makes you vulnerable to being hurt or rejected. But interpreting a situation as a personal affront when you do not know for sure that this is the case may cause you to try to avoid such situations. The result of this is that you are actually rejecting yourself before anyone else gets a chance to do it.

For example: Joe would like to develop a business as a computer consultant. But to do that, he has to let potential customers know what services he can provide. He sets up an appointment with a possible client, makes his pitch, and is turned down cold. "We have no interest in this at all," says the business owner. "I guess I just don't have it," concludes Joe. He has assumed that the business owner's conclusion about *the service* is a conclusion about *Joe's abilities or Joe.*

If he thinks that way, he isn't likely to continue to call on other potential customers, or to think about modifying the service he offers to make it more attractive.

It is entirely possible that this person turned Joe down for a personal reason. Maybe he didn't like Joe's looks. But by *assuming* that is the reaction—and further, that it will be everybody's reaction—Joe sets himself up for failure. Joe is marching down the path of generalization described in Chapter Two. He assumes that all future experiences will be a repeat of this one.

Here's another example:

"This place is chaos," gripes the boss. Betty hears this remark and concludes: "She means she doesn't like *my* work." The result: Betty broods about her own personal situation. She is angry at the boss. She complains to colleagues in the office. She has no time left to think objectively about the problems of the department and come up with recommendations to solve them. Betty may be bringing about a self-fulfilling prophecy. In time, the boss will complain about her work and Betty will think: "See, I was right."

Personalizing leads to feeling guilty.

There is a certain ego boost to be had in thinking of yourself as responsible for everything in the world—for the happiness of your spouse, your children, and your neighbors; the smooth running of your workplace; the cleanliness of the environment; the tenderness of every piece of meat; and the success of the local football franchise. It's gratifying to feel that, if not for you, everything would fall apart.

On the other hand, it's not as gratifying to feel that others hold you responsible for every possible unhappiness, unevenness, and imperfection. That burden is too heavy. When you find that you have taken on too much as your personal responsibility and can't handle it, you are likely to feel guilty.

Yet it would be unfair for anyone to put the burden of such total responsibility on you alone, and it's unfair to do it to yourself.

Personalizing can damage the ability to see other points of view.

Pete complained that his girlfriend, Tess, had embarrassed him by winning when they played tennis. That's the nature of the game—somebody wins, somebody loses. "Yes," he thinks, "but she should have made sure I won." In Pete's mind, Tess's win was a personal attack on him as a man. He is unable to understand that Tess might enjoy winning just as much as he.

Common Sources of Personalizing

Although it certainly is possible to personalize about any comment, action, or situation, there are a few areas where this particular mistake seems to flourish. You will probably find at least one of them very familiar.

Children

Children are one of the most common sources of personalizing. As the saying goes, "Children do not choose to be born." That means a pair of adults is responsible for a child's very existence. Or you may have chosen to bring a child into your home by adopting. You may become a stepparent when you marry someone who has children. You may well conclude that since you are responsible for that child being under your roof, you are responsible ever after for every single thing the child does. But that's not true, even though it may sometimes seem as if the child is holding you responsible.

The baby cries night after night. Her tired mother may well moan: "Why is that child determined to torture me?"—instead of reasoning (or discovering after inquiring of the pediatrician) that many teething babies cry night after night. That's just the way it is.

Three-year-old Rebecca says: "Daddy, you get off the couch. I want to be with Mommy." "Oh God," says Daddy, "my daughter is rejecting me. She doesn't want to be with me. What did I do to make her feel that way?" He ignores the fact that this is typical three-year-old behavior.

The fourteen-year-old is rude and sloppy and shows no gratitude at all for the efforts made and money spent on his behalf. "Why can't I have a polite, neat, obedient, and appreciative child?" groans his father. "Where did I go wrong? Why is this child doing this to me?" (Because he is fourteen, that's why.)

In each of these examples, the children are behaving the way children of their age tend to behave. We may not like it. But that doesn't mean the children are doing it to "get us." Undoubtedly, millions of parents through the years have treasured Dr. Benjamin Spock's book *Baby and Child Care* because Dr. Spock tells it like it is about child behavior. Babies cry a lot and they don't check the clock before doing so. Contrariness reaches new heights at age two. ("The one year old contradicts his mother. The two and a half year old even contradicts himself," writes Spock.) Three-year-olds who love being with either parent alone may protest when both parents are together.

Says Spock on the subject of adolescents: "Some of the tension that often shows at this stage between father and son and mother and daughter is due to a natural rivalry." The teen is trying to show independence—and doesn't yet know how to do it graciously.

Yes, a parent has responsibility for shaping the child, but if the parent takes every action of the child personally, the result can range from simply an added level of strain to, at the extreme, child abuse. Parents who hurt their children often explain later that the child "hurt" them first. "She didn't love me." "He wouldn't stop crying." The child becomes an enemy in the parent's mind although the child is only being a child.

Intimate Relationships

The mistakes of mind reading and personalizing have a way of combining when we are misinterpreting the act of someone we know very well.

This is a case of assuming that a person you know well is sending you a personal insult in code. Steve is in a bad mood. The dog wants to play. "This dog ought to be out in the backyard," Steve says angrily. He takes the dog by the collar and moves it toward the back door. Steve's wife, Laura, snaps: "How am I supposed to know you didn't want to play with the dog tonight?" Her angry tone matches his. She has simply assumed that Steve has assigned responsibility for the dog to her—and that his comment about the dog is a personal attack on her for not putting the dog outside. That could be the case. But it could also be true that Steve's bad mood is the result of something that happened at the office. That because of that bad mood, he finds the dog annoying. And because he finds the dog annoying, he wants to put the dog outside. All of this has absolutely nothing to do with Laura.

The error could also work this way: Steve, still in that bad mood, overhears Laura talking to her friend on the phone and catches the phrase: ". . . really behaved like a jerk." He jumps to the conclusion that she is referring to him, to the way he complained about the dog. He thinks: "Now she's complaining to her friends about me." Steve tells Laura later that he is furious about what she said to her friend. "I wasn't referring to you," says Laura. "I was talking about an employee at the supermarket who refused to cash my check even though I always cash checks there." Steve, caught up in his anger spiral, refuses to believe her. "That's a good story, but not good enough," he replies.

Between mind reading and personalizing, this couple can continue to escalate the battle until both are close to the breaking point. And the basic fact is that Steve does not really know whom Laura was talking about. All he gains by assuming she is talking about him (and rejecting her statement that she was not) is to create a division between himself and Laura or widen one that already exists.

Motorists

You get caught in a traffic jam and think: "Why are all these SOBs getting in *my* way?" A driver cuts you off and you become furious: "How dare he do that to *me?*" Driving a car is like being in control of a small kingdom, and when other motorists don't show the king or queen proper respect, most of us have a tendency to want to say: "Off with their heads." Here again, this is a case of combining two mistakes: mind reading and personalizing.

You interpret driving behavior as a personal message directed at you. You read the other driver's mind to find: "I want to get in that guy's way and make him miserable." Some people take an affront on the highway so personally, they quite literally become dangerous to others and themselves as they attempt to get back at one they perceive has insulted them. Angry motorists have been known to bump into other cars as revenge for some driving offense. There have been many news stories about motorists who pull a weapon and shoot another driver. There have been stories about shouting matches that end up with one motorist physically assaulting another.

Are there poor drivers on the highway? Yes. Are there jerks behind the wheel? Yes. Is that annoying? Absolutely. But it is not necessary to approve of every other driver to avoid the personalizing mistake. If you interpret the poor driving habits of others as mere incompetence or inattention, or as accidental rather than as a personal attack (even if that motorist really is playing games with you in mind), you are more likely to *protect* yourself from any confrontation with this idiot, rather than to seek one out.

The Cumulative Effect

The mistake of personalizing is very often made when bad things happen in a series—or in what seems to be a series. You may find yourself saying: "Why me?" It may seem as if God—or the fates or Lady Luck—has selected you to pick on or punish. Even people who rarely take things personally may find themselves doing it when bad events seem to be piling up.

"Seem to be" is the key phrase here. The brain has a way of assembling things for us that do not always truly go together. For example, Len's mother died at the age of eighty-two, and just two months later, his father, eighty-four, died as well. It was a difficult period for Len and his family. And then, on the way to his father's funeral, the muffler on Len's car falls onto the highway.

"What did I do to deserve this?" Len thinks. On top of grief, he now places anger and guilt. If Len would stop, look, and listen at this particular crossing, he could think about what actually happened and decide whether it was meant as a judgment on his personal worth.

Mom died.

"Elderly people die. It isn't likely I could have prevented it."

Dad died.

"I couldn't have prevented that either. And he seemed lost without Mom."

The muffler fell out.

"That really had no connection to the deaths at all. Mufflers fall out."

Why is this important? Because there is a difference between the unhappiness you feel when sad or merely unfortunate events occur and the deeper unhappiness that flows when you believe that these events mark you as a loser or as bad.

Analyze to Depersonalize

The key to reducing the problems caused by personalizing is simply to stop, review what you are thinking, and analyze those thoughts.

Personalizing is an automatic reaction. And as with any automatic reaction, sometimes it will be the right one, and sometimes it will be the wrong one. And you will very often be able to tell which is which if you simply s-l-o-w d-o-w-n and think about it.

When you feel that inner burn that says: "I've been hit," stop and ask yourself: "What am I thinking? What special meaning am I attributing to these words or actions? How do I know that this meaning is the correct one?" You might say: "I just know, that's all. I can tell. I can feel it." If that's what you are telling yourself, demand more analysis.

To analyze: Recall what was said or done—factually. The actual words. The precise action. He said: "This office is in chaos." Or: "The car broke down."

Consider whether there could be *any other explanation* for those words or that behavior except an insult to you:

- "Is he picking on me, or could there be another explanation for his feeling that the office is in chaos? Is he just blowing off steam? Is the office in chaos?"
- "Is this a general statement or one that could apply *only* to me?"
- "Is this person my personal enemy or just a jerk?"

You do not, in any case, have to prove beyond a shadow of a doubt that this person could not possibly have even hinted at criticizing you. The idea is to merely *make yourself aware* of when some other explanation is plausible.

Rhonda is disappointed because she was not picked to serve as a panel member at her organization's annual meeting. Her initial reaction may be: "They rejected me. They didn't think I was good enough." Or: "They wanted to hurt me." But if no one has actually said that, it may not be the case. It could be that if the panel had four members instead of three, Rhonda would have been asked. Those particular three could have been named for political reasons that have nothing to do with Rhonda.

"That's just making excuses for people," you might say. And that could be. But since the truth is not known, it makes as much sense to consider alternative explanations that do not imply a personal insult rather than an explanation that creates anger, hurt, or embarrassment. If you are aware that another explanation could be *as likely* as the personal insult you perceive, you will react differently. You will be less likely to feel hurt and more likely to give people the benefit of the doubt. You are less likely to be angry and more willing to investigate, explore, and try.

When You Are Right to Feel Criticized

Obviously, sometimes you feel you have been insulted because you *have* been insulted. Do people blame you for outcomes of all kinds? Of course. Sometimes it's deserved and sometimes not.

Sometimes taking a generalized comment as a personal attack makes a great deal of sense. Bigotry and prejudice exist in this world. A bigot who hates the group you belong to (because of race, ethnic background, or any other reason) is very likely to attack you personally just because you are a member of that group. There may well be places that would be dangerous for you to go because people who hate the group you belong to are in control there.

Sometimes you might be wise to accept personal responsibility for something even though, strictly speaking, you *alone* are not totally responsible for the situation. Following the crash of a Japan Air Lines plane in Tokyo Bay in 1982, the president of the airline personally visited the families of all the crash victims to offer apology and compensation. Not a single lawsuit was filed. True, the Japanese do not resort to courts as quickly as Americans, but experienced negotiators here contend that, quite often, all the injured party in a dispute wants is an admission that the other is sorry that the injury occurred.

But suppose you are right that the insult was meant for you and only you—and it is unjustified. You are right to be angry. Then what?

That's often a good question to ask yourself when analyzing your thoughts. It's a good way to help yourself to develop alternative reactions. Suppose a motorist on a busy highway with you not only cuts you off, missing your fender by an inch, but also shouts an insult at you as he goes past. Your first thought may be: "How dare he say that to me? Who does he think he is? I ought to teach that jerk a lesson."

Your internal dialogue might then go something like this: "Suppose I pull up next to him and tell him what a jerk he is. Then what?

"Then he might escalate the confrontation. Then what?

"I could end up in a shouting match or, worse, in an accident. Then what?

"I might not get to work today. I might even get hurt. There's a lot of dangerous people on the road today."

As you mentally review the possible outcome of teaching that jerk a lesson, you may well decide that, although you are fully justified in being angry, you could lose more than you gain by attempting to confront him.

Ellen might say to herself: "Suppose I am right that my teacher is accusing me of not working hard enough? Then what?" She must now decide what she can do about it. Ellen's personal schema may tell her that the only way to deal with an accusation is to fight back. That could lead her to confront the teacher angrily or file a complaint about her. But it is important to remember that the question "Then what?" may have more than one possible answer. It helps to think of as many as possible.

Ellen may well feel that she "should" have an angry confrontation with the teacher, but at the same time decide not to do so. This is just one class out of many, and she would prefer to concentrate her energies elsewhere. So then what? She might say:

- "I can ask for a conference with her."
- "I can work harder."
- "I can tell myself I'm just going to have to survive this semester because this teacher and I are not going to get along."
- "I can develop an alternative way of feeling. Instead of feeling discouraged because I can't please her, I can feel annoyed that she isn't doing a better job of teaching me."

It is always possible to pick your fights—emotional and intellectual as well as physical. And it is also a good idea to do so. If you are constantly at the barricades, you will be continuously exhausted. And tired people don't fight well. You will be able to respond better if you choose where you want to concentrate your fire.

Ask yourself: "Who is saying this? Does this person matter?"

If the insulter is a total stranger, a jerk, a sad case, it may be better to just shrug it off.

At a dinner party, Granny makes a disparaging comment about African-Americans (or Jews or Polish people or Southerners or some other group—none of which Granny is, but one of which you are). She is insulting your people and probably means to insult you, too. Do you rise to do battle? Or change the subject?

If Granny is a member of Congress, the leader of an organization, a prominent and influential citizen, you may decide not to let her get away it. On the other hand, if Granny is an individual with old ideas that probably aren't going to change, but who isn't in a position to harm you or anyone else and whose opinions do not reflect those of the others at the party, you may decide it's not worth disrupting dinner to straighten her out.

You may find that you can easily dismiss a minor insult or a major insult from someone who doesn't matter—the first time, but not the third. This is known as letting it get to you. Someone says something once. You ignore it. Twice. You ignore it. Three times. You explode.

Once again, the way to deal with this is to become aware if and when you do it. You can then determine not to let it get to you. If something is trivial once, repeating it does not make it more significant. And, indeed, if someone is repeating an insult in hopes of getting to you, why let them succeed? The critical question in picking your fight is: "Is there an advantage to me in acknowledging this insult and doing something about it?"

Picking Your Response

While you are pausing, while you are carefully considering rather than automatically responding, you not only decide whether to respond but, if so, how.

You are sick and tired of snide remarks about short people. You believe you have been personally denied opportunity because of bias against short people. Do you end up in one fist fight after another to uphold your honor? Or do you organize an association of short people who will campaign against height restrictions for police and firefighter jobs?

You may run into somebody who is even more of a personalizer than you are, and that person is spoiling for a fight. For example, suppose a police officer insists you went through a red light. "No, sir," you say. "That light was green." "Are you calling me a liar?" asks the officer, his voice rising. Uh-oh. You were merely stating the facts as you saw them. But the officer is taking your reply as an insult—and he has the power to put you in jail. So even though you feel he is wrong to take your comment personally, this may not be the time to get into a discussion of the matter.

Your son tells you that he doesn't like the salad dressing you went to elaborate lengths to prepare for him. You refuse to take it personally. You don't attack him as unappreciative. He has a right to his taste buds, and disliking your salad dressing doesn't mean he dislikes you or doesn't appreciate your effort to please him. You do not have to take personal responsibility for his inability to appreciate good food. And you know that he is not the ultimate world judge of salad dressing worthiness. But you don't think you'll go to that much trouble next time. You might even serve him a bottled salad dressing. And if *he* takes that personally, you can explain the error of his ways.

CHAPTER FIVE

BELIEVING YOUR PRESS AGENT

Many stories can be told of famous, accomplished people who, after riding high for years and garnering reams of good publicity, suddenly face financial or personal difficulty. Donald Trump comes to mind. Newspaperpeople have an expression that describes one possible explanation for such reversals of fortune. They'll say: "His problem is that he believed his press clippings." Or: "Her problem was that she believed her press agent's hype."

In saying this, the journalists are mocking themselves as much as the people they are writing about. They know that when someone seems to be doing well, the media rarely cast a critical eye. Most coverage tends to be favorable, admiring, even fawning. The word of press agents—who are paid to spread only positive information around—is taken with little or no investigation or debate.

But people in the press know from experience that it's one thing to have stories written about you that imply you can do no wrong—and quite another to actually believe those stories yourself! It's a press agent's job to spread information around that makes the client appear to be invincible. But it's a mistake for that client to believe that the press agent is telling the whole story. Alas, people who believe they can walk on water have a way of sinking over their heads.

Is this an argument against self-esteem, self-confidence, and a winning attitude? you ask. Not at all. There is a considerable body of research that says an optimistic can-do attitude is far more likely to bring satisfaction and success than a pessimistic it-will-never-work attitude. Looking on the bright side is likely to make you feel much better than would dwelling on life's darker aspects. Yes, optimism is a good thing. But just as a proper dose of vitamins is helpful but an overdose of those same vitamins can be toxic, too much optimism can get you into trouble.

Remember that avoiding any of the ten dumbest mistakes smart people make first requires *thinking realistically*. That means not erring on the side of being too negative—but *also* not erring on the side of being *too positive*.

How an Overdose of Positive Thinking Can Produce Negative Results

When things seem to be going well for you, it's easy to believe that things always will. It's easy to believe that life is good because you are so deserving—that luck and other people play only minor roles. It's easy to do what press agents do, which is to focus only on the positive things that can be said about you and ignore everything else. It's certainly harder to accept the notion that too much positive thinking can hurt you. How can that possibly happen? Here are some of the ways.

One-Size Talent Fits All Situations

If you are successful at everything you try, your reality is pleasant indeed. But most of us are not equally adept at everything. And if you simply assume that because you have been successful in one sphere of your life, you must naturally be successful in everything you do—*without making any extra efforts*—you may learn to your cost that you are wrong.

The reasoning might go something like this: "I've made a fortune in the cheese business, so now I'll buy a steel mill. I don't have to know anything about the steel business because my obviously good instincts will lead me to the right decisions."

The decade of the eighties produced one example after the other of high-flying business types who crashlanded before the nineties rolled around. One of the best known of these was Albert Campeau, a Canadian who earned both respect and a considerable fortune as a homebuilder. Then he decided to branch into retailing, a field in which he had no experience. Possibly he thought something like: "I succeeded brilliantly before, why shouldn't I succeed brilliantly again?"

He borrowed almost $10 billion to finance the takeover of two huge chains—Allied Stores and Federated Stores. And in so doing he incurred an annual interest bill that was larger than the most those operations had ever made in pretax profits in the past. Experienced retailers said Campeau couldn't overcome that much debt—and they were right. Shortly after completing what *Fortune* magazine dubbed "the looniest deal ever," both chains were in bankruptcy and Campeau lost control of his company.

A variation of that thinking could be this: "I'm so terrific at this phase of the business, I know I can count on everything else just naturally working out."

In his first book about himself, Donald Trump bragged about his ability to make deals in which he acquired hotels, casinos, and other assets. In his second book, Trump admitted that good though he was at deal making, he hadn't paid enough attention to running those assets after he bought them. He might have avoided a lot of grief if he'd thought about that earlier.

But the world of business is not the only place where this sense of one-size talent fits all situations can get you into trouble. For example, the same aggressive pushing-to-the-limits zeal that succeeds well in sports does not bring success on the highway. This has been proved tragically over and over again. In 1985 Pelle Lindbergh, star goalkeeper for the Philadelphia Flyers hockey team, died when, after a bout of drinking, he slammed his Porsche into a concrete wall. Two friends were injured in the same accident. Teammates said Lindbergh had been warned that he drove too fast but believed he lived a charmed life both on the ice and off it.

Being successful in one phase of your life does not automatically mean all other phases will just naturally work out. Dan was a young man who was very well thought of in his community. He had a responsible job that took more than eight hours a day, but he never complained. He earned a good living. He played the organ at his church. And he was active in civic affairs. He felt he was living a model life until his wife left him, taking the children with her. Dan was crushed. What had he done wrong? It wasn't what he had done *wrong*, said his wife, it was what he hadn't *done*. He hadn't spent enough time with her. She felt ignored. She felt last on his list.

Who, Me?

Too much positive thinking may also play out as a tendency to avoid taking responsibility for your own actions. That has a way of escalating problems.

Nelson knows that his second wife, Shirley, is angry about the money that he lavishes on his daughter from his first marriage. Shirley feels she is being asked to sacrifice to provide the daughter with luxuries Shirley doesn't have. Shirley complains that Nelson bought his daughter a new car. "No, I didn't," Nelson says. "I saw it," replies Shirley angrily. Nelson shifts his ground: "You said she has a new car, but it's not new, it's used. And I didn't buy it for her; it's not totally paid for yet."

What's going on here? Why does Nelson lie to Shirley? After all, a car is a pretty large item to keep secret. He lies because he believes that he doesn't feel he owes her *any* explanation. He feels it's his money and what he does with it is his business. When Shirley complains, he first attempts to put her off with a lie, and when that doesn't end the matter, he attacks the form in which she put her complaint. Nelson believes that being Nelson means never being wrong, never having to explain. But Shirley cannot accept that attitude. She feels it demeans her. Does such a marriage have much of a future?

You too may feel that others are owed neither explanations

nor apologies. You may feel that you do not need to answer to anyone for what you do. And if things go wrong, you do not even need to acknowledge that fact. How well that works for you depends on whether you want or need approval of others.

Historians believe that John F. Kennedy was able to maintain public support after the Bay of Pigs fiasco *because* he forthrightly took responsibility for it. The voters elected Grover Cleveland president in 1884 after he admitted that the opposition's accusations that he had fathered an illegitimate child were true. (And such an act was more scandalous then than it would be today.) On the other hand, it can be argued that President Richard Nixon's attempts to stonewall when asked about transgressions of his reelection campaign of 1972 helped turn public—and congressional—sentiment against him and hastened his departure from office before his term expired.

A belief in your own superiority can lead to blaming others when problems arise. ("It can't possibly be me, so it must be you.") And those who are blamed may well resent that fact. They may see you as pompous, arrogant, and unlikable—rather than as simply cleverer and harder working than they. Some might even be annoyed enough to seek ways to undermine your success—and that may not be what you want.

If you invariably blame others for the setbacks that occur in your life, others may see you as a chronic whiner and that, too, can be counterproductive. This may be so even when you are right that you are not appreciated as much as you should be.

Resting on Laurels

One of the great dangers that comes along with all the pleasures of success is the lure of resting on your laurels. When you have achieved something—and others recognize that achievement—it's easy to feel you no longer have to prove yourself.

Sometimes that is happily the case. One success leads to other successes. People call on you. You are given assignments that others covet even without asking for them. But, just as often, the world takes a harder stance that can be summed up as: "What have you done for us lately?" The Yankees traded Babe

Ruth at the end of his career. He had been the greatest Yankee ever, but he wasn't hitting so well lately.

That doesn't mean your previous accomplishments are forgotten as though they never happened. State governors are always accorded the honorary title of governor even after they leave office. But an honorary title does not convey the same power as an official one. Honors given you in the past may not necessarily carry you very far in the present or future.

This is a lesson commonly brought home to young people who were standout students at high school or college or professional school. When applying to another school or for a job, they have no difficulty assembling a sheaf of recommendations: "Lucy was the best student we ever had here. Her work was the finest I've ever seen." Lucy is used to being a star. And she expects that treatment to continue at whichever school—or firm—she deigns to honor with her presence. But then she finds that in her class, or among the other new hires at the firm, are the stars of a dozen other schools, who were also the finest *their* teachers had ever seen. In her new environment, Lucy is no longer a star—unless she proves it. She isn't going to get rewards based on her proud past, only on how she fares competing in this new—and tougher—situation. If she recognizes that she is, once again, starting from scratch, she may succeed. If she waits for recognition, she may wait a long time.

This is often the case when taking a new job, moving to a new town, moving to any kind of new situation. You may well ask: "After all I've done, do I have to prove myself again?" Unfortunately, the answer may be yes.

The laurels that are tempting to rest on may not necessarily have anything to do with accomplishment. They may simply be such attributes as good looks, youth, charm, and good luck. Someone with all those attributes may find it isn't necessary to go seeking a social life, because social invitations of all sorts just pour in. That was true for Wally. When he was young, he had a rich social life. Now a middle-aged widower, he is lonely and resentful. "My friends know my situation," he says. "They could invite me over more than they do. They could arrange some introductions for me." While Wally waits for the invitations he feels are his due, he does nothing on his own to meet anyone new.

Locked Into Strategy That No Longer Works

In recent years, many very successful middle management men and women have lost their jobs, not as a result of personal failure, but rather as the result of mergers, bankruptcies, takeovers, downsizing, and the like. (According to the American Management Association, 1,219 corporations eliminated roughly 81,000 positions in 1990, of which 45 percent were managerial or professional.) If two firms joined, there was no longer a need for two heads of marketing. If a firm was closed because the board of directors approved taking on too much debt, good people whose opinions were never asked found themselves out of work. Years of praise and promotion suddenly counted for nothing.

As cruel as that is, such people often found themselves out of the running for possible new posts on the grounds that they were "overqualified." But as bad as that is when done by others, it is made worse if done by and to oneself:

- "I used to make $100,000, and accepting a new position paying less than that is clearly beneath me, even if the job is interesting."
- "I was in charge of four hundred people at my previous post. I can't possibly work for a firm that has only a hundred employees, no matter what they pay me."

Lucy, the student who is used to being a star, may discover that in her new environment, she can't possibly be a star because the competition is too intense. Although many of her colleagues are happy just to be part of a group that is head and shoulders above most groups, that isn't enough for Lucy. She feels like a failure in this situation. She has decided that stardom is everything.

Some people react to having less than their previous standard of success by giving up too soon. If it takes longer than two months to line up a new job, they are devastated. They can't believe that finding what they want—or close to it—could take as much as a year of hard searching. ("If someone with my credentials can't find something in two months, there can't be anything there. It's hopeless.")

Some people react by taking up residence in the past. They talk only of past glories until the eyes of their listeners glaze over. They exist in the present, but don't truly live there ("My life used to be wonderful," sighs Lucy unhappily). Such people often refuse to consider an option that will improve their lives on the grounds that it would not totally restore all past glory.

All of this is not to say that if you suffer a setback you must always resign yourself to less. Definitely not. The point is only that if you are *too rigid* in defining what you can accept, you are likely to fail to see opportunities when they arise or mire yourself in constant mourning for what you do not have.

Press Agents in Everyday Life

The average person, of course, isn't likely to employ a real press agent to grind out hype for public consumption. But many of us have what might be called press agent substitutes in our lives.

It could be your mother.

Your mother has told you all your life how wonderful you are—and would she lie? No, of course not. Mothers believe their kids are wonderful, which is why mothers are wonderful. But some mothers, well, exaggerate. Tom's mother, for example, never stopped telling him how exceptional he was. And if something Tom tried went awry, she was quick to assure him that it was no fault of his. Others hadn't done what they should have. Others were undermining him because they were jealous. It was never Tom. It was always somebody else. And so Tom grew up believing he was always right. Negotiation, explanation, and compromise were for other people. Never for him.

It could be your friends.

Teenagers are particularly prone to both being—and believing—press agents. One teen may say: "We shouldn't be drinking and driving. We could have an accident." And the press agents will reply: "It will never happen. Don't be a party pooper." The unspoken message of these press agents is: "You are invulnerable. You don't have to be careful. Nothing can hurt you." It's a message many want to believe.

Friends are expected to flatter and praise. That's part of what makes friendship so wonderful. But there can be times when flattery is dangerous. Donna asked her friend Wendy for advice when she and Vince separated. "He wants to get back together and I'm torn," said Donna. "I feel I'm partly to blame for what happened." "Don't even think about it," snapped Wendy. "You did more for that man than any man has a right to ask. You are too good for him. Don't lower yourself to his level." Wendy feels she is loyally backing a friend who she really believes can do no wrong. But if Donna really *wants* a reconciliation, Wendy's praise makes that choice more difficult.

It could be business contacts who have something to gain.

Flattery will get you everywhere, so it is said. And salespeople take the lesson to heart. If they are to get a percentage of the sale, they may tell you how wonderful you look in an outfit (even if you don't), how smart an investor you are (even if you are not), how clever you are to put your faith (and money) in their judgment.

It could be people who work for you.

It is never pleasant to tell people something you know they will not be happy to hear. Yes men are more popular with some executives than subordinates who are prepared to argue. This, of course, is the point of the old story of "The Emperor's New Clothes." The emperor struts about naked while his attendants tell him only how wonderful he looks in his new outfit. It takes a little boy to whom the emperor is just another adult to blurt out that he isn't wearing anything.

It could be the people you work for.

In the best of all possible worlds, it would be possible to get accurate feedback about the work you are doing without having to make any special effort to obtain it. In the real world, however, many people so dislike being the bearer of negative news that they totally duck that responsibility. Instead, they adopt the policy of giving you enough rope to hang yourself. They go along as if everything is fine—until the situation has declined to the point where they feel forced to march you to the gallows.

It could be the voice of privilege.

One of Harvard psychiatrist Robert Coles's famous books about children cites a characteristic he found to be common among the children of the rich. He calls it a sense of entitlement. Most children, he said, when asked what they will do when they grow up, will say something like: "I want to be a doctor" or "I'd like to be a firefighter." They don't add: "If things work out, if the money can be found, if I can pass the test," but those phrases are implied. The children of the rich, Coles said, tend to answer the same question: "I'm *going* to be a doctor." "I'm going to be a nuclear physicist." The implication here is: "Whatever I want, I'll get."

Along with that may go the feeling that they are entitled to take personal credit for things they get only because of their money and connections. Former Texas commissioner of agriculture Jim Hightower once described a well-known multimillionaire politician by saying: "He was born on third base and thinks he hit a triple."

Does coming from a rich, well-connected family help in getting what you want? Who could deny it? Donald Trump's brains and ability helped him amass his real estate empire, but it hardly hurt him that his father was already a multimillionaire builder (the owner of 25,000 apartments in Brooklyn and the Bronx) with lots of capital and the kind of political connections needed to obtain a forty-year tax abatement for Donald's first project in Manhattan. Did Donald Trump believe that whatever he wanted, he could get? That certainly seems to be how he oper-ated—to a point that finally put his entire empire in jeopardy.

It could be the voice of religion.

Your clergyman might have told you that pleasing God and setting a righteous example to others will guarantee rewards in this world and perhaps in the next as well. And having faith, you believe you enjoy a kind of divine protection. That can be crush-ing when something happens to shake your faith.

Or, in time of trouble or tragedy, earnest friends assure you that you can rise above anything. "Everything happens for the best." "God never gives us a burden we can't carry." "It's a test." In the long run, they may be right, but in the short run, believing them may serve only to make you feel guilty if you feel you haven't passed "the test."

It could be people who only want to motivate you.

Many people think they do others a favor by being cheerlead-ers in a random, unfocused way. The teacher may say: "You can be anything you want to be." (Can you be a professional basket-ball player even though you are only five-foot-four? Very doubt-ful.) Well-meaning advisers may claim that if you just say: "I can do it," you will do it. Obviously, believing you can do some-thing is more likely to motivate you to try than believing you can't. But merely pumping yourself up with positive thoughts alone is *mistaking image for substance*. The student who says: "I can do it" and then doesn't bother to study will probably flunk the test.

The Press Agent Inside

The most important press agent of all is the one inside your head. If your internal press agent speaks too loudly, you may never seek the opinions of others or hear them when offered. You may be insensitive to the needs and desires of others. You may simply assume that others want what you want. ("You're just saying you don't want to go to bed with me. I know you really want to.") This kind of thinking leads to the breakdown of business and personal relationships and to the breaking of laws.

Two types of people are most prone to these internal hype artists: those who simply choose to believe that they are wonderful because someone—usually a parent—has told them so. And those who have legitimately achieved at a high level at one point in their lives and use that as the lifelong basis for everything they do:

- "Dad says I am wonderful, which means I am wonderful."
- "Why should I listen to anybody else? Every one but me is a moron."
- "I can do anything, have anything, steal anything, trick anyone, and get away with it." (When caught and hauled into court, this sort of person often says—as did junk bond king Michael Milken after pleading guilty to securities law violations—that his actions offended his own principles. Unfortunately, principles have a way of hiding when a strident internal press agent takes control.)
- "I'm not going to take that assistant buyer's job. I'm not going to be anybody's assistant. I'm going to wait until I get offered what I deserve even if I have to wait—in poverty—forever."

This is positive thinking gone amok.

It's not that revving up that can-do spirit isn't helpful. There is great power in what psychologists call positive affirmation. The coach's pep talk before the big game can pump up the players to produce an extra edge of effort that enables them to extend themselves beyond their normal limits. But this sort of thing works only for the short term. A jolt of adrenaline at the right time can produce a touchdown, but adrenaline alone won't get you from September into a Bowl game.

Yes, there are people who seem to make no effort and yet get along famously. And if that works for you, fine. You can probably point to times when you just winged it and won the day. But what is more usually the case is implied in the old joke about the young man who stops an older man on a Manhattan street and asks him: "How do I get to Carnegie Hall?" And the old man replies: "Practice. Practice. Practice."

Yes, we have all heard of so-called Renaissance types who can do it all. More accurately, they have multiple talents—like, for example, that true citizen of the Renaissance, Leonardo da Vinci. He was a magnificent painter, sculptor, anatomist, astronomer, and engineer. He had sketched his own version of flying machines and parachutes before either was thought about by others. Was he multitalented? Indeed he was. But even Leonardo couldn't do everything. He had no interest in history, literature, or religion. He lived a solitary, some say lonely, life. His faithful friend and heir, Francesco Melzi, became his companion only late in Leonardo's life.

Yes, some people get away with criminal activity. They don't get caught, or they get caught and still don't go to jail. But realistic thinking says, as jailhouse jargon puts it: "If you can't do the time, don't do the crime." The city may have just opened a new prison to relieve overcrowding when the judge is about to sentence you. And of all the judges of the bench, you may manage to draw Hanging Harry.

Reality Check

When people think of themselves as beyond the rules that apply to humans generally, we often say they have too much ego. We use the word *ego* to mean vanity, narcissism, or arrogance. But those are not the meanings Sigmund Freud ascribed to the word. In Freudian terms, the id is that part of us that reacts to pleasure, the superego is our sense of morality, and the ego is our ability to deal with *reality*. Thus people with healthy egos don't believe all their press clippings. They won't assume they are invincible just because that's what their admirers say. They don't assume that success in the past *guarantees* success in the future.

The Power of Practical Thinking

Peter Pan tells Wendy and her brothers just to think beautiful thoughts and they will fly. And you, too, can think beautiful thoughts and fly—as long as you have also taken the trouble to buy a ticket on an airplane or perhaps taken a course in flying and obtained a pilot's license.

Whenever you are considering a new venture, a new relationship, a new anything, ask yourself: "What do I know about this? What are the positives? What are the negatives?"

When clever investors decide where to put their money, they not only consider the potential for profit, they also consider the downside. How much might they lose if the investment goes sour? Considering the downside of anything is not a cheerful business. But it's part of facing reality. Only by recognizing the negatives you face can you plan how to deal with them.

You must also ask: "What have I done to improve the possibility of this being a success other than to think beautiful thoughts?"

The most wonderful idea in creation is just an idea until you find a way to make use of it. Practical thinking is not pessimistic thinking. It isn't a matter of talking yourself out of trying something new. It isn't saying: "This can't be done." It is merely an acknowledgment that what has worked in the past may not be suitable for the present, that new obstacles may require new strategies, and that you may have to work hard to make your dreams come true.

You may have to investigate. Study. Learn. Ask. Check your assumptions. What do you mean by what you say? What is the evidence that supports that conclusion? Practical thinking is not an argument against taking a risk. It is an argument only for fully exploring what is involved.

Advancing in a Different Direction

During the Korean War, Marine General Oliver Smith decided to pull his troops back from a battle that was not going well. A reporter asked him a question about this retreat, and Smith replied with a memorable line: "Retreat, hell. We're not retreating. We're just advancing in a different direction.''

In ordinary life as in war, one is sometimes forced to retreat. And it makes sense to look on it as advancing in a different direction.

It may be that the position you have achieved has, for some reason, been lost, and your efforts to find its equivalent have, for one reason or another, not succeeded. The company executive let go when the firm is merged does not find precisely the position he seeks. A divorcée, even in an enlightened age, may find she has lost the social status she had as a married woman. A star athlete loses fame when he is no longer on the team. Lucy, the student who was "the finest ever" in her school may find she ranks only fourth—or tenth—when competing with others who were the finest in their schools.

In each case, how the person thinks about the situation is critical to the effect it has on that person's life. Continuing to believe those press agents who say: "You can accept nothing less than your previous status" is a thinking mistake. Why? Because it allows you no flexibility. It is setting yourself up for failure. It is setting yourself up for a lifetime of regret, complaining, and bitterness.

Advancing in a different direction allows you all kinds of flexibility. It permits you to step back to proceed again. It permits you to compromise.

Countering Your Press Agents

The trick in dealing with press agents is learning how to enjoy all the compliments they pay without being controlled by them. That means recognizing that press agents are paid to focus on the positive and totally ignore the negative. They are paid to be experts in extravagant exaggeration, commonly known as hype. A press agent will describe a product as a new invention that is the greatest thing since sliced bread, and something everybody needs, when actually it is a modest improvement that will be of some benefit to a segment of the population.

You don't want to be fooled, and you don't want to fool yourself.

"Who is telling me this? How much does this person know?"

Your friend may be quite sincere in enthusiastically recommending that, given your color sense, you should become a decorator. Or, given your talent in the kitchen, you should open a restaurant. But unless your friend is a decorator or owns a restaurant, she will not be able to inform you knowledgeably about what such a business involves. You need to get more information.

"Does this press agent have something to gain?"

"Sir, it is obvious that you are talented, able, clever, intelligent, thrifty, clean, brave, and reverent, and therefore I know you will recognize the value of product X. Lesser people might not buy one, but you . . ."
The best deal is one that benefits both sides. And so it may be that product X is just as valuable as this person says. But if you are as clever and intelligent as described, you will buy based on your assessment of the product—not on the salesperson's assessment of you.

"Does the fact that I have not heard of (or thought about) a negative mean that none exists?"

Every emperor could use at least one child around who will let him know when he lacks a shirt. The wisest person can use at least one person who will challenge the rosy glow, point out a negative, raise a few questions.

- "He sounds wonderful, but what do your children think of him?"
- "The idea sounds wonderful, but can you get the capital it will require? Do you know how much capital it will require?"

Assigning Blame and Responsibility
When the people who admire you end up causing you a problem, the blame is partly theirs, of course, but also partly

yours. It's up to you to remember that just because *they* tell you that you can't miss doesn't make it true.

Back in the mid-seventies, the CBS network decided to create its very own Cinderella story. Sally Quinn, a talented writer for the *Washington Post*, was offered the very high-salaried job of co-anchor of the "CBS Morning News" show. Overnight, Quinn became nationally known. CBS literally had press agents spreading her fame. She was touted as competition for Barbara Walters, who then reigned at NBC's "Today" show.

However, Quinn bombed on TV. In her book about her brief, unhappy adventure, *We're Going to Make You a Star*, Quinn said she went on the air with no previous TV experience and no training. She made one goof after the other—each of which was duly noted by the press. The strain was terrible, she said. She developed a severe case of acne. She constantly threw up. And just six months later, she quit and returned to the *Post*.

She felt, with considerable justification, that CBS had thrown her to the wolves. As a newspaperwoman, Quinn needed no help in writing a good story. But she did need help in making a transition to TV, and she hadn't gotten any.

But Quinn acknowledged in her book that she hadn't looked out for her own best interests. She enjoyed the thought of big money, she said. She enjoyed the hype that preceded her first appearance. She enjoyed being told how great she was. She enjoyed being interviewed rather than being the interviewer. So she allowed herself to be swept along by the hype.

She admitted that, in effect, thinking beautiful thoughts was all she did to prepare herself for the new challenge. When she asked the man who hired her why he had not prepared her for what she would face, he asked her if she would have been willing to undergo training for three to six months at a local TV station. And Quinn replied: "Of course not."

In short, those who gave Quinn too much opportunity before she was prepared for it are partly to blame for her lack of success, but she recognized that she, too, bore responsibility.

Dad may decide to make Junior the head of a division before he has learned enough to do a good job. Dad thinks: "He's my son, isn't he? Of course he'll do fine." But Junior would do well to investigate just what his new job will require and take action to fill the gaps, lest his proud father set him up for failure.

The True Winning Attitude

The true winning attitude is a realistic one. It is confidence backed by an open mind. It is a willingness to take risks backed by a willingness to take responsibility for the efforts required. And sometimes all that is necessary when you feel that you may be making the Press Agent mistake is to tell yourself so. This is a technique known as *self-instruction*. If you sense that your superpositive outlook is not bringing you superpositive results, you can simply tell yourself: "I think I'd better back off a little." Or: "Try to be a little less aggressive." Or: "Give this some effort. It's worth it." Or: "Let others believe the hype about me—I'm going to operate in the real world."

CHAPTER SIX

BELIEVING YOUR CRITICS

No doubt many people will say that overconfidence is a problem they wish they had. Somehow, being surrounded by press agents who constantly tell you how wonderful you are doesn't sound terribly unpleasant—even if it does frequently lead to disaster. You may be thinking: "I only wish I felt that good about myself."

That's understandable because most people have the opposite problem. They feel themselves surrounded by critics who sum up their performance in a single word: *loser*. Even the experience of success may not keep these critics away. They lurk in what is sometimes called "the impostor phenomenon." That is, the successful person doubts that the success is justified. "A loser like me can't possibly be a winner," this person says. And this attitude undermines success.

But the fact remains that both patterns of thinking are mistakes that lead to more mistakes. You can get into trouble by never seeing a negative anywhere, and you can get into trouble by seeing—and believing—negatives *everywhere*.

The Tuning Fork Factor

Some of us are more sensitive to criticism than others. If just one person says: "You are wrong," that judgment is accepted as if it came straight from heaven. If just one effort fails, an internal critic proclaims: "That's it—give up." If the reaction received is merely less enthusiastic than hoped for, the conclusion is: "I just don't have it."

But it is very likely that this reaction does not occur all the time on every occasion. Most of us learn to screen out some criticism and are able to ignore it.

Imagine yourself walking down the street. You see a stranger wearing a sign that proclaims: "The world will end tomorrow unless everyone eats their brussels sprouts." He comes up to you and says: "You don't know what you're talking about." You would probably say to yourself: "Poor fellow, I wonder what *his* problem is." You would easily brush his criticism aside.

Unless, perhaps, you were walking along thinking to yourself that you had just performed badly, just bungled something, made the wrong decision, said something dumb—whatever. Now you hear the stranger's words and you think: "How does he know about me?"

Of course, he doesn't know anything about you. He has only accidentally touched an area where you feel insecure or particularly sensitive. Or, to put it another way, he has caused an internal emotional tuning fork to start vibrating.

When you strike a tuning fork, its tines begin to vibrate and give off a sound. If you have two tuning forks on the same frequency, an interesting phenomenon is possible. You hit one and start it vibrating, then just hold it near the other and the second will start vibrating too. Those vibrations are known as sympathetic vibrations.

Most people react to criticism similarly. They do not react the same way to all criticism. They begin to "vibrate" only if the criticism relates to an area where they feel particularly sensitive. In those areas of your life where you feel confident, you probably have no difficulty in dusting off foolish criticism. But if there are areas of your life in which you feel insecure—be it career, love, looks, whatever—then that is the frequency to which your internal tuning fork is set. Just one word or look on that frequency is enough to set off an automatic reaction. You hear it. You believe it. You add to it. You feel miserable.

Some people, of course, have such sensitive tuning forks that just about any critical noise sets them shimmying and shaking. Some people hear even the mildest comment as massive condemnation. To such a person, a comment like: "You have a thread on your sweater" is immediately translated into being called a slob or worse. And instead of just saying: "Thanks, I'll brush it off," they feel humiliated. If they are told: "You are too sensitive to criticism," the internal fork senses only that a negative sentence has been said and responds with negative feelings. Little kids have those feelings just right when they chant: "Nobody loves me. Everybody hates me, I'm goin' to go eat worms."

Where Sensitivity to Criticism Comes From

The earliest lesson most people get on the subject of criticism is simply to accept it. This may not quite reach the level of the maxim "Children should be seen and not heard," but it generally means children should not be heard "talking back" to their elders. Children are taught to believe that when parents, teachers, and other authority figures criticize them, those authority figures are always right. For example:

"Your hands are filthy. Go wash them before you pick up that sandwich."

"They are clean enough for me."

"Go wash your hands before I lose my temper!"

Or:

"Your work is unsatisfactory. You have given the wrong answer to this question."

"No, I haven't. That is the right answer."

"How dare you question me. Go to the board and write one

hundred times: 'I will not talk back to my teacher.' "

The idea, of course, is to help children learn the rules of the family, the community, and the society in which they are grow- ing up. The rules are not necessarily the same everywhere— different cultures have different mores, standards, and views. But in every culture it is understood that there must be some com- mon consensus about the proper way to behave (like stopping for a red light and going on a green light), or total chaos would result. If no one ever worries about the rules or what people will say, the culture itself is threatened. And in every culture, it is the job of the adults to pass this understanding on to children and to let children know when they are right or wrong.

Alas, in this effort to help children learn the ways of the world, adults—usually with the best intentions—often pass along a lot of wrong information.

It may be information that is right for the immediate situation but won't work in another, such as: "You are not going to succeed if you don't sit still and keep your mouth shut."

Or it may be information offered to scare a youngster into "behaving": "You will never amount to anything, Johnny Jones, because you refuse to do what you are told."

Or it may be a comment that is sincerely intended to motivate but only serves to discourage: "Yes, you did that well, but not well enough. I'm sure you can do better." (Fine if the youngster can do better, discouraging if the child either can't or has no interest in that particular subject.)

But whether in ways that are helpful or ways that are not, children receive the message over and over again that getting along means accepting, absorbing, and heeding criticism without questioning it:

"Why, Mom?"

"Because I say so, that's why!"

Learning to Question Critics

As we get older, we begin to realize—partly through the instruction or example of others, partly through our own observations—that all critics are not wise, just, or right, and that even those critics whom we love and who love us can on occasion be wrong. We realize that some criticism is justified and helpful while some is designed only to hurt. All these realizations come not as a single event, like a bolt of lightning, but as a process, like an extended voyage.

Just how long and difficult that voyage turns out to be depends on the circumstances of your life. The more heavily criticized you are as a child, the harder it is to develop the ability to evaluate criticism. And, of course, many different circumstances of life can create an area of special sensitivity to which your individual tuning fork responds.

Further, reaching adulthood does not mean all don't-talk-back/ because-I-say-so-that's-why critics disappear from your life. Your parents may still see you as a child they continue to have both the right and the responsibility to command. Certainly the world of work has its share of authoritarian managers who presume themselves to be always right—which makes anyone who disagrees with them wrong. The social world has its share of people who firmly believe: "I'm somebody and you're not, so what I say counts."

It's true that Americans are more willing to talk back in more areas of life than ever before. At one time, for example, if designers said women's skirts were to be two inches shorter, millions of women would rehem every skirt in the closet for fear of being criticized as out of fashion. Today, although a great many women—and men, too—delight in keeping current with style trends, the era of fashion dictatorship is definitely dead.

But, give or take a few subject areas, it's still fair to say that most of us grow up—and remain—surrounded by a multitude of critics and a variety of criticism. Thus the process of sorting out criticism that is constructive and worthy of attention from criticism that is destructive and worthless is a never-ending one. Successfully dealing with criticism means welcoming criticism that enables you to learn, to improve, or to correct while refusing to be beaten down by criticism that is designed only to hurt.

Filtering and Grading

Criticism must be filtered and graded. You separate out criticism that deserves attention from criticism that does not—and then determine just how much attention the filtered criticism deserves. This is something that you probably do easily—and without much conscious thought—in areas where you feel confident or with critics who simply do not matter to you.

But avoiding that beaten-down feeling means filtering and grading *all* criticism and *all* critics. And that requires *conscious* thought. Here, again, you must pause, reflect, and ask yourself a series of questions to give your own common sense a chance to help you.

Remember the discussion in Chapter Four about personalizing? That chapter described the way we often interpret generalized statements and opinions as personal criticism. That is surely the first filter through which criticism must pass. You must first decide if this is, in fact, a criticism of you. Assuming that it is, more filters are required.

Who Says?

The next question to ask is: "Who says?"

In his book, *In Search of Meaning*, Viennese psychiatrist Victor Frankl offers a theory about why some prisoners of Nazi concentration camps struggled to survive the terrible situation in which they found themselves while others lost the will to live. In Frankl's view, the difference is that the latter accepted the Nazis' view of their status in life. The survivors, he argues, refused to feel humiliated, despite their loss of former position, material goods, health, and freedom. The Nazis treated them like trash, but their internal response was: "Oh yeah? Why would I believe pigs like you?"

They asked the question: "Who says?" And the answer was: "Nobody worth listening to."

The question of whether your critic is credible applies to all sorts of situations. A *Wall Street Journal* story described the high-pressure sales techniques of a group of brokers selling stock of dubious value. Their pitch involved casting aspersions on the manhood of those called: "I understand you want to talk with your wife, but does she go to work with you every day? Does she make the decisions? C'mon, drop your pompoms and get into the game with the varsity." Or: "Take your backbone out of the closet." Or: "Put your wife on the phone, she's more of a man than you are."

Did this approach sell stock? Yes, it did . . . to men who did not ask themselves: "Who says?"

Who was this who was claiming that to reject their sales pitch was proof of being henpecked or having no backbone? It was simply somebody whose goal was to make a profit by selling something—not an expert on every potential customer's manliness or marital situation.

Certainly, everyone is entitled to an opinion, but not all opinions are equally credible. And you may fairly judge which opinions you choose to care about. Is the person an expert? If the subject was your car's motor, whose opinion would you value more: your accountant's or your auto mechanic's? On the other hand, whose opinion would you value more if the subject was your tax return?

The question "Who says?" also includes the query "How many say?" People who do not question their critics have a tendency to accept a single negative opinion as final. That is usually an opinion in an area of sensitivity—an area where an internal tuning fork is all set to vibrate.

Mary submits a short story to a quarterly literary journal, and it is rejected. "I knew it," Mary tells herself. "I have no talent." America's top-selling author Stephen King was routinely rejected by publishers until his novel *Carrie* was accepted and became a smash success. Luckily for King, he did not take the first rejection as final. Was it painful? Maybe. But not the last word on the subject.

The main problem with accepting a single negative as final is that there is rarely a way to be sure that this single opinion is expert, or right, or unbiased. The best way to check one opinion is to gather several with which to compare it.

When you ask the question "Who says?" the object is both to filter out critics who have no credibility and to grade the expertise of those who you feel deserve some attention.

Ava has a thirty-five-year-old son who uses drugs. He comes to see her to ask for money. He says he plans to go to a rehabilitation center, but meanwhile he needs money to pay rent and buy food. Ava gives him the money—and he uses it to buy more drugs. When he returns for more money, Ava refuses to give it to him. He tells her a truly loving mother would not reject her son. She offers to send rent money directly to the landlord. The son angrily accuses her of treating him like a baby. He warns her that he doesn't know what will become of him if she doesn't give him money. He says she will be responsible if he ends up in the street.

Ava feels that she must have already failed her son in some way or he wouldn't be an addict. This is her tuning fork. And her son knows how to get it to whisper: "Bad mother, bad mother, bad mother."

Who says? A junkie. Yes, he is her son, so she is going to pay some attention. But how much attention? How much attention does a thirty-five-year-old addict who lies to his mother deserve? Grading her son's criticism will enable Ava to consider a wider range of responses to it.

If she believes he is 100 percent correct, she will continue feeling guilty and continue giving him money until she runs out. She thus becomes an enabler—someone who helps the addict stay addicted.

If she believes he is correct that he deserves her help—but only to a degree—she may offer to help him seek counseling or go to counseling with him or seek counseling herself to determine what her best course of action is.

What Everybody Says

Possibly, the critic who has the most effect on the most people is that all-powerful critic known as "everybody." It is almost the worst thing in the world to have "everybody" think you are a jerk or to be embarrassed in front of "everybody." It's hard not to accept a verdict that "everybody" has pronounced. But the truth is that "everybody" does not exist. Yes, there are values on which this society has a consensus and to which most people conform. Certainly, we don't believe in murder or stealing or torture but, even here, you can't claim that "everybody" agrees. If everybody agreed, there would no need for jails.

Yet, all too often, we accept "everybody's" existence—and power—with not even a single question.

In third grade, Norma made a funny noise when she sneezed, and the other kids in the class started giggling. Norma was embarrassed and for years afterward, she suppressed every sneeze for fear of making a fool of herself in front of "everybody."

Who was "everybody"? One group of children, in one instance, in a third grade classroom. Norma gave those children a power that was greater—and lasted far longer—than their perceived criticism deserved.

Bob is another example. As a teenager, Bob suffered from an anxious tic that caused him to pluck his body hair nervously. He had pulled so many hairs from his arm that, years later, he ended up with a large, noticeable bald spot on an otherwise hairy forearm. Bob was so sensitive about this that he refused to ever wear a short-sleeve shirt. When his friends went swimming, Bob made excuses. He didn't want to take his shirt off. As long as his arm was concealed, Bob was outgoing and confident, but even the thought of rolling up his sleeve was enough to throw Bob offstride. He hated missing out on good times, but he felt he had no choice. Everybody would see, everybody would think, everybody would snicker or stare or say something.

Is this true? In most cases, some people will not notice at all. At any given time, some people are so wound up in their own thoughts and activities that they don't notice much of anything else at all: "Wow. Did you see that?" "See what?" they say.

Some people notice and don't care. They see and forget almost at the same time. They are more interested in something else: "Did you notice that the new supervisor has a scar across his nose?" "Yes. Do you think he'll change the accounting system? I heard that he might."

Some people notice, make a direct comment, and then let it go: "Hey, Darryl. How many pounds have you put on lately? Maybe you should tell Mary to cook some dishes you don't like. Now about these reports . . ."

And some people, it must be admitted, will insist upon making a point of noticing: "Say, Bob, why do you have that peculiar bald spot on your arm? Funny, I never noticed it because you always wear long sleeves. But I noticed it when you were changing into your jogging clothes in the locker room and I wondered . . ."

This is not "everybody." This is one somebody.

So the next question is, once again: "Who says? Who is this somebody? How much information is this somebody entitled to know?"

If this somebody is your physician asking questions to diagnose a condition correctly, you are only hurting yourself by not being truthful and complete in your answer. But if this person is merely a curious soul, you are entitled to decide how much, if any, information to impart.

If Bob doesn't want to say: "I plucked out my hair as a result of an anxiety condition," he breaks no law, offends no moral imperative by not saying it. He can choose to be evasive: "I don't know. It's been that way since I was a kid." He can decline to answer: "It's no big deal, I'd rather not go into it."

However he decides to answer, the point is that Bob is now dealing with a specific critic—rather than what "everybody" says. By opting to deal with a specific critic if and when one appears, Bob allows himself to go swimming rather than staying at home because of what "everybody" would say.

Dealing With Prejudice and Bias

Prejudice and bias do exist, and many people—even if not everybody—may join to criticize you on the basis of race,

creed, color, sex, sexual orientation, disability, appearance—
you name it.

The question is still: "Who says?"

Just because they say it, do you have to believe it?

How expert are they?

Do they have an ulterior motive?

Do they benefit in some way by making you feel inferior or
by denying you opportunity?

The Internal Critic

The internal critic not only accepts all perceived outside criticism as correct, but also both adds to it and invents more. The
internal critic is the harshest critic of all—even tougher than
"everybody." The internal critic says: "I'm no good, and if you
disagree, there must be something wrong with you." This belief
was immortalized in Groucho Marx's famous line: "I wouldn't
belong to any club that would have me for a member."

The mind reader, described in Chapter Three, observes
someone looking in her direction and says: "That person is not
really interested in me." The internal critic observes someone
looking in her direction and says: "That person is interested in
me. I can't understand why. There must be something wrong
with him."

To say that internal critics tend to judge on very little evidence is an understatement. In the unforgiving world of the
internal critic, just one false move and you're dead.

Ernie believes he dares not hope for a social life because he
has some visible bumps on his cheek. His internal critic tells him
he is too ugly to appeal to anyone. (Robert Redford has several
skin imperfections, but luckily for his career, his internal critic
apparently hasn't noticed.) What Ernie does is rule out all other
attributes that anyone else might like about him—his sense of
humor, his intelligence, his interests. His internal critic says *only*
perfect skin counts.

To accept this internal critic uncritically is the same mistake as accepting any single external critic without checking on whether that critic's opinion is expert, right, or biased. You may well find you are biased against yourself. You then deny yourself opportunity before anyone else has a chance to do it for you.

In the sixties, civil rights leaders felt that only part of their battle to assure equal opportunity for African-Americans was to convince the white majority. Another part lay in convincing the members of the minority group itself. And leaders of the woman's movement of the seventies also felt that part of their campaign lay in raising the consciousness of women themselves that they were equal, deserving, and worthy. The message of the "black is beautiful" campaign and the consciousness-raising groups were similarly aimed at internal critics who were echoing the opinions of the wider society at the time.

How do you question the internal critic?

Ask: "How do I know for sure?" The usual answer is: "I feel it. I just know it." Sometimes the internal critic puts the blame on "everybody," whom we already know doesn't exist.

More evidence is required. Look for other people who share your situation. What is their experience? It is common for people with harsh internal critics to believe that they are alone: "I am the only person this has ever happened to, so no wonder everybody thinks I am a jerk." But it would be a rare case indeed if you were alone.

The fact that books about problems and support groups for people with like problems have proliferated in recent years makes this point. If you wore a sign that said: "I think I am a loser because I'm working in a job that I feel is beneath my ability," a dozen people would probably come up to you and say: "You too?" Discovering that others share your problem is often very helpful. It may disarm the internal voice that says: "Everybody else but you is doing just fine." Meeting with others who share your problem can be very helpful—if, that is, the goal of your meetings is to offer mutual support in dealing with the problem, rather than merely to form a whining chorus.

There's a joke about three elderly women who meet each day at the same park bench. The three sit down, and the first woman heaves a sigh. "Oh my," she says. The second woman sighs and says: "Oh my goodness." The third sighs and says: "Oh good-ness me." At which point the first woman says sternly: "I thought we had agreed we were going to stop complaining about our children."

Determining When Criticism Is Helpful

The next question is: "What is the content of the criticism?" Praise is obviously always more welcome than criticism, but *some criticism is helpful.* And some criticism is meant to be help-ful, even if it is not. Thus it is important to focus on exactly what was said, done, or implied.

It's important to get a fix on exactly what the criticism is to stop the tuning fork effect. Once you start vibrating, you will add levels of criticism to any that was actually offered, and every level you add makes you feel worse. A critical statement such as: "Jones, this report you gave me is too short" can, in seconds, be expanded in the mind to: "He doesn't like my report, I'm failing at work [here comes Chicken Little], my job is threatened." Or you might think: "He is saying that because I'm a woman." Or: "He is saying that because he likes to hassle people."

By focusing in on *exactly what is said*—not what *emotions* those words touch off in you, or the imagined motivation of the critic—you are better able to determine how to respond to it. If the problem is strictly as stated ("The report is too short") you may easily be able to say: "Okay, I'll make it longer." Or you may decide to say: "I disagree. In my opinion, it's perfect just as it is."

Laurie is an artist. She has invited a fellow artist whose work she respects to her studio. The colleague looks at a painting that is still in progress and comments: "I think the sky would be enhanced if you deepened the blue on the left-hand side." There is no doubt that this is direct criticism of Laurie's work.

If Laurie assumes there is hidden meaning in this remark, there is no limit to the negative interpretations that are possible:

- Angry: "She really means I'm not a good artist, that I don't know what I'm doing. I'll never let her in here again."
- Hurt: "That's just her subtle way of saying the whole painting stinks. She's probably right, too. I might as well throw it away."
- Sad: "All that work for nothing."
- Frustrated: "No matter how hard I try, I'm never good enough."

If, however, she judges the comment by *content* alone, she allows herself to decide whether the criticism is *useful*.

"Is she right? Hmmm. No, I don't think so. I like it better the way it is." Aloud she might politely say: "Thanks for the suggestion, Helen, I'll give it some thought."

"Is she right? Hmmm. Yes, I think she is. The sky would look better that way." Aloud she says, "Thanks for the tip, Helen. I agree with you."

To be helpful, criticism has to have some value. And that is something else for you to determine. For example, if you buy an expensive watch because you like it, you'll probably view the money as well spent. But if you buy it because you feel you *have to* to avoid criticism, you are only investing in dissatisfaction. Thus responding to this particular form of criticism may have no value for you.

Delaying Your Response

It is not always necessary to react *immediately* to criticism. Your first impulse may be anger: "How dare they criticize me?" Or your first impulse may be passivity: "They're right and I'm wrong—as usual."

But your first impulse may be wrong. And you may well realize that fact once you have given yourself a chance to think about precisely what was said, to question the critics and the criticism. Postponing your response to both internal and external criticism may help you sort out what is helpful and what is not. Just because somebody says jump doesn't mean you must ask: "How high?" You can say: "Thanks for the suggestion. I may try that next time." Or: "I appreciate your input. You may be right. Let me think about it, will you?"

Delay helps because it enables you to get your automatic responses under control. Delay enables you to think over what was said, who said it, and what response is required.

Dealing With Criticism

There are many possible responses to criticism:

You can simply reject it.

If the critic is not worth listening to, if the content is not helpful, if accepting the criticism in no way improves you or improves your life—forget it.

Some people feel they have to endure critics who are harsh, nasty, and mean. These critics are unforgiving and unrelenting for reasons that are not clear and usually have nothing to do with the person they criticize. Thea's mother is such a critic. Nothing Thea does pleases this woman. If Thea spends two dollars on a birthday card for Mom, Mom says: "Is that all I'm worth to you, two dollars?" And if she spends five dollars, Mom says: "Five dollars for a card—that's ridiculous. You have no idea of the value of money."

How to deal with such a critic? Accept her for what she is: impossible! And refuse to fight with her.

Don't attempt to argue. Don't worry if you have not succeeded in pleasing her, since she cannot be pleased. Simply do what you think best—and when she complains, ignore the complaint. "That's how she is," you tell yourself.

Many people find this difficult to do because, having learned as children that whatever elders say must be accepted, they feel guilty ignoring Mom—or any other critic, for that matter. Or they are afraid that rejecting the critic will cause that critic to reject them. Or they are afraid that the critic will escalate the stakes in the battle. Ava wonders whether her son really will end up on the street. Adolescents may threaten to run away—and some do.

Lil's elderly mother lives with her and complains bitterly if Lil has to work late and doesn't make her dinner on time. Lil tries to explain, but her mother doesn't want to hear. A friend suggests: "Why don't you just tell her that if she doesn't like living with you she can try a nursing home . . . or a tent?" Lil is scandalized. "I can't say that to my mother. She would never speak to me again." Indeed, if Lil tries to get tough, her mother may escalate the battle by playing on Lil's desire to be a good daughter: "How dare you say such a thing to your mother? After all I've done for you." Or: "You know I'm not well. You are aggravating my condition. You don't care if I die."

What could Lil do then? Exactly the same thing. Ignoring such a complaint is the best policy. Don't respond. Let the criticism roll over you.

"Easier said than done," you might be saying. And you're right. There is no denying the difficulty of maintaining such a policy. But look at it this way: For reasons that are not clear, some people seem determined to go fishing for trouble. They want to catch you on a hook and play you on the line the way a sports fisherman reels in a trout. When the trout puts up a fight, it's more fun for the fisherman. It's certainly not fun for the trout. And, what's more, it's useless. Once the poor fish is well and firmly on the hook, all that struggling is in vain. And that is just as true when the poor fish is a human who allows herself to get hooked by a critic who enjoys watching the fish struggle. Such critics usually know exactly the right bait to put on the hook. They know what will catch you. A morsel of guilt. A tasty accusation. A nice, fat threat. Gotcha!

Lil's mother says: "You don't care about me. If you cared about me, you'd make sure you were always here on time." Lil does care for her mother, but if she agrees that the only way to show it is to be home when her mother wants her there, she can't do her job properly. Nor does she *want* to be totally at her mother's beck and call. Therefore, constantly responding to her mother's criticism solves nothing and only makes her feel angry, frustrated, and guilty.

Lil's mother is certainly a critic whose opinion Lil values. But the *content* of her criticism is neither helpful nor possible. There is *no value* in heeding it. If you don't want to become a poor, struggling fish, you have to learn to keep your mouth shut when that tempting bait is dangled in front of you. Because underneath that bait is a big, sharp hook.

Lil can help herself by thinking in terms of alternatives in thought, action, and feeling. Taking the bait helps no one and makes Lil feel both guilty and angry. If she thinks: "That's just how Mom is," she can take pressure off herself. If she feels resigned rather than guilty, she can better endure the situation. If she ignores the bait, rather than taking it, she can avoid endless, useless wrangling.

She can tell her mother: "Mom, you're right, but nothing can be done and *I'm not going to discuss it again*." Her mother may object. Her mother may accuse her of not caring. Her mother may cry. Her mother may threaten. Her mother may drag others into the discussion: "Your sister, if she were here, wouldn't fool around after work, knowing that I'm here all alone." Lil must instruct herself: "Don't take that bait."

How easy it would be to get into a new and equally useless argument over whether Lil is "fooling around after work" or whether the sister would or would not adhere to her mother's schedule. But once Lil has decided on the alternative action of *not* getting hooked, she must forgo the temptation to explore that territory. ("Mom, if you want to talk about something else, fine. If not, I'm tuning out.")

You can accept and reject it at the same time.

Some criticism you accept because you feel you have no choice.

Pete's boss says: "I don't like the way you are doing this. Only an idiot would do it that way. Either do it my way or leave."

If Pete does not choose to leave—or does not choose to leave immediately—he may well say: "Yes, sir, your way is the only way." That doesn't mean he has to accept the boss's view that he is an idiot. Indeed, he may well think the boss is an idiot and yet still accept the practical necessity to do things the boss's way.

Some people feel it's a matter of principle to fight when a critic is clearly wrong. A policeman stops you for going through a red light and says: "I'm not going to give you a ticket. Just a warning. Don't do it again." And you feel you must straighten the officer out. The light was yellow, not yet red. So, instead of saying: "Thank you, officer," and driving away, you get into a debate that very well may continue at the local jail.

No law says you must act on all criticism or correct all unfair criticism. As discussed in Chapter Four, you can pick your fights. Pursue some. Ignore some.

Linda comes from a small blue-collar town where it is not the custom for young people to go to college—and certainly not for a young woman. Linda understands that if she breaks with custom and goes off to a college, her family, neighbors, and friends will think she is odd. They may take it as rejection of everything they stand for. If she leaves, she sets herself apart. Thus to leave is a conscious choice to bring criticism on herself—but also to ignore it.

You can minimize it by surrounding yourself with like-minded people.

A great many people distrust others who are not like themselves and are likely to criticize them. One way to deal with this is to join together with people who are more like you—support groups for people in a particular situation, an ethnic neighborhood likely to have stores selling your favorite food, a club for people with your interests.

You might ask: "Why should I have to surround myself with people like me? I insist that others accept me as I am." You don't have to surround yourself with people like yourself, and you may well decide that it's worth fighting to convince your critics to accept you. But if you want to find allies in your fight, if you want to locate an island of acceptance amid the battle, you can often do that by joining together with people who share your concerns.

You can make use of it.

Criticism is essential in a democracy. Only in a dictatorship are all citizens expected to say: "What a wonderful idea" every time someone in authority issues an order. Open criticism of policies, programs, and projects can lead to compromises that contribute to overall success.

Criticism can help you improve your individual performance. If you learn that you lack certain needed skills, you can do something about obtaining those skills. If you never learn—or if you refuse to believe—that you have a gap in skill that needs filling, you won't do anything to solve the problem.

You may find you benefit from seeking criticism. By asking others to give you an opinion, you can double-check the views of other critics, and also obtain suggestions that you find helpful.

Listening to Criticism Is Not a Mistake

Listening to criticism is not a mistake. The mistake is to *believe all* criticism—or to *reject all* criticism—without pausing to think about it, without ever questioning the expertise of the critic, the motivation of the critic, the content of the criticism, or the value of the criticism.

There is no shame in taking advantage of the experience and ideas of others. There is no guilt in deciding that even though their way may work fine for them, it doesn't suit you.

There is really no way to avoid the barrage of criticism that comes at all of us. Sometimes it seems to come from everywhere. In recent years, corporate managers were subjected to an insistent message that if they were not on the fast track they might as well lie down on a track and be run over by a train. Ads announced that if you didn't have the right car or the right watch, you were revealed as a nerd. And on top of that, you were nobody unless somebody loved you. When you feel you don't measure up, it's hard not to feel down. But you can avoid being trampled by criticism if you simply take the time and trouble to analyze it, to analyze your own reaction to it.

Merely pausing to *question* criticism has the same effect on your internal tuning fork as does simply placing a finger on a real tuning fork. It stops the vibrations cold.

Stopping the Vibrations

Several techniques described earlier are very useful when dealing with critics, either internal or external, in addition to those already mentioned. You can *de-catastrophize*. When an external critic or your own harsh internal critic predicts that if you don't measure up the worst will happen, you may find yourself believing it. That is the time to ask: "What is this worst? What makes me agree that it will occur?" When, for example, you begin thinking: "Everybody will think I am a fool," you can ask: "How likely is it that *everybody* will have this same opinion?" You can play *defense attorney*. That's only fair, since your critics are playing the role of prosecutor. Before the judge renders a verdict, what can you say in your own defense? What rebuttal, what mitigating factor, what alternative explanation is possible? Finally, it is also helpful to *assign responsibility*: Are the critics being too harsh? Are you being overly accepting? When a salesperson tells you that if you don't buy you are stupid, do you have to believe that? The salesperson bears some responsibility in making unprovable accusations. But you bear some responsibility if you accept that accusation without proof. You may not be able to prevent that tap that starts your tuning fork vibrating, but you can act to bring it under control.

CHAPTER SEVEN

PERFECTIONISM

From earliest childhood, we are taught to strive for perfection. For example: Whose papers does the teacher pin up on the classroom bulletin board? The ones turned in by pupils who got all the answers right, of course. Who do we hear praised? Who do we see admired? Those who do everything perfectly—or at least *seem* to.

But whoever invented the phrase: "Nobody's perfect" really put it perfectly. Sure, some occasions seem perfect. Some specific efforts, like that spelling test in fifth grade, are judged to be perfect. But as a general rule of life, there is good, there is great, there is nearly perfect—but perfection doesn't exist.

Statisticians express this concept by drawing a bell-shaped curve with tails that extend into infinity. This curve represents the law of probability and chance. If, for example, you dropped a quantity of beads through a grid so that all beads had an equal chance of falling to the left or right, you'd end with a pile of beads shaped like a bell. Most of the beads would end up in the center, with smaller quantities on either side. The bell shape is never perfect—that is, you can't precisely place the outer rim of the bell—because, unless you have collected every bead on earth, you can't be sure how each and every one will fall. In life, as in statistics, you can get very, very close, yet still not achieve 100 percent certainty.

Perfection's Imperfections

Sometimes it seems as if the very notion of perfection was invented just to torment us.

Quite often, what we call perfection is simply a matter of opinion.

As we've discussed before, so much of what we do in life is judged by others. And others don't always agree with us—or with each other. How many times have you read two movie reviews that made you wonder if the critics had really seen the same movie? One critic says: "This is the best movie of the year." Another says: "Save your money, this is a bomb." One calls the acting "beautifully restrained," but the other finds the same acting "dull."

Perfection is sometimes just a matter of timing.

Back in the 1940s, a highly popular advertising jingle for Chiquita Bananas ended with the line: "Bananas like the climate of the very, very tropical equator, so you should never put bananas in the refrigerator. No. No. No. No." According to a former vice president of the company that marketed Chiquita, the only reason the word *refrigerator* was mentioned in the jingle was that it rhymed with *equator*. The company wanted shoppers to be reminded that the bananas came all the way from Central America. The truth was—and is—that bananas can be put into the refrigerator, yes, yes, yes, yes, and indeed last longer if they are cold.

However, that didn't matter in the forties when refrigerators were tiny and the majority of women went grocery shopping almost daily. What mattered then was that people loved the Chiquita jingle, sang it everywhere, and bought lots of bananas. (The jingle became so popular, recordings of it appeared in jukeboxes. And the U.S. government borrowed the tune for a song about conserving water during World War II.) However, what had seemed to be the perfect ad campaign began costing the company sales in the fifties when the suburbs boomed, refrigerators doubled in size, and shopping became a once-a-week event. Shoppers would buy a dozen apples or a dozen oranges but only three bananas because they "knew" that bananas should never go in the fridge. The company tried in vain for years to counter the jingle's message but finally gave up.

Perfection can involve imperfection.

Imagine you are at the World Series. The two best pro baseball teams in their leagues are fighting for the championship. It's the last inning, possibly the last pitch, the count is three and two and the game hangs in the balance. It's possible that the pitcher pitches the ball "perfectly." But the batter does a perfect job and hits the ball. Then an outfielder does a perfect job and catches the ball. The result of all this perfection? The batter's team has lost the game. In their view this is not perfect. If the batter had hit a home run, the pitcher's pitch would not be considered perfect no matter how good it was.

Of course, if you are a baseball fan, you may well consider this imperfect situation to be "perfection" because the suspense of waiting to see how the game comes out is what makes it so much fun to watch.

Too much perfection can be a bad thing.

This is a most important point. Just as you can overdo overconfidence, you can also overdo perfection. British transportation unions have made very practical use of this fact in getting around a law that prohibits them from striking. They came up with a perfect solution called "working to rule."

Instead of walking off the job when negotiations over a new contract broke down, the transit workers resolved to follow every single rule in their work manual—perfectly. Each and every rule was be observed meticulously, flawlessly, and to the letter. For example, if a rule said the engineer must be sure that all doors are closed before the train leaves the station, the engineer would physically leave the train and carefully look at each door—instead of just sticking his head out of a window and looking back. No train left the station with open doors. No train left the station on time, either. Simply following the rules perfectly has, on more than one occasion, been enough to cause the complete collapse of British transit.

High Standards Are Fine

Hold on, you might be saying now. Are you actually recommending an absence of standards? Would you like to be operated on by a brain surgeon who says: "Don't bother to check the instruments. They're probably all there"? Would you want a lawyer representing you who says: "I really know nothing of the procedures in this court"?

The answer is no. But there is a difference between someone who simply doesn't care about doing a good job and is indifferent to any need for careful preparation, and someone who, feeling pressured to be perfect, is immobilized by the fear of doing something wrong. You would not want to be operated on by a brain surgeon who is a nervous wreck.

It's true that in some professions perfection is more sought after than in others. The diamond cutter and the dentist, like the surgeon, must work within critically close parameters. A good accountant is meticulous in preparing an audit. A good reporter double checks facts and makes sure that names are spelled correctly. The trapeze artist must have precise timing to catch a partner flying through the air.

But even these can run into problems with perfectionism. Take the trapeze artist. Admittedly, the performer can't often get away with saying: "Well, I came close." On the other hand, if in pursuit of perfection the trapeze artist practices for twenty hours straight and then, come performance time, is too tired to concentrate, that perfectionism becomes self-defeating.

Further, the same level of perfection may not be required in all phases of life. The trapeze artist may well have a more relaxing, less exacting standard when joining friends for a round of golf. The level of perfection we aspire to and admire is not likely to be obtained without going through a less-than-perfect period of practice first. The trapeze artist is not going to do a quadruple loop on the first attempt.

In sum, a striving for high standards only becomes the mistake of perfectionism when it is *carried to an extreme.*

The Perfect Amount of Perfection

Alas, because we are taught from childhood to aspire to an ideal that is illusive, we are frequently caught in a tug of war between what we feel we should do and what we actually can do. We are told stories of people who succeed because they refuse to accept second best. We hear about the motivating power of reaching for the stars. And those stories are true—up to a point. But a law of diminishing returns applies to the quest for perfection. Yes, it can motivate you to do your best. But carried to an extreme, it can bring about exactly the opposite. It can lead to constant dissatisfaction, to failure, to giving up, to procrastination, and to just not trying. As the nineteenth-century French poet Alfred de Musset wrote: "To understand perfection is the triumph of human intelligence. To desire to possess it is the most dangerous kind of madness."

It is dangerous because, all too often, when we insist upon perfection, we end up with nothing at all. Therapists call this the all-or-nothing syndrome. When we set terms of all or nothing, what we generally end up with is nothing.

If you decide that if you cannot do something perfectly, there is no point to doing it at all, you may not do it.

Take Ted, for example. Ted is bright and capable—he always got top marks in school. His parents bored the neighbors by constantly boasting about Ted's ability to accomplish "anything he puts his mind to." Most recently, Ted has put his mind to developing a two-day course for new employees in his firm's marketing department. Naturally, Ted wants this project to turn out brilliantly. He wants the new employees to be impressed. He wants the higher-ups to notice him favorably.

He wants this so badly, he is numb. Every idea he has seems second rate. Every attempt to write his thoughts down is blocked by his sense that they aren't "good enough." So Ted arranges to be busy with other less pressured projects. He continues to promise that the course will be completed on time, but he isn't going to hand in just anything. It has to be right. All he has to do (as his parents would remind him) is put his mind to it. Unfortunately, Ted's department head does not appreciate Ted's determination to do a perfect job, since, from his point of view, Ted simply hasn't done any job. All Ted has produced is promises.

Perfectionism is not just a work-related issue, it applies to social situations too.

If you feel that unless you have the mate who meets your specifications down to the last detail, you would rather be alone, you had better get used to your own company.

Cheryl has a checklist for her soul mate. He has to be of the same race and religion. He has to be slightly older than she—but not too old. He has to be good-looking, have a business or profession. He has to have a sense of humor. "I'm not getting any younger," says Cheryl, "so there is no point in wasting time with anyone who isn't a real prospect for a long-range relationship." But real prospects are few and far between because Cheryl checks the list and writes them off. Sam seemed to meet most of her specifications—but unfortunately, says Cheryl, "He's going bald."

If you put off completing a project, hosting a party, taking a trip, or making a decision until the perfect time and the perfect plan is in place, you will probably be waiting forever.

It may be hard simply to pick a date arbitrarily and say: "That's it. My standard will be the best that can be done by that date—not the best that can be done if I had all of eternity in which to do it." There are times when the ability to compromise, to adopt a second-best decision, to develop an alternative plan, or simply to let a toss of a coin decide which way you'll go can be invaluable.

Mary and Steve decide to stop at an ice cream stand and get cones. There isn't any place to park, so Mary goes in while Steve stays in the car. "What flavor do you want?" she asks. "I don't care," he says. "Vanilla fudge, if they have it." They don't have it. And Mary dithers and dallies and debates which flavor Steve might like. Plain vanilla? Chocolate? Chocolate mint? She doesn't want to bring the wrong thing. It has to be *exactly right*. Meanwhile Steve, waiting in the car, gets annoyed. What is keeping Mary? Others who had entered the shop after she did had already come out. When he later gripes about being kept waiting, Mary feels hurt that he doesn't appreciate her effort to please him. What started out to be a pleasure trip turns into a source of friction between them.

If you feel you must be perfect in every single thing you do, you may be wasting time on something very minor when your energies could be more wisely invested.

Stan had one paper to finish to qualify for his master's degree. It was just a short paper, but he had difficulty with it. And he wasn't satisfied with his work. He asked the professor for an extension of time to complete it. The extension meant that Stan wouldn't graduate on time, so the professor assumed Stan had asked for the extension because he was ill. But Stan was simply determined that, after getting A's on every other paper, he wasn't going to settle for a B on this last one. Yet the mark on that one paper would have little if any effect on his final grade. Certainly getting a B on that paper would cause less harm to his future career than failing to graduate on time, but Stan isn't looking at the big picture. He wants to be perfect on the small paper.

Why It's Hard to Compromise

Why is a perfectionist so determined to do it right? Partly out of fear, partly out of fantasy. The fear is that others will find us out—that if we just once do something that is not wonderful, terrific, out-of-the-ordinary, we will lose the respect of others.

Our internal critic will start to complain. The famous "everybody" will disapprove.

Perfectionism manifests itself as a desire to avoid embarrassment. You might say to yourself: "If I miss a word in that speech, I'll be humiliated." Then that thought becomes: "I'd better not even try to give a speech, because I might make a mistake and be humiliated."

This can lead to a belief that it is better to do nothing than to be found out and embarrassed. Doing nothing makes it possible to cling to the comforting fantasy: "It would have been perfect—if I had done it." And some people are perfectly willing to *settle* for fantasy. For example, Max is a waiter and good one, but he likes to tell people that he is also a novelist. He says he is writing the great American novel in his spare time. Has he shown it to a publisher? "Not yet," says Max. "I'm not ready. I'm still polishing. I'll know when it's ready." Max is just enjoying himself. The novel will never be ready, if indeed it has even been started. It exists only to enhance Max's image. There is no need for Max to set a limit on his novel's "perfection" since fantasy has no limits.

Opening the Way to Change

But you know whether you find a fantasy of perfection satisfying or not. You know whether your desire for perfectionism is helping you or hurting you. You might not care if others complain that you are too exacting or a fussbudget if being that way helps you reach your goals. But if sticking to your standards is causing you to fail, to delay, to miss deadlines, or to be lonely, you may want to adjust your perfection settings.

You might feel that isn't possible. "That's how I am," you may say, "and I can't change." However, if you admit to yourself that this is how you are, that is the *first step* on the way to change. You might say: "Hold it. I'm being perfectionistic again. And it isn't helping me." When you label what is going on, you open the way to doing something about it, just as a physician must first diagnose a condition before determining what course of treatment would do the most good. It may be that you are not only being perfectionistic but also making another thinking mistake at the same time. No matter. By naming one mistake—and taking an action to overcome it—you begin the process of gaining control.

The "Perfect" Point of View

Becoming more aware of how perfectionism affects you may be helpful. First, let's examine your feelings about perfectionism in others. Have you, perhaps, said these things:

- "They get away with low standards—but just because they have low standards doesn't make it acceptable for me."
- "It's okay for them to goof up occasionally because they are so successful (or well liked, or fabulously rich) but I can't get away with that."
- "*They* do everything perfectly, so I should be able to, too."
- "I expect perfection from my children [or employees, or spouse, or friends] only because I want the best for them. I am trying to motivate them to be the best they can be."

Let's look at these views more closely because they very often get perfectionists in trouble.

"They have low standards."

Yes, some people have low standards—some seem to have no standards—and get away with it. No one suggests you should sink to their low level. However, sinking to a low level may not be at issue at all. The questions you must ask yourself are:

- "Does deviating *to any degree* from my standard mean I am abandoning standards entirely?"
- "Does the fact that others may deviate *to any degree* from my standard *prove* that they have low or no standards?"

The answer to both questions is no. To accept the fact that sometimes you may do work that is less than your best—because you don't have sufficient time or resources or background to do better *at this time*—is not the same thing as having low standards. Sometimes you need to adjust your goal for a given project or experience. Yes, it would be great to do a perfect job. But sometimes simply meeting a deadline—even if that means doing less than perfect work—may be a more important goal. That does not reflect a lowering of your standards, but merely a realization that, in this instance, a different goal has priority. And, of course, others may also have a need to temper a given standard to meet specific goals.

"It's okay for them."

No doubt it is much easier to goof up and get away with it if you are successful and popular and *also* fabulously rich. Obviously making a mistake that results in the loss of $10,000 is of less importance to someone who starts with a million dollars than to someone who starts with $10,001. But succeeding even though less than perfectly is not a luxury allowed only to a favored few. It is something all of us can experience.

In other words, the fact that some people have more slack than others is not proof that you have none. That's another example of all-or-nothing thinking: They have all, you have nothing. But that's rarely the case.

"They do everything perfectly."

You may believe "they" do everything perfectly—whoever they are—but how can you know for sure? To repeat what was said at the beginning of this chapter, nobody's perfect. It is very unlikely that those others you admire do *everything* perfectly . . . or always did perfectly the things they seem to do so perfectly now. We tend to look at those we like and admire through rose-colored glasses. Other people seem to accomplish difficult things easily and effortlessly. But that's rarely true—and certainly not of everything they do.

If it's possible to get into a conversation with such a paragon, you might ask if that person ever made a blooper, ever suffered through an embarrassing situation, ever settled for second or third best—and you will probably hear a cheerful confession. Many people delight in recounting their Great Moments in Humiliation History—now that they are history, of course.

What people who reach goals do best is not let setbacks *get them down*. Okay, so the speech did not go flawlessly. In fact, it was a disaster. Does that mean never giving another speech? Not at all. They might seek coaching or rehearse more or just choose the topic more carefully, but rather than viewing this imperfection as a character flaw, they see it as a learning experience.

"I expect perfection."

When you demand perfection from others, are you asking for their best or are you asking for more than they can possibly give? Are you willing to pay the price that demanding perfection of others requires?

Gabriel says he's only trying to motivate his son, Ben, when he chastises him for failing to catch a ball or not getting 100 percent on his arithmetic test. But Ben does not feel motivated at all. He feels no pleasure in playing ball. He sees no benefit in getting a 98 percent on a test because he knows nothing less than perfect is good enough for Gabriel. Worse, even when Ben does produce a 100 percent result, he knows that Gabriel may not even notice, because Gabriel is not perfect himself. Thus, Ben realizes that even when he does do everything right, he won't necessarily get credit for it. As a result, he just stops trying.

Parents put pressure on their children to be perfect for many reasons in addition to the quite natural desire to see them succeed. Many people see their children as a reflection of themselves ("If a child I created does well, that means I have done well"). Some see their children as a means of settling old scores ("You thought I wasn't good enough to marry your daughter; watch how well my child does"). Some feel a need to compete at every level ("My child must do better than all other children"). If the children feel they cannot measure up to their parents' wishes, they may, like Ben, just give up. Or they may spend their lives trying to please—suffering long after their parents are dead, because they can never live up to those impossible expectations.

There is a line between pressure that motivates and pressure that crushes and, unfortunately, teachers and school counselors as well as parents sometimes cross it.

This is another instance in which too much perfectionism brings about very imperfect results. Don is a workaholic. He's at the office six days a week—sometimes seven. He works late, he works hard, and he can't understand why others are not as dedicated as he. He concludes his co-workers are lazy, and it makes him resentful of them. He doesn't have any friends in the office—and he resents that, too.

Somewhere there is a middle ground between setting a good example and setting unreasonable standards. That middle ground is not always easy to determine. One way to seek it is by actually writing a list of advantages and disadvantages of doing things your way. Don, for example, realizes that his co-workers resent his obvious low opinion of them. That is why they are not friendly to him. And that, he has found, is a disadvantage. It's more than a matter of not having company for lunch. When Don needs his colleagues' help on a project, they claim to be too busy. They may be saying to themselves: "He thinks I'm a goof-off anyway, so there is no reason to knock myself out for him."

And, too, being an all-or-nothing perfectionist, Don may have lumped all his co-workers into the same do-nothing category. By taking the time to consider them one by one, on a scale of, say, 1 to 10, he may find that a relationship with some co-workers—even if not with all—is possible.

Of course, Don may think it through and decide that he is willing to sacrifice the goodwill of his co-workers—every single one of them—to follow his own rules on how work should be done. He needs to recognize the trade-off he is making. It is one thing to say: "I realize the consequences but I choose this route anyway." It's quite another to later have to say: "I didn't think it through—I should have known better."

Setting Your Standards

Each of us has to come to an individual conclusion about how important a personal standard of perfection is. But that conclusion should be drawn only after we fairly consider the *reasons for our choices*. That doesn't mean the reasons given to you by your internal or external critics.

"What do I have to sacrifice to do it right? Is it worth it?"

Joanna and Margaret are sisters who were jointly left their mother's jewelry after her death. Their mother left no instructions on how the jewelry was to be divided, but each sister feels she knows what Mother would have wanted. Unfortunately their views do not agree. Each feels she should have their mother's pearl necklace, for example. To Joanna, Margaret is simply being greedy and stubborn to insist on having the necklace, while Joanna is simply insisting on doing the right thing. Joanna feels that to accept a less than perfect distribution of the jewelry would be an affront to their mother's memory. Alas, Margaret feels exactly the same way—in reverse. Others might flip a coin, sell the necklace and split the proceeds, donate the necklace to a niece they both adore—but those are compromises. And perfectionists find it difficult to compromise. A compromise means admitting that what you believe may not be the single, perfect solution.

Yet arguing over the necklace puts a terrible strain on Joanna and Margaret and their families. They finally have to ask themselves: "Is owning Mother's necklace worth breaking family ties?"

Many principles are worth fighting for stubbornly, no matter what. If you believe that you are in such a fight, more power to you. But you owe it to yourself—and to those around you—to take the time to write down the pros and cons, the cost of winning as opposed to the price of losing. And make a reasoned decision.

It's not unusual for perfectionists to get into fights just be-

cause they automatically want to win—a normal enough feeling—without a second thought about whether the cost is worth
the prize.

"Am I correctly interpreting the response of others?"

Maybe you hold back from completing a project or initiating
a relationship because you think that another person thinks you
aren't perfect enough. But thinking is not knowing. Maybe what
you deem less than your best is seen by others as fantastic.

Perfection, as was mentioned before, is a matter of opinion.
So the response of one is not necessarily an indication of the
response of all. What one person rejects, another may welcome.
You may have to kiss a dozen frogs to find your prince, and a
dozen otherwise noble types may think you are a frog until your
prince finds you.

How can you find out how others judge you? Only by doing
your best and *taking a chance*. Yes, that creates anxiety. Yes, that
creates some discomfort. But sometimes, as they say in the Nike
ads, you have to "just do it." You can't win a contest if you
haven't entered. You can't fall in love with someone you haven't
met. You can't get praise for an assignment you haven't turned
in. At some point, you have to just do it.

But, you may ask, what if it turns out that what you view as
less than perfect, others see the same way? You would like to do
100 percent, but you feel 75 percent is the best you can manage
now, and they say: "It's not good enough."

You go on from there. You learned something. Most likely,
you now know where another person thinks the gaps are, and
that may not be where you thought they were. It isn't easy to
learn by trial and error. But learning something is better than
simply wishing you knew—and meanwhile getting nowhere at
all.

A recent study showed that physicians in health maintenance
organizations miss the diagnosis of depression 78 percent of the
time, and psychiatrists miss it 50 percent of the time. This is
dismaying—we would prefer a standard a little closer to perfection in such cases—but mental health professionals view this

statistic simply as a signal that better means of diagnosis are needed, not that they must turn in their licenses or go into hiding.

People often say: "I'll be so embarrassed I'll die." Will you really die? Can you remember the last time you were embarrassed? Has it had lasting effect? The trick is to think past possible initial embarrassment to the future—to long-range goals like learning, improving, keeping the job, finding true love. The trick is to say: "I will take a chance on this—even though I'm not sure it's absolutely right—because the only way I'm going to find out whether I can do this is to try."

"Am I being fair to myself in dismissing the positive comments of others?"

Maybe you've said: "I'm my own worst critic." Many people are that way. Someone will tell them: "Wow, that was great." And they'll reply: "Thanks, it really wasn't good enough." When compared to the opinion of the harsh internal critic, other people's comments are dismissed as ill-informed or "just being polite."

And that may be true at times. But if you find yourself rejecting the good opinion of others with great frequency, you are probably holding yourself to unfair, unrealistic standards that leave you always feeling unfulfilled and unsuccessful. And, as you have probably already discovered, that leads to feeling discouraged more than to feeling motivated.

"Am I being too hard on myself? Can I find anything to praise?"

Perfectionists tend to see the glass as half empty, rather than half full. For example, Michael, a psychologist, always receives good reviews for his books and articles. They are called helpful, useful, valuable contributions. But never scholarly. He had at one time hoped to be renowned as a scholar, but what he achieved instead was renown as a clinician. Should he spend his life tortured by the fact that his colleagues do not find him scholarly—or take satisfaction from the fact that his colleagues find his work welcome on other grounds?

Developing Flexibility

Perfectionists often get into trouble because they define perfection as 100 percent, *100 percent of the time,* when a repertoire of "perfection styles" would serve them better.

Yes, it's a good idea to check that business proposal for spelling errors and punctuation mistakes because you don't want your prospective client to think you do sloppy work. You want that first impression to be a good impression—a correct impression. But once you are launched on the project, maybe the best response to a query from the client is to scribble an answer on the note the client sent you and fax it right back. In this instance, *perfect* means "clear and quick," and waiting for a secretary to type up your reply so that it looks nicer might not be as good a solution.

Similarly, you don't always have to maintain the same level of perfection in a relationship. When you first meet someone, here again you want the first impression to be, well, impressive. But if you never relax, never allow the less-perfect you to be seen, you never allow that other person to know you—and you never allow yourself to really get to know that other person. And that puts a strain on any relationship.

Or if you work in a field where a demand for perfection is high—such as a scientist conducting an experiment, an assembler of delicate instruments—the standards of the workplace do not have to be duplicated at home.

"Is there more than one way to do this?"

Perfectionists admire the philosophy Frank Sinatra made famous: "I did it my way." You may be right that your way is the best way. But maybe not. It helps to ask the question: "Is this the *only* way?"

Usually, you know other ways to do things—you know how this one or that one does it. But you reject any other way but your own. Developing flexibility means thinking about the ways others do things. You might want to adopt just one aspect of another person's style. Another person's way may work better in some situations, while your way works better in others.

Sometimes we get an idea in our heads about how something is done that simply isn't correct. There are those who believe— because they read it in a novel—that when sex is done "right" the earth moves or lights flash. And when that doesn't happen, they assume some flaw in themselves or in their partner. They can't enjoy any part of the process because they are too busy noticing how imperfect it is. Such people would benefit from some research into sexual responses that might help to redefine their expectations and understand that there is no one single "right" way to experience sexual satisfaction.

Or let us say that Max the waiter decides he really would like to get his novel published and assumes that he can't show it to a publisher until he has completed and polished it to perfection. He then struggles for perfection all alone. But if Max asks other writers, or reads up on the subject of how books are published, he would discover that it is the accepted custom to approach a literary agent or a publisher after writing only a few chapters and an outline. The writer then benefits from getting professional feedback at the beginning of the project, and that generally leads to a better finished work.

If you never *question* whether "my way" is the only way, you may never discover better ways, much less the "best" way.

> *"Might it not be better to do it somebody else's way this time—just to please them, just to humor them, just because it's a practical solution to a current problem?"*

The city editor of the daily newspaper for which Debbie works thinks that Debbie has the makings of a star reporter. "She's smart, she knows the right questions to ask, she writes well, but . . ." That "but" is a big one. The editor complains that Debbie doesn't meet deadlines. She doesn't want to turn the story in until it's perfect in every aspect. But timeliness is important on a daily newspaper. The story that doesn't get in the paper today becomes old news tomorrow. Or what might have been an exclusive—a scoop—appears in another paper or on TV.

Some people who refuse to meet another person's time schedule do so because they are angry, because they are determined to assert control—"I'll do it when I'm damn good and ready," they say. But this is rarely the case with the perfectionist. And Debbie isn't angry, merely determined to present herself and her work in the best possible light. However, the city editor wants things done his way—which means turning in a story that may be less than perfect (interviewing only six people instead of seven, rewriting it only three times instead of ten)—but turning it in *today*—not tomorrow and not next week.

Debbie has three choices:

1. She can continue to do things her way
   - even though it means many of her stories never get printed at all.
   - even though the city editor is obviously annoyed with her and no longer gives her the best assignments.
2. She can quit her present job and look for another that is more tolerant of her need to take time to perfect her writing—perhaps a publication with monthly rather than daily deadlines—although this will work only if it is really more time she needs. If her desire for perfection causes her to miss *monthly* deadlines as well, the change of job won't help.
3. She can agree to please the city editor by turning in at least some stories his way
   - even though she thinks he is wrong.
   - even though she hates to have her name on a story she thinks is less than perfect.
   - even though she believes deeply that the readers are not well-served by getting less than her best.

It's not easy to do things other people's way. It's not easy to say: "This is the best I can hand in, even if it's not the best I could do if I had more time." But sometimes you do yourself a favor if you do *someone else* a favor. Be generous. Let someone else win. This time.

Sometimes it's not even easy to watch *other* people do things the "wrong" way. Fran groans as she watches her mother-in-law do dishes. "You are supposed to wash the glasses before you wash the plates," Fran says. "Here, let me do it." Her mother-in-law does not appreciate the instructions. "I've been washing dishes since before you were born and no one has been poisoned from eating from them," she says angrily.

Fran has two choices:

1. She can provide her mother-in-law with two dozen books on housekeeping practices that prove she is right about the order in which dishes should be washed
   - even though this will damage her relationship with her mother-in-law.
   - even though this will upset her husband.
2. She can close her eyes and let her mother-in-law do things her own way
   - even though she thinks she's wrong.

You may decide to take a stand on principle, but you must be willing to pay the price (annoying the boss, fighting with a loved one, devoting your energies to battling). If Debbie wants to succeed as a reporter, she must learn to do things a different way—she must incorporate the city editor's concern for timeliness into her definition of perfection. This may cause her some discomfort when she turns in the story—but probably not as much discomfort as losing her job.

If Fran wants to keep the friendship of her mother-in-law, which she truly enjoys, she must decide whether it is worthwhile to pick a fight with her over how to wash dishes.

You may think that failing to be perfect is the equivalent of failing to do your best—and that causes a crisis of conscience for you. You have been told—and you believe—that you must always go for the top, never settle for second best. And yet sometimes the best policy is to go for the middle. Not all the time, just sometimes. Go for that bulge in the bell curve—this time.

Here again, it may help you to rank this particular project on a scale of 1 to 10. How important is it that this specific task be perfect? Or this person? Is this the most important project you will ever handle? Is this *the* crucial turning point in your life? Or is this one project of many? Is this person, who may not be the perfect person to fall in love with, an interesting addition to your circle of friends? If the importance of being perfect *this time* is only a four or five, why worry about it?

A Step-by-Step Approach

Deciding to be less than perfect may mean living, at least for a time, with some discomfort. The sensation of not being perfect can cause some anxiety. But the end result will be less discomfort and less anxiety as you find yourself actually achieving more than you have in the past.

You may have to take it in steps. Start by deliberately doing some small thing imperfectly. Make the bed and don't tuck the corner in. Or wash all the dishes but one. Or wash the car but don't wipe the bumpers. It doesn't matter what you choose to do imperfectly. The idea is to do something imperfectly and then evaluate the result. Did you survive? Do people point at you in the street? Do your loved ones leave you?

This may sound like making light of a serious matter. But it isn't. If you feel you must do things perfectly, deep down you are convinced that terrible things will result if you are not perfect. You must prove to yourself—in small ways—that this *isn't* so. In earlier chapters, we discussed the need to test your perceptions and to take intermediate steps that can suggest ways to solve problems. That can be equally important here.

Taking a step-by-step approach to any kind of goal will help you reach it—and you might not even have to lower your standards to do it. Often what seems impossible to be done perfectly when viewed in its entirety becomes perfectly easy when you take it a step at a time. People will say: "I can't possibly get this project finished the way it has to be in the time I have." And then they spend time fretting that might otherwise have been devoted to the project.

It may be true that the project cannot be done "the way it has to be" in the time available. On the other hand, one way to find out is to break the project down into smaller steps—steps that are much easier to do well. You then begin working on one part at a time, until the job is done. And you may be amazed at how well it turns out.

Say you want to write an article. But you are stopped because you can't think of the perfect beginning. The beginning is just one piece of the whole. Go on to a piece that you find easy to work on. Finish that. An idea for the ending may come to you. Work on that. If you have a lot of material that has to be organized, write a rough draft about each topic in turn. You can put it together later. You can polish it later. Think in terms of a process, not a single act. Think in terms of pieces, not of the whole. It's easier to get something small right. And then that small piece can be used to build something bigger.

The important thing is to do something, to begin somewhere, and not to let the overwhelming possibility that the end result won't be perfect stop you before you start.

We are often told that the "best" and "fastest" way to get from one place to the other is the direct route. But that is not always the case. If you were to try to run straight up a steep, icy slope, you might find yourself sliding back. You might never reach the top—or you might get there only after many frustrating tries. But suppose you were able to chop a series of steps in the slope. Each step gives you a firm foothold. One step at a time, you get exactly where you want to go.

Something, Not Nothing

As long as you think in terms of all or nothing, perfection or nothing, "my way" or no way, leaping tall buildings at a single bound, you are likely to end up frustrated and defeated. But if you think in terms of improvement, of discovery, of adjusting your sights to the more important goal—which could be completion as opposed to perfection—you are more likely to make progress.

Everything becomes easier if you think in terms of moving closer to your goal rather than of finally accomplishing it. Yes, it is difficult to fight a lifetime of messages, but the only way to do it is to do it.

CHAPTER EIGHT

COMPARISONITIS

In the fairy tale "Snow White and the Seven Dwarfs," a queen who is very beautiful likes to look into her mirror and ask it: "Who is the fairest of them all?" For years this talking mirror is able to reply truthfully: "You are." But then Snow White is born and as she grows up, it becomes apparent to everyone, including the mirror, that she is even more beautiful than the queen. And so there comes a day when the queen asks the mirror: "Who is the fairest of them all?" and the mirror has to inform the queen that she has been displaced.

The queen is so consumed by vanity, anger, and jealousy that she attempts to murder Snow White, not just once but again and again. She is foiled each time, of course. And, as everyone who grew up with this story knows, Snow White lives happily ever after and the queen remains miserably unhappy until the day she dies. Unfortunately, the queen was afflicted by a common variation of the thinking mistake this book calls comparisonitis. This mistake causes a great deal of misery and unhappiness—and not just to queens who attempt to remove their rivals by tricking them into eating a poisoned apple.

The suffix *-itis* means "inflammation." We know that appendicitis is an inflammation of the appendix and bronchitis an inflammation of the bronchial tubes to the lungs. So if you suffer from an inflammation of your ability to make comparisons, it seems fair to call that comparisonitis. This is a condition that exists when you make comparisons that are unreasonable, when you make too many comparisons, or when you make them too often.

The Ability to Compare

It's hard to imagine how we could function if we *never* made comparisons, because comparisons function as a point of reference, as a means of bringing order out of chaos. We note that the economy this year is better or worse than last year, that the rainfall this spring is heavier or lighter than usual, that we enjoyed this play more than that one.

We don't live abstract lives. We need to get a fix on the situations we face. If it is colder today than yesterday, we may decide to wear a sweater in addition to a jacket. Comparing allows us to put things in a context. The situation, if not perfect, is improving. The situation, if not disastrous, is getting worse.

A great many choices—which job to take, which person to hire, which car to buy, which entry wins the contest, which candidate should be elected to office—are made after we compare one possibility with another or one with many others.

Comparing enables us not only to make choices but also to solve problems. If the turkey you bought last year was sufficient for six guests—but this year twelve are coming for Thanksgiving dinner, you need a turkey twice as large—or you need to expand the menu with more side dishes. The title of Chapter One in this book is a comparator—we speak of knowing better, not of knowing perfectly everything there is to know. Does anyone know *perfectly* everything there is to know? As the last chapter tried to make clear, that's doubtful. But—as you have probably told yourself—sometimes you could and should have known better.

We are surrounded by meters, gauges, rankings, and other measures, the better to help us compare. We are offered lists: the ten best, the ten worst, the Fortune 500 (biggest corporations in America), the Forbes 400 (richest people in America.) We are offered editorial opinions comparing values and policies. Consumer publications keep us posted on comparisons of quality and price. And all of this can be very helpful indeed.

The Ego Factor

But in the comparisons with which we could use the most help, we seem to get the least. These are comparisons involving the ego—that is, comparisons we make that help us define to ourselves who we are or get a fix on our own personal realms.

Sometimes you make positive comparisons. "I did a better job than she did." "I look younger." These are usually not the comparisons that get you into trouble. It's true that if you flaunt your comparison, people may find you arrogant—and that can be a problem. If you are so pleased with yourself that you decide to rest on your laurels ("I'm so terrific I never have to do anything again"), you might find others don't share your view—and that can get you into trouble.

But, by and large, negative comparisons cause the most grief. The negative comparison is most vulnerable to the dread comparisonitis. These tend to occur in one of three ways.

You compare yourself to others.

Unless you live the life of a hermit who never sees another human face, you undoubtedly compare yourself to others—to very specific others.

• You compare yourself to those have more than you do, rather than less.

Yes, even if you have very little, there are probably times when you see someone who has less and say to yourself: "That could be me. Oh, how fortunate I am." But more often than not, you probably compare yourself to those *who seem to have more.* It may not be admirable, but it is human nature to compare yourself to those who have what you feel you are missing—while taking for granted all that you already have.

• You compare yourself to those with whom you feel in competition.

You may well heartily applaud the success and good fortune of an eminent scientist, a top-level statesman, or even a clever colleague at the office. You might enjoy reading about the love life of a famous star. You enjoy listening to a famous violinist play. It may be that the only emotion you feel for these people is admiration or awe. You don't bother to compare yourself to them—or them to you—because you simply do not feel in competition with them.

But what if you and the scientist are directly competing for a grant? What if you and the movie star are cousins? What if the statesman was your high school classmate? What if you have been practicing the violin for years? You might feel differently.

• You compare yourself to others in several ways.

You might compare personal traits. You might say: "I wish I were as comfortable with women as my brother is," or "as witty as Mary is," or "as tall as the other guys at the office," or "as thin as Jane Fonda."

You might compare family or possessions or power or some other indication of what you think they have compared to what you have. You might say: "It bothers me that he has a bigger house than I do," or that "her children get A's in school and my children are having problems," or that "my brother-in-law has ten million dollars when I have only one million." Or, you might say: "I know my parents didn't love me the way other parents love their kids. I grew up watching 'Ozzie and Harriet' and 'Father Knows Best' on TV, and so I know how other parents relate to their kids."

You might compare status and awards. You might say: "When I went to high school with that guy, he was a nothing—now look at him getting honored, while I am not noticed at all." Or: "I worked much harder than she did, I was more loyal to the company—but they gave her the job and not me."

You compare yourself today to a view you have of yourself in the past.

A. E. Housman's famous poem "To an Athlete Dying Young" makes the point that a young man dying in his prime will never face the realization that he can no longer achieve what he once did. "Eyes the shady night has shut . . . cannot see the record cut." Death is a drastic solution to the problem, of course, but it is often difficult to come to terms with changes in your life that make you feel less than you were before. A divorce can change your sense of yourself and of your place in society. So can the loss of a job or a particular position. So can a permanent injury that makes it impossible for you to do something you enjoyed doing before. So can the loss of fame. Housman's poem speaks of a name that dies "before the man."

You may see yourself as diminished or—doing a little mind reading here—believe others see you as a has-been, a loser, a sad case in one way or the other. This is prime comparisonitis territory.

You compare yourself today to the dream you had for yourself that has not come true.

This kind of comparison is similar to comparing what you are now to what you were before. It too can result in a sense of loss, a feeling of defeat. It too has a tendency to produce comparisonitis. Exactly this kind of comparison provides the plot for the movie classic *It's a Wonderful Life*. Jimmy Stewart plays a character who as a young man dreamed of traveling to exotic places, making a career away from the small town in which he grew up. Instead he ended up as a bank officer in that small town, and the bank has problems. When he compares the life he has lived with the life he dreamed of living, he sees himself as a failure. He becomes despondent and wants to end it all. At that point, Clarence, his guardian angel, steps in and shows him how bleak his hometown would be had he not lived there. Clarence helps him to realize that even though he didn't achieve his youthful dreams, he has led a wonderful life.

Sometimes the dream involves romance. Expressions like "man of my dreams," "my dream girl," "dream lover," "dreaming of love" go back for generations. Most people grow up with the expectation that they will fall in love and live happily ever after. Of course, that expectation may not work out. Making comparisons with such a dream can trip you up in a variety of ways:

• That dreamed about love simply doesn't happen. And instead of focusing on all the positive aspects of your life—friends, family, job, freedom to pursue all kinds of interests—you focus only on the dream that did *not* come true and count your entire life as a failure.

• Those who loved you did not measure up to your dream qualifications. This gets back to the perfectionism problem. You may reject potential mates with whom you have a great deal in common because they cannot compare with that perfect mate you pair yourself with in your dream. You insist on all or nothing and end up with nothing.

• Your dream love came along—but didn't stay "happily ever after." Perhaps your loved one died but your feeling of loss, even after many years, is still very much alive. When you compare those you meet now with the one you lost, the newcomers never measure up. Often you remember only the good things about the person who is no longer around, editing out all the negatives. No one in your present or your future can possibly compare to that idealized memory. Thus you never give new love a chance.

The Role of Outside Comparers

You may say: "I wouldn't feel the way I do when I compare myself with X—or with what X has that I do not—if it weren't that *others* make me feel this way."

Yes, others may compare you unfavorably and let you know it. It's certainly common enough:

- "Look at little Johnny. His desk is neat. Why isn't your desk as neat as Johnny's?"
- "Your sister Marie can do that and she is younger than you—I don't think you are trying hard enough."
- "All the Patersons are engineers—how dare you even think of becoming an actor?"
- "If only you were half as smart as Margaret."
- "Didn't you used to be somebody important?"
- "Jim and Carrie were able to save *their* marriage—but they really worked at it."
- "Snow White is the fairest of all—not you."

We have already talked about dealing with the criticisms of others in an earlier chapter. Negative comparing is just another form of criticism. The critical issue is whether you *internalize their comparison and make it your own.* Assigning responsibility is important in dealing with comparisonitis. Just because *they* think so, does that mean *you* have to think so too? You may not be able to do anything about them, but you can do something about you.

Jerry's mother says to him: "Look at your cousin, Ned. He is more successful than you even though he's ten years younger." Jerry may be able to say to himself: "No, he's not. She's wrong." But suppose what his mother says is true. Jerry can choose how to react to that.

Jerry might think: "Mom is right. I am a failure." In this case, it's clear that it isn't what Mom has actually *said* that matters, it is the *meaning* Jerry has attached to her words. He believes that she thinks he is not merely a little older and a little less successful than Ned, but a total failure—and he agrees with her. This quite naturally makes him feel terrible.

Actually, Jerry doesn't have to agree with his mother to become upset. Suppose, for example, Jerry sees his mother talking to Ned at a family party. And he thinks: "Ned is so much more successful than I am—and younger, too. My mother won't say anything to me, but I know that deep down she is disappointed in me. She wishes I were more like Ned." Now Jerry feels guilty about disappointing his mother even though she has never said a word.

Does Jerry have any other choice? He has lots of choices. He can react to what his mother thinks (or what he thinks she thinks) by saying to himself: "So what?" Or: "Who cares?" Or: "Ned's type of success does not appeal to me." Or: "Ned's welcome to his success—I wouldn't want to put up with what he has to put up with to have it." Thus, even if his mother intended to criticize him, Jerry hears her remark as just a piece of family gossip.

It's only natural to *prefer* to be compared favorably to others, of course. Advertisers take advantage of this desire for favorable comparison when they imply that we can improve the way others view us by using a particular product. "See this terrible nerd? Does he remind you of yourself? Well, now see what happens to him after using our mouthwash [or deodorant, or shaving cream]. Women now find him irresistible." "Look at that crowd of self-confident, buoyant, boisterous, laughing, happy cola drinkers—if you would be like them, you know what you have to buy."

Comparison as a Motivator

To be told—or to believe others think—that we are something less than we see ourselves, or would like to see ourselves, can be a powerful goad. That's why comparisons are so commonly used to motivate us to better performance:

- "Do you want this ball club to be in last place?"
- "Look how nicely your sister cleaned her room. Why can't you manage to do that?"
- "You children are a disgrace. I have never in my entire career taught a class as noisy as this one."

Thus are we intimidated into practicing longer, cleaning up, or quieting down.

Jerry's mother may hope that by holding him up to comparison with his younger, more successful cousin, Ned, she will inspire Jerry to work harder, to go back to school, to accept a job offer he has been dithering about. She hopes Jerry will say: "Mom's right. I'm a failure. But I don't have to remain a failure all my life. *I can do something about it* . . . and I will, starting right now." And, indeed, Jerry may be galvanized to action *because* he thinks his mother is disappointed in him. It happens all the time. This is an example of how you can often turn a disadvantage to an advantage.

Psychiatrist Alfred Adler argued that the human striving for superiority is one of the prime motivating forces in life. Adler broke with Sigmund Freud over this because Freud was unwilling to accept the importance of this influence, while Adler contended that this striving for superiority enables us to develop. Adler, who invented the term *inferiority complex*, said we all have feelings of inferiority at some time, and we tend to cope with them by finding ways to overcome what we lack or by finding substitutes.

As babies, Adler said, we feel inferior to those around us who can communicate, and so we learn how to talk. Other theories on why babies learn to talk have been propounded, but that doesn't refute Adler's main point, that comparing is both a normal and a necessary part of the process of growing up. Adler stressed the importance of role models—people you believe are superior. He felt that the desire to be more like those people motivates you to grow and learn.

A role model does not have to be somebody you know personally. Society sets up role models for us. Your father may have told you that a certain action is not what "nice" people do. You learn what is admired behavior in your school, your community, your place of business. Few of us manage to get through life totally unaware—or uncaring—of the many standards against which to measure ourselves. The urge to fit in, to measure up, or to excel is a powerful motivating force.

Many accomplished people tell of being motivated to succeed in order to show people who said: "You don't have what it takes." They think: "Sez you. Someday I'll come back and *you'll* be jealous of *me.*" "Oh yeah? Just step back and watch my dust."

The Prod as Blunt Instrument

In murder mysteries, the blunt instrument is a tool of some kind that has been used to beat somebody over the head. It's usually a tool that has an innocent and useful purpose when in the right hands. Like a fireplace poker. Anyone with a fireplace knows how useful that is. But anyone who reads murder mysteries or watches a lot of TV knows how lethal a poker can be when used as a weapon.

So it is with comparisons. Yes, they can be useful tools to prod, motivate, move, and inspire. But they can also be used with great effectiveness to destroy.

Consider how many insults are comparisons. Dense as a stone, dumb as an ox. "You're no better than a pig." "You're like an animal." "You are acting like a baby." "You are not the man your father was." Presumably the purpose of such insults is to shame us into more acceptable behavior. But would anyone deny that these are blunt instruments with the power to hurt?

Depending on how you take them, negative comparisons can damage your self-confidence and warp your judgment.

If you say: "I want to do as good a job as Leslie does, so I'm going to work harder," the comparison is motivating. If you say: "I'll never be as good as Leslie, so there isn't any point in trying anything," the comparison stops you in your tracks.

If you say: "Nothing I can do now is the equal of what I did before, so there is no point in doing anything," you condemn yourself to a lifetime of inaction and dissatisfaction.

If you think over and over again: "I don't have what certain others have, therefore I am a failure," you cancel any opportunity you might have to become aware of and enjoy the positive aspects of your life. Thus, if Jerry internalizes his mother's comparison, he may become discouraged rather than motivated, disgusted rather than determined. "I just can't cut it. I obviously don't have what it takes. There's no point in trying." Depending on how you take them, negative comparisons may prod you *in the wrong direction*: to give up, rather than to try; to ignore any positive possibilities that may exist for you, rather than search them out. Or, like the queen, to focus your energies into undermining a rival rather than doing something to help yourself.

If the queen had been able to say "Well, I'm still one of the two fairest of all, and that's pretty good," she might have avoided a lot of grief. If she had been able to say "That may be the mirror's opinion, but I don't agree," she might have lived happily ever after, enjoying all the admiration that surely came her way.

Which Way Are You Affected?

You know how you are affected. When you compare yourself to some specific other person, or to your past, or to your dream, does it make you *more* determined to succeed, or does it seem only to discourage you?

Does thinking about another person or what that other person has inspire you to believe "If he can do it, I can do it too," or does it only bring on a bout of jealousy that is so all-consuming you can barely think of anything else? "I should have what he has. The thought of him makes me feel like a failure."

Suppose your goal is to become as slim as Jane Fonda. Would it help you to put a photograph of your role model on the front of the refrigerator? Would you look at it and say: "If I keep to this diet, I'm going to look as slim as that"? Or would you look at it and say: "Every time I see that photo, I feel bad because I realize that, given my inherited skeletal structure, I'm not going to look like that even if I stopped eating for a month"? Or put another way: Would you look at the photo and forgo the chocolate cake or look at the photo and say: "Oh, what's the use? I might as well eat the cake and the pie too"?

Suppose your goal is to become the best salesperson in your organization. Would you be energized if your company named a best salesperson of the week? Would that spur you to greater effort? Or does hearing the number of sales required to make "best of the week" leave you feeling dispirited and worthless?

Even if you revel in competition and comparison in some areas of your life, do you find that in other areas—perhaps in the social arena—comparing yourself to others gets you down?

If comparing and being compared is painful to you, it's likely you have a case of comparisonitis. Your comparing ability may be out of kilter.

When You Have Comparisonitis

Comparisonitis has a way of making people feel inadequate, insecure, even hopeless. That is bad enough, but just as comparisons can goad us to take positive actions, they can also get us into trouble. For example:

You give up all attempts to reach a goal.

One of the most common results of comparisonitis is giving up:

- "I'll never be the top salesperson, so there is no point in trying."
- "Because of my age, I'll never be able to get as good a job as I had in the past, so there is no point in trying."
- "I'm taller [or fatter, or less witty] than all the others here, so nobody will want to talk to me. I can't face it. I'm going home."

You undermine others rather than improve yourself.

We often talk scornfully of people with "superiority complexes" but Alfred Adler would argue that there is no such thing. He contended that people who have a need to diminish others in order to look good themselves suffer from an overinflated *inferiority* complex.

This theory distinguishes between positive and negative ways to excel or stand out in a crowd. Normal striving for superiority involves improving your own efforts, abilities, and achievements. But, of course, that's not the only way to get noticed. You can cause trouble. You can inflate your opinion of yourself by deriding everyone else: "Joe, you haven't had a good idea in ten years." "You are naive, Nancy." "You must come from another planet, Pete." One by one, you dismiss others until only you are left. The perceived need to undermine others is at the root of all forms of bigotry, of course.

If others are content to accept your views, this might not be a problem—but if those you deride decide to fight back, you may find yourself in trouble in a wide spectrum of relationships, from getting along with a spouse to dealing with colleagues or employees in a work setting.

Keeping up with the Joneses becomes so important you do almost anything to match them—even if you can't afford it, even if you suffer terrible consequences.

In his book *Getting by on $100,000 a Year*, financial writer Andrew Tobias told the sad tale of David Begelman, who, when president of the film division of Columbia Pictures Industries, Inc., was caught forging some $80,000 in checks. At the time—in the mid-seventies—Begelman was earning $234,000 annual salary, plus bonuses, plus elaborate perquisites (the studio leased him a home with pool in Beverly Hills). Why, Tobias asked, would such a successful man risk his career for $80,000? Tobias offered this theory: To the rest of the world a quarter-million-dollar-a-year studio head's salary "looks rich," but when your friends are all multimillionaires, you "feel poor." A high income, Tobias explains, is not Real Money. Begelman, he said, was trying to keep up with people who thought nothing of spending $1,000 a day after taxes—and he didn't make $1,000 a day *before* taxes. But once the forgery became public, Columbia fired Begelman, and the story got a great deal of publicity.

This particular variety of comparisonitis is by no means confined to those who compete with millionaires. The urge to keep up with the Joneses—to be seen by others as equally prosperous or brave or smart or whatever—gets a great many people into trouble.

When Pete started dating Alyce, he met her friends and liked them. One night, one of the group says: "Let's arrange to take our vacations together. I know a great place we can go." Pete knows he cannot afford either the money or time off involved. But he doesn't want Alyce or her friends to know that. He doesn't want them to know he doesn't have the same freedom to take off from work as they do. So he says yes. And borrows money that he knows he'll have difficulty paying back—and makes excuses at work that he knows will not do his career any good. Then he doesn't enjoy the trip. He is too worried about money, about what is happening at the office. "This vacation is not worth what I've had to give up for it," laments Pete. "I'm not enjoying it."

The problem of keeping up with the Joneses is not exclusively a matter of spending money. It could be that you are so determined to outdo a rival that you interpret everything that person does as a challenge. "She is taking dancing lessons? I'll take them too and dance better—even though I have absolutely no interest in dancing." "He has been assigned to the marketing department? I'll put in for a transfer—even though I have no interest in marketing."

The desire to be one of the gang, one of the group, part of the in crowd is a powerful force that can easily lure the unwary into everything from stealing cars ("If you don't, everybody will think you're chicken") to overspending on credit cards, to all sorts of acts or activities that you would not personally choose—and that lead you later to say ruefully: "I should have known better."

Introducing Reality

It is certainly unpleasant to come out on the short end of a comparison. It is dismaying enough when that comparison is undeniably accurate. But it is even more dismaying when, because of an attack of comparisonitis, that comparison is distorted, exaggerated, and downright unfair. The restoring tonic of reality is needed here.

The first step to curing the pain of comparisonitis is to weed out comparisons that are simply wrong. To do this, you must ask yourself a series of questions.

What are you comparing?

This will require some introspection on your part. When you feel less than another, what in particular do you focus on? Is it looks, success, power, celebrity status, popularity, happiness, family life?

How accurate is your comparison?

Are you comparing what you know for sure about that other person—or what you *think* is true? You may be engaging in a little mind reading here.

It's easy to believe that other people have no problems, achieve easily, and are totally happy, especially if you don't know those other people well—if at all. When you compare your own life to this life you have invented for another, it's only too easy to feel inadequate.

It certainly doesn't help that in this age of communication we tend to be bombarded in newspapers, magazines, and TV with success stories—the lifestyles of the rich, the famous, the thin, the gorgeous, the honored, the powerful, the have-it-alls. Their lives may seem so much easier, so much happier, so much better than your own. Maybe that's true, but maybe it's not. Sometimes real press agents are at work in their cases—emphasizing the positive, hiding the negatives. Or perhaps you tend to skip over those articles and interviews in which the supposed have-it-alls admit to or are described as having their share of problems too. TV's Barbara Walters once told an interviewer that if she is your idea of somebody who is always in control, don't believe it of anybody. A reporter once asked actor Tom Selleck whether he ever worried about his career ending, about losing what he had. And Selleck replied simply: "Yes."

But the person with whom you are comparing yourself doesn't have to be a celebrity to set off misinformed comparisons. Edward, for example, remembers well that when he was a child, he envied his classmate Billy because Billy had such a great mom. "All the kids wished that Billy's mother, Esther, was their mom," recalls Edward. "She always seemed so full of fun. She used to tell us dirty jokes. None of our mothers ever told us dirty jokes." Only years later, Edward learned that Billy had always been terribly embarrassed by his mother, that he longed to have their kind of family. Throughout Billy's childhood, Esther was in and out of mental hospitals. It was not easy being Esther's child.

Are you drawing conclusions about all of that person's life based on the one *fact you are sure of?*

Yes, the person has a million dollars—therefore she is healthy, secure, relaxed, surrounded by adoring loved ones, and happy in her career. That may all be true. Surveys indicate that people with lots of money do report greater satisfaction with their lives than people with little money—and that is hardly surprising. But that old cliché, "Money can't buy happiness," may also be operative. We often read of people with enviable wealth and fame who develop drug habits, go through successive divorces, spend years in therapy. You learn—maybe only late in some famous person's life—that they have endured decades of pain. The point is, if you don't know the whole story, why simply *assume* that they are so much better off than you—if the *only outcome* of that assumption is to make you feel bad?

When you make your comparison, do you chalk up every positive that exists on the other side but ignore any positive on your own side? Do you fairly tote up the negatives on both sides of your comparison?

Often if you have comparisonitis, you view the attributes of others as if looking at them through a pair of binoculars—which, of course, magnifies them. Then, before looking at your own attributes, you first turn the binoculars around. Have you ever looked through binoculars the wrong way? Everything looks smaller and farther away. Often you don't only minimize your own attributes, but ignore them completely. When gamblers talk about how much they've won, they often cheerfully forget to mention how much they've lost in the process. When you suffer from comparisonitis you do just the opposite. When you compare yourself to other people or to a past "better" version of yourself, you tend to focus on losses and ignore winnings.

Here's an example:

Martha is about to retire and so, naturally, talks about it with others of her age. This one and that one talk about the investments they had made, about all the money they had tucked away to cushion their retirement years. Martha feels sick. She has no such nest egg. She berates herself: "I should have saved my money instead of throwing it away."

But did Martha throw it away or enjoy it? While the more frugal among her friends were investing in long-term securities, Martha was investing in having a good time. She took trips that she enjoyed. She ate at expensive restaurants. She liked buying clothes. Perhaps Martha invested too much in enjoyment and too little in long-term security. But on the other hand, if one of those careful investors died the day after retiring, Martha would probably say: "It's a shame she never got a chance to spend any of that money. I'm glad I spent some of mine while I could still enjoy it."

The point here is not to determine who made the wiser choice, but merely to show that there are pluses and minuses to every choice and to make a fair comparison, you must include all of the them.

Here's another example:

Physician William A. Nolen, who wrote the best-seller *The Making of a Surgeon*, said years later that despite the success of the book and the fame it brought him, he suffered a serious mid-life crisis. He was chief of surgery at a county hospital in Litchfield, Minnesota, he had money, he loved his wife and six children, but, he said, he began comparing himself to others who in his opinion had done more with their lives. "One of my medical school classmates pioneered in kidney transplants.'' Nolen felt he'd made a mistake staying in Litchfield (population 5,000) so long. He began to have trouble sleeping. He hated to get up in the morning. He calmed himself with Valium, Quaa- ludes, and liquor. His medical practice and personal life suffered. He felt he had to get away. "I put an ad in a medical journal describing my current practice and stating my desire to relocate within 50 miles of Boston.'' He got dozens of replies to that ad, all of them from physicians who wanted to take over his position when he left. What he wanted to flee, they found highly attrac- tive. "It made me see my situation differently,'' he said. And he stayed.

Do you confuse "getting there" with "being there"?

It makes sense for a young trumpeter just starting out to aspire to reach the level of a Wynton Marsalis or for a would-be actor to model himself after Dustin Hoffman. But if after only a few lessons, the newcomer *gives up* because "I don't play as well'' or "I don't act as well,'' then that comparison is self-defeating and foolish. It eliminates the motivation to grow and improve.

Handling Outside Opinions

Sometimes getting an outside opinion is beneficial. Sometimes it helps to ask someone whose opinion you trust: "Was I as bad as I thought?'' "Do people really see me the way I think they do?'' You might say: "That doesn't do any good because the people I know are too polite to tell me the terrible truth.'' And you may be right. But if you explain to someone that you want a warts-and-all opinion because you cannot improve unless and until you get accurate information about your flaws, they may either relieve your worst fears or by confirming them set you on the path to *doing something about them.*

If you get positive input, you might as well take it at face value. If you get a negative reading, accept it graciously and don't argue, or you'll never get an opinion again.

The So-What Solution

When you fall victim to comparisonitis, it is usually because, as with all thinking mistakes, you have simply come to a conclusion too quickly. You have let those thoughts that fly through your brain below the level of awareness take over from your common sense. When you rethink that comparison, taking the factors mentioned in this chapter into consideration, you will probably discover that you are being too negative. You may not be giving yourself sufficient credit. You may be making assumptions about others for which you have no proof. Or you may be focusing on only one element of the comparison instead of the whole picture.

However, you may be totally right about the comparison you make. That person is happier than you are. That person is more successful. Your celebrity status is part of the past. A reasonable question to ask at this point is: "So what?"

That may sound frivolous, but it is not. What *meaningful difference* does your comparison make? What meaningful difference does it make if your old classmate has just won a prize and you have not? Does it affect your work, your ability, or your life in any way? Do people stop and point at you on the street? Will friends stop calling? You may feel a pang that you did not accomplish whatever your classmate did, but does that have any *other* kind of impact on your life?

If not, so what?

What meaningful difference does it make if you are not as pretty as your friend, Marie? Do only beautiful women enjoy life? Look around and you will notice that is not the case. Oprah Winfrey has said that she realized she was not as pretty as many of her classmates, and getting by on looks was not going to be a good plan for her. So she concentrated on improving her education and her communication skills—with obvious good results.

What Are You Willing to Give Up?

If you are *not* willing to say: "So what?" you might ask yourself: "What am I willing to give up to get what I want?" When you compare yourself to others, do you factor in the sacrifices they may have made? Do you know whether they had to make any sacrifices? If so, are you willing to make them too?

When most people are asked: "What price are you willing to pay?" they reply: "Nothing." "I want the same kind of job I had before . . . but I'm not willing to move to city X to get it." "I want what she has but I don't want to work fourteen hours a day as she does." "I want the status he has—but I need more money to live on than he gets." "I want what I want when I want it—and where and how I want it." If you say you are not willing to give up anything to get what you want, don't be surprised if you don't get it.

Changing the Comparison

Suppose you are right when you conclude that you will never be as happy in the future as you were in the past. Perhaps your spouse has died. Perhaps a business to which you devoted most of your life has folded. Suppose you are right when you conclude that you can never have what that other person has. She is the heir to a multimillion-dollar fortune. You have to work for every penny you own. He has had an incredible amount of plain good luck. And you haven't. You are not doing as well now as you did in the past.

You have two choices: You can dwell on the hopelessness of ever having what you had before, or what that other person has, and resign yourself to a lifetime of depression, despair, and self-recrimination. Or you can change the basis of your comparison. Instead of comparing what you had then with what you have now, compare what you are now with what you can be a year from now. Instead of comparing what someone has that you do not, compare what you have now with what you may be able to get if you do thus and so.

Superexaggeration is a good technique to use in comparisonitis. That means deliberating exaggerating your comparison. Don't say: "Compared to what I had before, I'm a failure." Say: "Compared to everybody in the whole world, I'm a failure. Nobody's life is more disastrous than mine. Nobody has messed up more than I have. An amoeba has more success than I do." Does that sound ridiculous? It's supposed to. Exaggerating can help you gain a more realistic perspective. Deliberately exaggerating can help make you aware of the exaggerated thoughts that are already flying through your mind and making you more upset than you need to be.

One Step at a Time

Beware of combining perfectionism with comparisonitis. Remember that if you take an all-or-nothing stance ("If I can't have everything I had before, I'd prefer to have nothing"), you are likely to end up with nothing. Say instead: "I'm not happy now but I'm going to try to change that. *Something more* than I have now *is better than nothing.*" That changes the basis of comparison in a way that allows you to move forward and, ultimately, improve the comparison. You may not be able to go as fast as you like. But here too, you can go one step at a time.

When a back injury forced Stan to give up outdoor construction work, Stan felt he'd lost his very identity. Stan's work had also been his favorite recreation. He liked being outdoors. He liked physical activity. He was good at it and enjoyed the esteem he received from others for his ability. Friends point out to him now that he still has his family and his friends, and no one can take from him his past accomplishments. Stan agrees, but he's still miserable. Because Stan defines himself by his work—as most of us do—he sees himself as a has-been.

That's true as far as his old job goes. But the question for Stan is where he goes now. He must seek something else to do.

Admittedly, he may not enjoy this *as much*, but he will surely enjoy it *more* than endlessly wallowing in his sense of loss. Stan must change his comparison one step at a time.

Here are some suggestions for Stan that might also work for you:

1. Brainstorm ideas. Get out a pencil and paper and write down everything you can do, might like to do, or know that others do that seems interesting or possible. If you can get friends to join in the brainstorming, so much the better. Write down any idea, no matter how silly it sounds initially. You never know when the germ of a good idea may be found in a joke. The greatest barrier to solving problems is not failing to come up with a solution, it is coming up with a single solution and stopping there. If that solution doesn't turn out to be feasible, you then say: "Well, I tried. And nothing works." Give yourself a list of possibilities—a menu of options—to choose from.

2. From this list, select one to check out. Suppose Stan had said: "Well, I'd like to stay in the construction business in some way. But with this back injury, there probably isn't any way I can do that." Stan can elect to check out staying in the construction business.

3. Back to brainstorming. What steps can Stan take to check this out? Who can he call? Where can he search? Who might know? Construction companies? The state employment office?

4. Break down the list of steps into smaller steps. Perhaps looking up phone numbers. Listing addresses. Developing a schedule for following up all leads.

5. The resulting investigation may lead to job possibilities. Or it could prove that Stan is right that the construction business is out and he must now investigate another alternative on his first list. Or the investigation may indicate that a job is possible only if Stan acquires skills he doesn't have now. That would establish a new goal: acquiring those skills.

Stan might say: "No way. I'd have to go back to school. I don't have the money." But Stan can check that out on a step by step basis too. He can investigate: How much schooling? How much money? Does any place offer financial help? Can he go part-time?

6. This search might result in a couple of alternative choices. At that point, it may be necessary to use those well-developed comparison skills in a positive way—that is, to compare the advantages and disadvantages of the alternatives. One alternative might call for moving to a new city, for example. The other might offer lower pay. There may be a dozen differences between them.

Advantages vs. Disadvantages

Here's a helpful hint when doing this kind of comparison: Don't just compare two ways (alternative A vs. alternative B), compare four ways. Here's how that works: Take two pieces of paper and draw a line down the middle of each. The heading of one will be the advantages and disadvantages of alternative A. The heading of the second will be the advantages and disadvantages of alternative B.

You will find that such lists often overlap—but at the same time, you will find that when you think about advantages and disadvantages of each alternative *separately*, you develop more facts about each than you will by comparing one directly against the other.

After you have listed advantages and disadvantages on those two sheets, go back and give each one a score from 1 to 5. The score is meant to reflect how strongly you feel about each one: 1 means this is a minor point; 5 means this is very important to you; 2, 3, and 4 indicate positions in between.

Your comparison will take on additional meaning. Now when you study the advantages and disadvantages, you will see which points are most important to you.

Comparing Less

You will never stop making comparisons, and of course you don't want to give up those comparisons that are helpful. But you may find that your life becomes more comfortable if you simply start comparing less—and less often. Pay attention to what happens when you do this. If you stop measuring yourself against others, does your productivity slow down? Or does your discomfort diminish? That's not a bad comparison to make.

CHAPTER NINE

WHAT-IF THINKING

Worry. Worry. Worry. That's what what-if thinking is all about. It's worrying about things that don't exist or are highly improbable *in addition* to worrying about threats to health and happiness that are of real concern. And it is worrying about real threats to a degree that diminishes your ability to deal with them instead of increasing your coping power.

The what-if person is similar to Chicken Little in that both can clearly see a catastrophe that hasn't happened, but the what-if sufferer reacts in a different way. Chicken Little is so sure that something terrible is happening, or is about to, that he becomes so flustered and panicky he can't focus on what is really happening. The what-if person doesn't claim anything terrible *has happened*—but focuses attention on the fact that *it could*.

Worry. Worry. Worry. "What if they reject me? What if the bridge collapses? What if the medical report is bad? What if I make a fool of myself? What if something terrible—I don't even know what—happens to me? What if the gloomy situation I am in now doesn't improve? What if my current success doesn't last?"

What-if questions make you feel vulnerable and exposed, like someone clinging to the edge of a precipice by the fingertips. Worse, what-if questions increase your vulnerability when you are clinging to a precipice. If there was a tree branch near you to hang on to you probably wouldn't see it because all you can think about is: "What if no one hears my cries? What if the ledge breaks? What if my fingers slip?"

What-if thinking is paralyzing. It saps your ability to do anything new because the mind conjures up all kinds of terrible things that *could* happen if you dare to move. It saps the pleasure that might be possible when things are going well because the mind imagines all kinds of terrible things that *could* go wrong.

What-if people find it difficult to take risks because the potential dangers of failure loom so much larger than the potential gains of success. What-if people have no energy left to take a risk because they are so busy warding off anticipated disaster.

Rewriting Murphy's Law

You might ask: "But isn't it true that bad things *do* happen?" The answer, of course, is yes. Many people are fond of quoting Murphy's Law, which holds, "If anything can go wrong, it will." And, of course, things *can* go wrong. Almost no problem or complication is absolutely impossible under any and all circumstances. But even if the probability is only a million to one, the what-if worrier will pay more attention to that one chance that things will go wrong than to the 999,999 chances that things will go right.

When you are consumed with worry, the implausible seems all too possible. You can literally see in your mind's eye how the disaster could happen—in fact, you are likely to visualize that disaster in the process of happening. What-if thinkers tend to be very creative, very imaginative—they are like playwrights able to conjure up one disaster plot after the other.

But although bad things do happen, it is demonstrably, statistically true that they do not happen *as often* as we worry about them happening. And the things we worry about often turn out to be nowhere near as serious as we feared, or we can handle the problem more easily than we thought. Thus, a more accurate stating of Murphy's Law would be: "If anything can go wrong, it may—under certain conditions, at particular times, in some places, to some people, but most of those people will find that they are quite able to cope with the problems that result."

Not as catchy maybe, but much more realistic.

The Flawed Premise

What-if thinking generally springs from a flawed premise. This flawed premise provides the foundation on which we then construct a tower of fear.

Here's an example: George, a biology professor for more than forty years, knows he was very foolish when he kissed and fondled his long-time secretary, Phyllis. He had always been able to confide in Phyllis. She had a sympathetic ear for his personal troubles. But this time he did more than confide. She hadn't objected. It wasn't that. But George knows full well that what he did was unprofessional. It was unfair to his wife—and to Phyllis. Then the thought strikes him: "What if she becomes pregnant?"

His mind begins racing, one thought automatically following the other. "It will be all over for me. My wife will divorce me. My colleagues will ridicule me. I could be ruined. I could lose everything."

All of this is possible *if* Phyllis becomes pregnant. And was it possible for Phyllis to become pregnant? That is the question George does not ask. He is too busy constructing his what-if scenario. Had he asked it, he could easily have answered no. Phyllis had had a hysterectomy. In addition, although George had kissed and touched Phyllis, they had not consummated the sex act. It was close to impossible for Phyllis to be pregnant, and who should know this better than a professor of biology?

But as example after example in this book shows, knowing better will not necessarily prevent a mistake in thinking. No doubt, George will eventually look back and ask: "How could I have been so incredibly stupid?"

The answer is that George allows himself to become a what-if victim. Merely *asking the what-if question* sent his mind racing along to envision all the results that might be possible if the *original premise* was correct. When his mind raced forward, it left his common sense behind. He never stopped to ask himself whether the premise itself was flawed. And that omission is all too common.

Here's another example: Emily has had a tough day. She is impatient and grumbling when she gets into her car, and it certainly doesn't help her mood any that the road is covered with ice and snow. Then when she pulls away from her curbside parking place, she bumps into the car ahead! "Oh, no." She gets out, checks for damage, finds none, and so proceeds to drive away.

But the bump stays in her mind. It launches a what-if procession of thoughts. "What if there was a baby in the back seat of that car? What if the baby was knocked from the seat? What if the baby is hurt? What if the parents don't return to the car soon? What if I'm arrested for hit-and-run? I could lose everything I own if I'm sued. I could be imprisoned. My life is ruined!"

This scenario assumes that someone would leave a baby all alone in the back seat of a parked car on a cold, icy, snowy day. And it further assumes that if someone was foolish enough to leave the baby there, the baby would be injured by a slight bump to the car. Yes, it's possible—but also highly improbable. But as Emily thinks about the bump, her mind sees that baby, hears it cry, and pictures the police coming to take her to jail. These pictures are so real that she feels sick.

What-if thinking can also work this way:

A tree branch, moved by the wind, raps against a window in your home. You were in bed, fast asleep, but now are awakened by the noise. "What was that?" you ask yourself. Maybe you think: "What if somebody is trying to get into the house?"

That is a scary thought. You can feel yourself getting tense. Your heart starts to pound. Your mind starts racing. "What if it is a burglar? Will he be content just to steal from me? Or will he hurt me, kill me, harm my family, harm my pet?" Your brain goes on automatic—and it automatically starts writing a horror story. You feel trapped. You are unable to move. You want to scream but no sound comes.

If, however, when you are awakened by the noise, you think: "That sounds like a tree branch hitting the window," you may be concerned that the window might break, but you will not be frightened. Clearly the difference in how you interpret the noise makes a great deal of difference in how you react to it.

You might argue that in this instance, you couldn't possibly know that your premise was flawed—since that noise at the window *could* have been a burglar. Burglars do exist. Fair enough. However, all you really know is that you heard a noise. There could be several explanations for that noise, a burglar being just one of them. And although an intruder trying to get into your house is certainly the most frightening explanation, it isn't necessarily the most likely. But once you start your mind racing to answer the question "What if it's a burglar?" you have laid the foundation on which your fears can climb ever higher. The result? Your brain is too occupied in imagining scenes of disaster for it to concentrate on more accurately assessing the meaning of the noise.

To be flawed, a premise does not have to be *impossible*, but simply *not very likely*.

Harris has heard about an opening at a local TV station, and he would like to send his resumé to the station manager there but does not. He isn't asking himself: "What if I don't get hired?" He can live with that. He recognizes that there may be a hundred applicants for that job. No, what Harris asks himself is: "What if the station manager thinks I am foolish for daring to apply for this job? And what if he jokes about me to others at the station? What if he tells my present boss that I applied? What if my boss then gets angry and fires me? What if . . ."

These things are possible, but they are *not very likely*. More likely the station manager is going to look through a hundred resumés, pick the best candidates for the job from among them, and then schedule interviews. Period. Harris may be one of them. Or he may not. But even if the manager does think that

Harris was foolish to apply, it isn't likely that this information will become public. The unwanted resumés will be tossed into the wastepaper basket, and that will be that.

Borrowing Trouble

What-if behavior is simply another means we use for focusing on the negative rather than the positive, for talking ourselves into being more miserable rather than talking ourselves out of being miserable and into feeling more confident.

We do often face potential threats that can go either way. Sometimes the threat is much greater than simply having your resumé thrown away. And sometimes just listening more carefully won't help. Suppose, for example, you are about to go into surgery. The surgery may be successful and you will live happily ever after. Or the surgeon may have bad news for you when you come out of the anesthesia. It is only natural to worry about the latter. But frequently the patient *begins* by focusing on the negative possibility ("What if the news is bad?") and continues to pile one disaster scenario on the other.

What if the news is bad?

- "It probably will mean I'll have to stay in the hospital for months."
- "It probably will mean I'll lose my job."
- "It probably means I will never work again."
- "It probably means my family will be destitute."
- "It probably means I will die."

Pretty soon it is hard to tell where what-if leaves off and the Chicken Little syndrome with its accompanying all-is-lost feeling begins. This is known as borrowing trouble. You don't know and can't know that the news will be bad, but you start imagining all manner of terrible outcomes that you will be helpless to avoid. In other words, since you do not know whether you will be in trouble later, you borrow some trouble to worry about now.

Here again the premise is flawed, because until you actually get the surgeon's report, you do not know whether the news will be good or bad or somewhere in between. Further, you may not have complete knowledge of the options that you will be given along with the precise diagnosis. Nor are you likely to consider your ability to cope with any of those options, since you don't yet know what those options will be.

Many people put off seeing a doctor about some symptom that concerns them because they are so worried that their worst fears will be confirmed. And thereby they cause themselves harm in one of two ways: Either they spend a lot of energy worrying for no reason, or, failing to get an early diagnosis, they allow the problem to become worse and harder to treat.

The Positive or Realistic What-If

It must be said that what-if thinking is not always a mistake. It is certainly possible to use it in positive and realistic ways. After all, the imagination can conjure up optimistic images as well as pessimistic ones. And sometimes the ability to spot potential problems in advance enables you to do a better job of preparing for them.

Leonard is a positive what-iffer. He psyches himself up to go to a singles bar by thinking: "What if I see a woman there I like? What if I start a conversation with her? What if it turns out that she just happens to be looking for a new relationship? And what if I am exactly the type of guy who appeals to her?" Leonard can envision himself having a wonderful time. It's possible that despite his optimistic outlook, he will be disappointed on this occasion. Leonard recognizes this. He thinks: "What if she isn't interested in me? Well, she isn't the only fish in the sea. What if I came on a Wednesday night—I hear there's a different crowd here then."

Mimi, who was assigned to assemble materials needed for a meeting, uses what-if thinking to prepare herself for a challenge. She thinks: "What if Smedley comes to the meeting? He'll probably ask for a profit and loss report for the past five years. So I'd better make sure I have that ready. And what if Forsythe asks a question about how many new people have been hired this year? She is interested in that kind of thing. I'd better get that number before the meeting." By anticipating areas of potential difficulty, Mimi is ready for anything. After the meeting, she receives compliments for how well prepared she was.

What-if thinking clearly is not a mistake when it is used to spur the imagination toward envisioning options or preparing for a challenge. But, unfortunately, the power of the human mind to imagine what-if scenarios is too often used only to worry, worry, and worry some more. What-if thinking becomes dysfunctional when it serves only to pile negative improbabilities upon possibilities that are either unknown or very slim to begin with.

Selective Worrying

In dealing with what-if thinking, it's important to recognize how selective it is. Although an almost infinite number of what-ifs are possible (even if not probable) you probably do not worry about them all. You may worry about being embarrassed in a particular situation or about your job security or about your health—and yet not give two seconds' thought to the possibility that a piano may drop on your head if you walk down the street.

Worry is a very individual matter. Theresa is afraid of airplanes. She asks: "What if the plane crashes? What if I'm killed?" She skips over the fact that plane crashes are quite rare. (When did you ever see a banner headline in the newspaper proclaiming: PLANE ACTUALLY LANDS SAFELY AT AIRPORT!) She skips over the fact that even when planes do crash, passengers are sometimes able to walk away. And so when faced with the need to get to a city 150 miles away from her home, Theresa refuses to consider flying and instead drives the entire way. As it happens, there are more deaths from automobile crashes than from airplane crashes. Theresa *knows* that autos are not totally safe, but she doesn't indulge in what-if thinking when she is behind the wheel. She just drives.

Judith is such a terrible worrier that she is agoraphobic—that is, she is too fearful to step outside her house. Her mind spins a never-ending scenario of: "What if I am run over as I cross the street? What if I am mugged as I walk down the street? What if I feel faint and no one is near?" Judith feels safe only inside her house—even though statisticians tell us that most accidents occur inside the house. But Judith isn't worried about suffering a case of food poisoning or falling down the stairs. Like Theresa, she has made her what-if selections, and she is sticking with them.

Tom is undeniably brave. As a fireman, he has won citations for rescuing people from burning buildings. His hobby is sky-diving. He loves to maneuver around in the sky using his arms and legs as rudders, only pulling the ripcord to release his para-chute when his altimeter tells him he is getting close to the ground. Yet Tom becomes tongue-tied at the thought of con-fronting his wife with his anger about her methods of disciplin-ing the children. "What if she leaves me? What if I never see our children again? What if . . ."

Questioning the What-If Question

Just as you can talk yourself into worrying more, you can talk yourself into worrying less. And that starts with questioning your what-if question.

What-if thinking is grounded in the view that merely know-ing that something is not very likely is not good enough. If someone says: "That just doesn't happen," you probably reply: "How can you be sure?" If someone says: "That has never happened," you probably reply: "There is always a first time."

What you want is absolute certainty—and that is impossible. If you are determined to worry as long as there is even one chance in a zillion that what you fear will happen, you are building a prison cell in which to confine yourself. If you cannot move as long as there is any chance in the universe of something going wrong, you will not move. If you cannot take a risk, no matter how small, you forsake all possibility of change because all changes involve some risk. (Not changing involves risk too, of course, but that is seldom considered.) The most important question you must ask about what-if thinking is whether it helps you or hurts you. Has it improved your life or truly protected you? Or has it made you unhappy?

You know that in what-if thinking you tend to focus selectively on one risk while ignoring other risks. You receive a letter from the Internal Revenue Service, and your mind begins conjuring up all the terrible things it might contain. As a result, you can't bring yourself to open it. And yet not opening it and not dealing with the problem (if indeed it even is a problem) may be a still greater risk.

So you must ask yourself whether by avoiding certain risks you are actually creating greater risks to your health, your career potential, or your future happiness in general.

Since what-if questions involve events that have not happened—and, for all you know, may never happen—it helps to question the evidence that convinces you to maintain your pessimistic outlook. Questioning your evidence is important in dealing with all mistakes in thinking. Suppose George, the professor, had stopped and said: "Why am I getting so upset? What exactly makes me feel that I am facing great danger?" He would confront his original premise: "Because I am worried that my secretary may be pregnant."

"Do I have any evidence that she is, in fact, pregnant?"

"No."

"How likely is this to be true?"

This last question forces George to review the facts to determine not whether this is a scientific possibility given all sorts of extraordinary circumstances but rather whether it is a likely event in his case. Probably then he would remember that no sexual intercourse took place, that his secretary has had a hysterectomy—and thus he has very little to worry about.

No matter what scenario you have spun for yourself, you can

always stop and say: "How likely is this? Is this really true? Is there any other possible explanation for this? Is there any other possible outcome?"

The very act of questioning a what-if scenario slows down the automatic process that escalates tension, builds fear, deepens worry, and immobilizes the thinker.

You may want to do more to gather evidence than question your own thoughts. Suppose you coughed a lot today. You might say: "I have a cough. I hope I'm not getting a cold." Or you might say: "What if that cough is the first symptom of tuberculosis?" What evidence are you working with? A cough. What can you do to pin down a diagnosis one way or the other? You could get a chest X-ray. Some might say that's a lot of trouble to go to for a cough. But if you are going to worry and lose sleep about this cough, you may be willing to take the trouble.

Of course, if you are determined to continue what-if thinking, you can always say: "What if the X-rays and examination that show my lungs are healthy and my throat is irritated from dust are wrong?" You can go from one physician to the next, never believing anyone who gives you a diagnosis that you are fine—if, that is, you combine perfectionism with what-if thinking and demand a statistical certainty of zero. And if you accept the condition that the risk of failing to diagnose a cough properly is greater than the risk of eliminating all pleasure from your life.

Diverting Your Thoughts

If questioning the evidence doesn't resolve your worries, you can try to interrupt your what-if thoughts by means of a diversion.

You can, for example, consciously search for an alternative question for your mind to focus on. Instead of thinking about: "What if he rejects me?" try thinking: "What if he likes me?" What would that mean? You can change: "What if the plane crashes?" to: "What if the plane arrives early?"

Or you could attempt to answer your own questions. Suppose you are nervous about a planned trip to another country. Your mind launches into the fretting refrain: "What if I become ill? What if I lose my money? What if I get lost and can't find anyone who speaks my language?" Instead of simply repeating these thoughts over and over in your mind, get the answers. Get a book about traveling in foreign lands. Ask a travel agent. Get specific information about the country in which you will be traveling. If you are worried about whether there is a hospital to treat a condition you have, find out—and put your mind at rest.

You could also divert your mind with a relaxation technique. That can range from simply finding a book that takes your mind off whatever is bothering you, to listening to a tape that guides you through a formal relaxation process. (A sample script that you can read into a tape recorder to make a relaxation tape of your own can be found in Chapter Thirteen.)

The object is to give yourself a break from your what-if thoughts. Anything that enables you to focus your attention on something else will help you. A very good technique is simply to think about every part of your body, one part at a time, and visualize it relaxing while steadily breathing deeply.

For example, you start with your toes and tell them to relax. Picture your toes going limp. Feel them going limp. Then move to your feet . . . then your lower legs . . . then your upper legs. As you relax each part of you, you may feel a heavy sensation. That's an indication that your body is relaxing. When your arms, legs, and whole body feel as if they weigh a ton, and you have no interest in moving, you will absolutely delight in the feeling of comfort that provides. All the while you breathe deeply, in and out.

It takes concentration to do this, to picture each part of your body relaxing, to focus on feelings of heaviness and warmth. It takes concentration to continue breathing in a rhythmic manner. It takes concentration to absorb the spreading sense of comfort that relaxation exercises bring. But while you are concentrating on these things, your mind is not churning up more what-if thoughts to torment you.

Scheduling Worry Time

Another very useful technique when your thoughts are making you miserable is to schedule a specific time to let those miserable thoughts out—and then refuse to allow them to intrude at any other time of the day or night. This is much easier to do than most people think.

Postponing worry to another time is done frequently. A surgeon ready to operate is notified that the Internal Revenue Service wants to schedule an audit. "I am not going to worry about that now," the doctor says. "I have to concentrate on what I'm doing in the operating room." Your report is due in another hour and you are scrambling to get it finished. The phone rings. It's your auto mechanic, who wants to talk about the problems in your car. "No time for that now," you say. "I can't worry about anything except finishing this report."

When you schedule worry time, you simply make a point of not being able to worry now—it will have to wait until later. It's artificial, but it works. Many people find that hard to believe because of an erroneous belief that life is basically spontaneous: "Things happen and that's that." But although many things in life are beyond our power either to foresee or to control, that is not the case with everything. Much of life is routine. Much of life can be planned. Meals don't just show up on tables. Somebody cooks them first. Somebody plans what to cook. Somebody buys the ingredients.

You can treat your need to worry the same way you treat your need to do the laundry, mow the lawn, or see your dentist. You make time for it—and then use the rest of your time for other activities. You may think: "I'm already overwhelmed. I already have too many things to do. I can't just set aside time to worry." But you can—and you will find that, over time, you become more comfortable doing so. The act of scheduling helps to give you a better fix on just how you are spending your time. When you put down in black and white exactly how you do spend your time, you will find that you can make time for other activities. You can make time to worry if you feel that need. But you will also be scheduling time in which you *will not allow your what-if thoughts to intrude.* If you have too many things to do, worrying around the clock cannot help you get those things done, because worrying makes everything harder to do. You will find that you get much more done in your scheduled worry-free hours than you are getting done now.

In Chapter Thirteen, you will find a detailed description of how to draw up a schedule of your daily activities. In Appendix B, you will find a form you can fill out to help you do that.

Planning Mastery and Pleasure

Even if you are overwhelmed by the things you have to do—plus the worrying you feel you have to do—it is important to make time in your schedule for activities that help you improve your life or that simply help you enjoy your life more.

The experiences may also not appear spontaneously. They will have to be thought about. They will have to be planned. Planning, scheduling, and having such experiences will help divert your mind from its what-if worry pattern, but more than that, they may help you to attack the very problem that is bringing on your what-if thinking in the first place.

For example, let us say that the specter of economic recession raises very real questions about whether you will be laid off from your job. You quite naturally are worried about this. "What if it happens? What if I can't get another job right away? What if I run through my savings? What if I never get another job? What if I lose my house?"—and on and on and on.

You can schedule time for relaxation—to give your body a chance to feel normal. It isn't going to help you do the job that you have or find another if you get sick, if you feel so tensed up you can barely move.

Schedule things that you like, that you might have put off. Why? Because your what-if thinking can create a feeling that there is nothing you can enjoy now—or ever. And you can prove to yourself that isn't so by scheduling something that will engage your attention in a pleasurable way.

You can schedule time to prepare for the problem you fear, just in case it does arrive. You can get information about how best to stretch your current finances so that you will feel less pressure if your salary stops. You can get information about the job-search procedure so that you will know what to do if the need arises. You might decide to take a course that will enable you to switch gears and careers if that seems beneficial. And if you decide to take a course, you put that in your schedule, too. Scheduled activities can get you moving when what-if thinking has stopped you cold. Scheduling other activities will make it easier for you to box your what-if thinking into its own corner of your day because when your mind is fully engaged in accomplishing these other activities, it won't be free to wonder: "What if?"

CHAPTER TEN

THE IMPERATIVE *SHOULD*

Saying *should* can be a big mistake.

Most people will find that hard to believe. After all, when you say: "I should do this," "I should not do that," or "I know I should feel that way about this," you are simply referring to all the behavior and feelings you have learned to think of as the right way, the proper way, the only way. We use the word *should* as shorthand for the difference between right and wrong.

And certainly most of us agree on what that means, starting out with the Ten Commandments. "Thou shalt not" is just another way of saying: "You shouldn't." Most of us accept the Golden Rule that we should "Do unto others as we would have others do unto us." Most of us believe in being law-abiding and clean.

Thank goodness for that, you might say. This world we live in would be even crazier than it already is if there were no standards, no laws, no common consensus on proper behavior. Indeed, it's not unreasonable to wonder whether humankind could survive at all if murder were accepted as nothing more than an individual whim, if thievery and viciousness were no more than the common everyday standard of how people *should* live their lives.

So how could saying *should* possibly be a mistake?

Amazing but true, this common, everyday word has an enormous potential for stirring up trouble. To be precise, it isn't the mere saying of the word that is the problem, it is the *meaning* that most of us associate with it.

The Nature of *Should*

Should is action without thinking. *Should* is a finger waving under your nose. *Should* is a command that carries a warning label: "Don't you dare deviate by as much as a millionth of a millimeter or you'll be sorry, you'll feel guilty, you'll feel ashamed, others will point their fingers at you—and they *should*."

It's true that *should* does not always carry such a weighty meaning. You might say: "I really should learn to knit" or "I should get out more" when all you mean is that would be a good idea. But, more often, *should* is used when we are referring to the concept of right and wrong in concrete, perfectionistic, black-vs.-white-with-no-gray-in-between terms.

Often, these are values that our parents worked hard to convey to us when we were small. According to the famed French child development expert Jean Piaget, the ability to make abstract judgments increases with age. Very little children do not do this well because their nervous systems are still growing, and abstractions require a neurological integration that is rarely complete before the age of eleven or twelve. To small children, then, the line between right and wrong, yes and no, here and gone is very, very sharp. Cover a baby's feet with a blanket, and as far as the baby is concerned, those feet have disappeared. If you can't see them, they aren't there. Right? Two-year-olds will cover their eyes and say: "You can't see me." If it's too dark for them to see you, it must be too dark for you to see them.

Many sharp divisions remain even as children begin to develop the ability to draw abstract distinctions—among them the division between what you should do and what you should not do. Children are taught that if they are not being good, they are being bad. Adults pass this lesson along for a few reasons. One is that it helps adults handle the difficult responsibility of raising a child. Another is that it is less confusing for a child to have simple, clear guidelines for living. It's safer to tell a young child: "Do not touch the burners on the stove—bad, bad, bad, never, never, never." Later, that child will learn that sometimes the burners are hot and other times they are cold, so that sometimes you can touch them with your bare fingers but other times you'll get burned.

But even after we are able to handle abstractions intellectually, it's common to maintain a certain core of *shoulds*. Some are brought along from those days when we were too young to understand that such a thing as in between could even exist and others are absorbed in the process of learning the various rules that govern our particular family, social circle, community, nation, and world. These *shoulds* become our givens—that is, the concrete no-margin-for-error standards—that we impose on ourselves and others. When we say *should*, we usually mean: "Don't think about it, don't question it—just do it. This is right. Anything else is wrong."

A Customized List

You might think that everyone would have the exact same list of *shoulds*. After all, if there is only one right and proper way to do or think about certain things, how could there possibly be two different lists? But of course we know that there are as many different lists as there are different people.

Shoulds differ by culture. Americans value individualism. We say: "The squeaky wheel gets the grease." The Japanese value concern for the group. They say: "The nail that stands out gets pounded down." *Shoulds* differ by local law, by religious belief, by political ideology. When people feel very strongly about a particular *should* that they think everyone should believe, we tend to refer to them as dedicated if we agree and fanatics if we disagree.

Your *shoulds* may change. Even those *shoulds* that are common to many people have a way of changing with the passage of time. Today it seems quaint to recall a time when good girls did not display an ankle. (The males in the family bought shoes for the females lest a shoe store clerk get a glimpse of that forbidden territory.) That particular *should* seems in no danger of being restored to prominence, though it's possible somebody thinks it *should*.

Kathleen waxes nostalgic when she remembers her teen years when the rule was: "Never kiss on a first date, much less do anything else." She feels that took some of the anxiety out of blind dates. And since young men also knew the rules, they didn't take the lack of a kiss as a permanent kiss-off of a relationship. But Kathleen's daughter thinks that is quaint. Which only means her *should* is different: A young woman should decide how she feels about a young man and respond accordingly.

The Comfort—and Virtue—of *Should*

Having some fixed rules about what you should and should not do offers great comfort and virtue. It is often much easier simply to do things "the way they are done." Most of us don't want to have to think about, investigate, and question every single thing we do. Who has the time? We would like to believe in some external verities we can count on. "We hold these truths to be self-evident," says the Declaration of Independence.

We admire people who just automatically do the right thing. A man sees a child in danger of drowning and jumps in the water to rescue him. "You might have drowned," friends say later. "I didn't think about that," the man says. "I couldn't just stand there and let that little boy die without even trying to save him."

Automatic responses can smooth your way in social situations or even save your life. Your parents may have drummed into you that you should look both ways before crossing the street, and you continue to do that even when crossing a one-way street. And why not? You can't be sure that some unthinking motorist won't drive the wrong way on that one-way street. And every year, there is a story about an American tourist who is struck by a car when crossing the street in England or Jamaica or Australia or Japan. In those countries traffic moves in a pattern opposite to that of the United States and most other countries. Thus, if you look for a car only in the direction that a car can be expected to come from in New York or Paris, you may be surprised.

In many ways, we find comfort in having stability and structure built into life. And we are talking about stability and structure when we use the word *should*. Flexibility can be scary. Too much flexibility is chaos. The more choices you have to make, the more opportunities you have for choosing "wrong." When you are sure of what you and others should do and how you and they should feel about things, you have a fix on the universe. You have a sense of your role in life. Your mind is free to think about other things.

Identifying the Troublemakers

But even though routinely responding to a command is sometimes the easiest thing to do, the belief that there is only one path—with no alternatives, no options, and no latitude—can also bring you *unnecessary* misery. That's when it's time to give the *shoulds* in your life more thought.

Shoulds become troublesome:

- When you fail to do something that you think you should—and end up feeling guilty or unworthy.
- When you did (or failed to do) something in the past and now feel yourself mired in regret.
- When others have done or failed to do something they should have—leaving you hurt or angry or both.
- When you are doing what you believe you should—but deep down wish you didn't have to and therefore feel both resentful about having to do it and guilty about feeling resentful.

- When you intend to do something that you shouldn't— and so feel guilty, anxious, and stressed all at the same time.
- When what you believe (your *should*) conflicts with what another believes.

You can identify the particular *shoulds* that make your life more difficult. The first step in dealing in a constructive way with the *shoulds* that make *you* feel guilty, angry, anxious, regretful, or stressed is to make a list of them.

- What should you be doing that you are not?
- What should you have done that you didn't do?
- What are others doing wrong where you are concerned?
- What duty are you fulfilling that makes you angry?
- What act are you contemplating that you know violates your values?

When Your *Shoulds* Pinch

Maybe the way you think about the *shoulds* you list actually makes it harder for you to live up to your own standards. In theory, a rigid application of the rules ought to make life less complicated and therefore easier. In practice, it doesn't work out that way.

In a way, *shoulds* are very much like shoes. You need a certain amount of structure in shoes to give your feet proper support, but if your shoes have no give at all or if they are laced too tightly, they'll begin to pinch. They'll begin to hurt. Instead of helping you to walk further, they force you to sit down.

To carry the image a little further: When you do everything you should and properly abstain from doing anything you should not, that's usually defined as walking the straight and narrow path—an admirable accomplishment.

But imagine now that you are walking across a bridge. This bridge is straight and *very* narrow. In fact, it is only as wide as your foot. To get across this bridge safely, you have to carefully place one foot in front of the other. You have to concentrate on keeping your balance. One wrong move and you are over the side. Imagine trying to negotiate this bridge when your feet hurt.

That is exactly what you attempt to do when you define your *shoulds* and those of others in very narrow, inflexible, concrete terms. It's a strain. Just one wrong move and you feel guilty or angry or stressed.

If you can make that bridge just a little wider, your progress is made easier. You still need the structure of the bridge to get from one side to the other, but if the bridge is wider and your shoes more comfortable, the trip will be less stressful. If your feet don't hurt and you don't have to worry so much about falling off, you might even enjoy the walk more. You can look around and appreciate the scenery. You can spend time thinking about which direction you might want to head in once you reach the other side. You could even pause—or trip—on the way over, and it wouldn't be such a big deal.

Widening the Bridge

To widen the bridge that you walk on requires thinking anew about each and every should you have listed.

When you use the word *should,* you are saying in effect: "*Don't* think. *Don't* consider alternatives. *Don't* consider consequences. *Don't* weigh and balance pros and cons. *Just do it.*" But it is precisely when you just do it—with no thought, no consideration of mitigating circumstances, no possibility of compromise, no consideration of other courses of action, that *should* so often becomes more hindrance than help.

It is not merely a coincidence that the word *should* popped up in the discussion of mind reading. When you feel angry because someone who you think *should know* what you want doesn't respond to your unspoken wishes, you are not merely *wishing* that person could read your mind, you have already found that person guilty of failing to do so. Thinking in terms of what others *should* know and *should* do closes the door to all benefit of doubt. No discussion required. Case closed.

Should also plays a role in the power we hand over to our perceived critics. We translate what we *assume* they are thinking into a command. You might, for example, be invited to the wedding of a couple who has much more money than you do. You get upset as you consider what gift you *should* give them because you think: "I have to give them a gift commensurate with their position in life. If I don't give them something as nice as the other things they will get, people will think I am a cheapskate. But I really can't afford an expensive gift. I wish I hadn't been invited."

Psychologist Albert Ellis believes we would be better off if we simply banished the word *should* from our vocabularies. He suggests substituting the expression: "It would be better if . . ." That phrase, according to Ellis, offers greater latitude for internal debate. *Should* offers only two choices—should or should not. "It would be better" is more open ended. It offers a broader array of choices such as: "It could be a little better, or not much worse."

It might be better if you could give this couple a very expensive gift, but if you don't have the money, then you can't. What will people say? Which people? How important are those people? The idea is to get out of the command mode ("Do it or else") and into the thoughtful consideration mode ("What is the best way to handle this?").

There is no *should* so powerful that you may not thoughtfully consider it. Most people would cite: "Thou shalt not kill" as one of the most powerful commandments of all, and yet as a matter of national policy we make exceptions for soldiers fighting for their country in time of war; as a matter of law we make exceptions for self-defense. Should you obey the speed limit? Well, yes—but suppose you are rushing somebody to a hospital emergency room and there is no other traffic on the road?

There are many *acceptable* and *responsible* ways to widen bridges, beginning with some innocent little tricks of language. People who would never swear or utter a four-letter word might say: "Gosh darn!" (which is no more than a bowdlerized version of "God damn") or "Shoot!" (the "polite" version of a four-letter word with *i*, instead of *oo*, in the middle). You might not think of that as a way of modifying a *should*, but that's what it is.

Once you begin paying attention to the word *should*, you may be amazed at how often you use it or an equivalent like: "I have to" or "That's the way it's done." You may be amazed as well at how often you simply accept a given *should* and take your punishment, without ever wondering if punishment is deserved.

People often berate themselves for not taking an action even when they haven't any idea what that action might have been.

Gordon cannot forgive himself for not doing something to prevent his brother from committing suicide. He tells himself: "I should have known how serious the situation was. There must have been some clues that I should have read. I should have been able to help." He isn't saying: "I wish I had known. I wish I had been able to help." Instead, he piles guilt on top of sadness. He is rendering a judgment: Guilty.

When you stop, write them down, and analyze them, you may well find you are enforcing *shoulds* that don't even exist. Sound strange? It's really quite common.

Here's an example that combines mind reading critics and then believing them without question: When Julie takes maternity leave, she tells her friends at the office that she plans to return to work. When she asks for an extension of the maternity leave, she explains that she is having difficulty in making child care arrangements. Finally, she admits she really doesn't want to come back to work. She wants to say home with the baby. She knows her husband supports this decision, but she is sure her friends at the office will look down on her. They all manage to combine home and career. She is sure that's what they think all women should do and so will view her as a traitor to the cause of equality for women. But when she confesses that she wants to take a few years off, her friends take it in stride. "You should do what's best for you," they say. "The women's movement seeks to open up options for women, not to close any off."

Analyzing Consequences

The first step in thinking anew about your particular list of *shoulds* is to analyze the consequences of maintaining them as opposed to the consequences of giving them up or modifying them.

You are not wrong to believe that if you violate a *should*, there will be consequences. All actions have consequences. But those consequences may not be the ones that you automatically assume.

The inner voice says you should finish everything on your plate (even if the restaurant has heaped so much food on the platter that finishing it means adding a pound you can do without). It says you should send holiday greeting cards. It says you should be a perfect parent. What will happen if you fall short? Will you be shot at dawn? Tarred and feathered? (A little deliberate superexaggeration will help reveal the exaggerations you are already thinking.)

Once you begin to think in terms of the advantages and disadvantages of specific consequences, you will find that you begin to think in terms of the *best*, rather than the *only*, solution. Suppose, for example, that Julie personally believed that as a modern woman, she is about to do something (stay home with the baby) that she should not do. To analyze this, she gets a piece of paper and writes down the consequences of maintaining this *should*:

- "I will feel guilty about not living up to my standards."
- "I will feel guilty about letting other women down."

(You might point out that she also will have less money since she is giving up a salary, but since that is not a consequence that *bothers* her, there is no point in listing it.)

What are the consequences of ignoring this should?

- "I'll be home with my baby."
- "I'll feel good about being able to give her my undivided attention."
- "I can go back to work later if I choose."

Julie now has a basis for comparing advantages and disadvantages. She can make a conscious choice rather than just automatically reacting in a guilty way.

Marty lives with his mother, who scolds, complains, and objects to any and all of his friends. Marty thinks about getting a place of his own. But he feels guilty. She has no one else. How can he possibly leave her? Marty has locked himself in by thinking of his *should* ("I should take care of my mother") in terms of an "only" solution rather than in terms of working out a compromise that might be best for both. Does having a place of his own mean he will never see his mother again? Not necessarily. By brainstorming alternatives, comparing advantages and disadvantages, Marty is more likely to come up with a solution that makes his life better and doesn't leave his mother totally alone.

Woulda, Coulda, Shoulda Thinking

"Woulda, coulda, shoulda" is an expression favored by sportswriters who, on Monday, review all the plays that would have, could have, and should have won the football game on Sunday if only the crucial pass had been caught, or the opposition blocked, or a better game plan executed.*

What's fun in football, however, is not so enjoyable in life. Ruminating about a mistake that you cannot now undo, or bitterly remembering how another person hurt or failed you, can—to borrow a football metaphor—stop the clock on your life.

Becoming overwhelmed by regret or guilt about something that happened in the past is a major consequence of this particular mistake. When you contemplate something that you believe should or should not have happened in the past, you are in a particularly vulnerable position, because the past cannot be

---

Woulda, Coulda, Shoulda is also the title of an earlier book by the authors. Subtitled *Overcoming Regrets, Mistakes, and Missed Opportunities*, it focuses specifically on the problem of putting the past behind you and improving your present and future.

changed. You cannot go back. You cannot relive what happened and have it come out some other way.

You might say today: "I married the wrong person. I should have waited." Or: "I should never have gotten married." It might have been better if you had not wed, but the reality is that you did marry the person you married. And that is the consequence you must deal with now.

You might say: "He should never have left me. I lie awake dreaming of the terrible things he deserves to have happen to him." It might have been better if he'd stayed (maybe not), but the reality is that he didn't. And devoting all your thoughts to what *should* happen to him will not improve your life at all.

You might say: "I should have taken that job in California when I had the chance. If I had taken that job, I wouldn't be in the mess I'm in today." It may well have been better if you had taken that job, but the reality is that you cannot possibly know what your situation would be today if you had. If you could change one fact about the past, other facts might change, too. If you took the job, you might have had a fatal accident as you drove to work. Devoting all your thoughts to what might have been will not move you an inch toward what still might be.

Moving Out of the Past

People often say: "I can't stop thinking about what happened in the past. I'd like to forget it, but I can't." That is an indication of the strong hold *shoulds* have on us.

The best way to deal with a *should* of the past is to learn from it (you may resolve to be more careful in your choice of marital partner or job in the future)—and then *push it to the back of your mind*.

How do you that? You replace one set of thoughts with another. When one set of thoughts occupies you, it's difficult to concentrate on something else at the same time. If you constantly review what should have happened in the past, you will find it hard to concentrate on what to do next. But, conversely, if you force yourself to think in terms of what to do next, you will find you think less and less about what should have happened in the past.

The process of pushing the past to the back of your mind begins with selecting just one thing that would make your life better—a new job, a better social life, an activity outside of work that you would enjoy—anything.

Follow the steps suggested for Stan in Chapter Eight: If something doesn't occur to you immediately, try brainstorming with a friend. Write down anything that you think you might enjoy, write down your friend's suggestions, no matter how silly, no matter how seemingly impossible.

When you feel guilty or angry or depressed about something you feel should be and isn't, your first thought may well be: "There's nothing that could make me happy." But what you really mean is: "I believe that nothing I can do now will make me as happy as I believe I now *should* be." And in saying this, you may very well be right.

If you have suffered an injury that bars you from your previous employment, if the love of your life has died, if you missed the opportunity to play pro football when you were young, if you never get what you would have, could have, should have had if life were fairer, if you were luckier, if a million things . . .

But remember: Even if it's true that you cannot be as happy as you would have been if things had gone as they should have in the past, it may still be possible for you to be happier in the future than you are now. Happier may not be as good as happy— but it's better than a lifetime of anger and despair.

Besides, unless you can predict the future—which is about as easy as reading minds—you really don't know what it holds for you. What you do know is that you have the choice of either trying to make the future better or continuing to bemoan the past. You can either focus your attention on a project or activity that will occupy both your mind and your time or you can continue to feel bad about what should have been.

Dealing with Guilt

You may choose to continue to bemoan the past because you feel you *should*. You have done something wrong. You have sinned. You have hurt another. You have not just bent a should, but smashed it to pieces. And you may well feel that you deserve the misery you now experience. You may think: "If the milk is spilt, you must live with the guilt."

However, there is more than one way to make amends for past offenses. To do no more than feel miserable will neither change the past nor improve the future. If you have hurt someone in the past, you might want to think of what you can do to help that particular person—or even someone else—now. If you have sinned in the past, you might want to think of what you can do now to help others avoid that same mistake. This last is a common pattern for former drug addicts. They have made a choice to stop blotting out their problems with drugs, and rather than spending the rest of their lives feeling bad about the years they have wasted, they work to help others kick the drug habit.

Here, too, the way to push the past behind you is to do something to improve the future.

When *Shoulds* Collide

When dealing with *shoulds* of the present and future, the greatest turmoil usually arises when your *should* conflicts with the *shoulds* of others. This is only to be expected when so many different lists of *shoulds* abound.

Shoulds have a way of creating havoc when they collide—even when the subject of the *should* seems minor indeed. Angela says dishes should be rinsed before being put in the dishwasher. Husband Jim says that's silly. Angela says the soup bowls should be stored on the first shelf of the closet. When Jim unloads the dishwasher, he sticks them on the second shelf. Result: constant squabbling. The quarrels sometimes escalate to drag in every other *should* on which Angela and Jim disagree. ("You should be nicer to my mother." "Yeah, since when is she nice to me?") There are basically only two choices when dealing with the *shoulds* of others: Accept or reject them.

Accepting the *Shoulds* of Others

It's not easy to accept the *should* of another—particularly when that person is a critic of your *should*. When your gut says you are right—why accept what is wrong?

The answer is that you do *not* have to accept that the other person is right when you agree to do things that way. You need only accept the idea that other people may have *shoulds* different from your own and that sometimes the consequences of going along with their *shoulds* are preferable to the consequences of going to battle with them.

For example, Ron is a resident in training at a large metropolitan hospital. This hospital has a rule requiring residents to request permission if they wish to make a change in the duty schedule. When Ron wants a day off, he doesn't bother to get permission but does arrange for a fellow resident to cover his duties for him while he is gone. When Ron returns, he learns that the hospital medical director has suspended him for breaking the permission rule. Ron argues that the suspension is undeserved. He points out that the purpose of asking permission is only to make sure that no shift is left uncovered, and he had made sure his shift was staffed. Ron is correct about the reason for the rule, the medical director agrees, but the suspension stands. Why? Because he believes that residents should follow the rules, not make up their own. And he is in charge.

Ron has to decide whether the consequences of fighting the rule are worth the effort. If not, he may still think the rule is silly, but he can decide to go along.

Rita is a lesbian who wants to bring a woman friend on a weekend visit to her father's house. Her father, who believes his children should all marry and produce grandchildren for him, refuses to invite Rita's friend.

Simply by acknowledging that her father may have *shoulds*

different from her own, Rita *expands the choices* open to her. That is, if Rita believes that her father should accept her way of life, and he believes she should change her way of life, each one puts the other in a do-it-or-else position. The likely result is that the relationship between father and daughter will end, with neither one feeling very good about it.

If Rita can accept the idea that her father feels as strongly about his *should* as she does about hers, she adds a second possible consequence to their situation: She could agree to visit him alone. Admittedly, that isn't as satisfactory to her as bringing her friend, but then she isn't doing exactly as her father wishes either. That opens the possibility of still a third consequence: At some point, her father may change his mind. (He, of course, may continue to hope that at some point *she* will change.)

In every case, when *shoulds* collide, you may say it would be better if we agreed, but then you must review the consequences of maintaining your *should* as opposed to the consequences of either going along with the *should* of another or finding a way to compromise.

If you want to travel in certain circles or advance to certain corporate levels, you may have to learn the *shoulds* that apply there, which may be in the form of a dress code, a set of regulations, or simply an accepted pattern of behavior. You don't have to agree that these are the best ways to go about things to decide the consequences of going along are more favorable than the consequences of rejecting them.

Rejecting the *Shoulds* of Critics

Rejecting a *should* seems like a contradiction in terms since the very idea of *should* implies: "Do it and don't think about it." But once you begin thinking in terms of analyzing consequences, you will find that you are not only better able to modify the way you respond to a given *should,* but you may also simply decide to reject *shoulds* that an external or internal critic wishes to impose on you.

Suppose Julie, who wanted to stay home with her baby, had been right that her friends would disapprove. Suppose part of her agrees that if you are a modern woman, working is what you *should* do. She must ask herself how important these critics are to her. She must ask herself: "What are the consequences of adhering to what they—and I—think *should* be done as opposed to what I really want to do?" Julie allows herself room to maneuver simply by acknowledging that there can be *a choice.*

Other people may not want you to believe this.

Burt's mother asks him: "Have you spoken to your sister lately?"

"No," says Burt.

"You should give her a call."

"Let her call me. I don't enjoy talking to her."

"That's a terrible thing to say. She's your sister."

"She is my sister, and she has been obnoxious for all the years I have known her."

"It doesn't matter. Members of a family should stick together." ·

It might be better if members of a family stick together—but you may decide that the price of sticking together is not one you wish to pay.

On the other hand, if someone in power says you should not be allowed to vote, or you should not be paid a decent wage, or you should not be free to practice your beliefs, you may feel the price of sticking up for what *you* feel is the better way may be high, but you are willing to pay it. You are responsible for yourself. What do *you* think is best? What are *you* willing to do?

Thinking "Better"

Avoiding the *should* mistake is simply a matter of giving yourself permission to consider, to weigh evidence, and to decide among alternatives rather than just reacting automatically. As you consider the *shoulds* in your life, you will undoubtedly decide to hang on to some because they make you feel comfortable. You may well decide to accommodate some of the *shoulds* of others because it makes *them* comfortable. And there may be *shoulds* that you decide to modify or give up. The critical word here is *decide*. In each case, you make the decision. You decide what's better. You decide what's possible. You have the power to loosen those *shoulds* that pinch so tightly that they impede your progress through life.

"Allow yourself some latitude" may be a platitude—but it's good advice.

CHAPTER ELEVEN

YES-BUTISM

There's an old story about a grandmother who takes her beloved grandson to the beach. He is playing on the sand when a huge wave crashes on the shore and sweeps him out to sea. The grandmother is naturally distraught. She is overcome by grief at the loss of her grandson and overwhelmed at the thought of facing her daughter and son-in-law with such terrible news. She cries out to God to help her. "Please, please," she begs. "Return my grandson to me. He is a good boy. His mother and father are wonderful people. I will do anything to have him back."

And lo, another wave crashes onto the shore and drops the child right back where he was before, none the worse for his watery trip. The old woman looks down at the child, looks up at the sky, and says: "Thank you, Lord . . . but where's his hat?"

That's yes-but. Yes, that was wonderful . . . *but not wonderful enough.*

Yes-but is a technique that acknowledges positives but follows up—sometimes immediately, sometimes after a short pause—with a negative that cancels out all satisfaction, all pleasure, all sense of accomplishment in what has gone before. It works this way whether you say it to others or say it to yourself:

- "Yes, it looks good, but . . ."
- "Yes, he did say he liked me, but . . ."
- "Yes, it could work, but . . ."

But . . . but . . . but . . . here come all the reasons why there is no point in hoping, no point in trying, no point in taking any pride in what you have done so far.

Yes-but is like a club that hangs over your head to beat you down every time you try to stand up. It snatches defeat from the jaws of victory. It surrounds every silver lining with a cloud. In its mildest form, it is like a bitter pill placed in the middle of a chocolate bonbon—just enough to spoil the treat. At its worst, it is like being given a medal before facing a firing squad—it is very difficult to appreciate the medal when all those holes keep appearing in your chest.

Around the world, therapists testify to the terrible power of those two little words, whether they are pronounced *yes-but* or *sí-pero* (Spanish) or *oui-mais* (French) or *ja-men* (Swedish) or translated into any other language. Whatever yes—or *sí* or *oui* or *ja*—gives, but, *pero, mais,* and *men* takes away.

The Kitchen Knife

Yes-but can also be used in situations where the meaning is merely informative. Take these examples:

- "Yes, I would like a chicken sandwich, but without mayonnaise, please."
- "Yes, I would like to go to the movies with you, but not Tuesday night because that's the night I work late."
- "Yes, that is a wonderful system, but it's too expensive for me."
- "Yes, Justin is a very nice man, and yes, he is rich, and yes, many of my friends feel he is a better catch than Larry, but I am in love with Larry, and he is the one I want to marry."

In these cases, yes-but is used in a reasonable way to cite both the positive and the negative in a given situation. There are also contexts in which yes-but can even be motivating. Such as:

- "Yes, what I have now is bad, but I'm going to do better."
- "Yes, I am unhappy now, but I know that if I struggle, I can improve things."
- "Yes, I know that project didn't go well, but that experience has taught me lessons that will benefit me in the future."

However, yes-but becomes a thinking mistake of major proportions when it becomes a *dominant mode of reacting* or when, as is so often the case, it is *carried to ludicrous extremes*.

Like every other thinking mistake described in this book, yes-but is somewhat in the position of an ordinary kitchen paring knife. When used properly, the kitchen knife is innocent, helpful, and quite necessary. But if used thoughtlessly, emotionally, angrily, or maliciously, that same kitchen knife can do a lot of damage. The same knife that peels the potatoes can become a lethal weapon. Yes-but thinking has that same potential for destruction.

Put in its simplest form, yes-but is a dogged determination to find a negative somewhere, somehow, or someway to minimize or cancel out whatever positive exists. It is sometimes used to undermine your own power *or* to assert power over another by finding a way to cancel out some positive in that person's life.

Alan's mother buys him two shirts, one red and one blue. The next time he visits her, he is wearing the red shirt. "Didn't you like the blue one?" she asks. Yes, he is wearing the red one which indicates he likes it, but he is not wearing the blue one. Therefore something must be wrong. This is a two-blade yes-but knife. Alan's mother stabs herself ("He didn't like my gift") while stabbing her son at the same time ("There is no way I can please my mother"). Whatever pleasure might have been possible either in the giving or in the receiving of the gift is destroyed.

There is almost no limit to how far a yes-but thinker will search to find a negative. If twenty people say: "That's a great-looking shirt you are wearing"—and then one person says: "I don't think red is a good color for you," the yes-but person will tuck the shirt into a drawer, never to be worn again. Yes, twenty people liked the shirt, *but one did not*. Yes, twenty people had positive opinions, *but only the negative opinion counts*.

If the yes-but weapon is aimed at other people rather than at yourself, the comment would likely be: "Yes, that's a great-looking shirt, but do you really think red is a good color for you?"

A Poor Substitute for Power

Why do so many people use yes-but in ways that hurt others or hurt themselves? Generally, yes-but arises from a perception of powerlessness. You may feel that you *can't say no* to anything or anybody. Thus, you have to accept a single negative opinion, even if you have received twenty positive ones. Or you may feel *unable to assert yourself* in any meaningful way.

Saying yes-but enables you to avoid a direct confrontation. You are afraid to say no, so you seem to agree while qualifying that agreement. That enables you to back away from a situation without giving up self-esteem, but backing away rarely changes anything.

Or you may resort to yes-but as a way of expressing anger when you are unwilling to deal with the real source of that anger. For example, Alan's mother may well be angry at her son because she feels he doesn't visit her often enough. But she is afraid to confront him directly. She fears he might say something like: "I don't like visiting you. I only come out of a sense of duty." So instead she expresses her frustration in yes-but. She gives a gift but then makes sure he doesn't enjoy getting it—even though that means she won't enjoy giving it either.

In short, in one way or another, when you use yes-but, you are admitting that you don't have the power to change anything.

When You Say Yes-But to Yourself

When you say yes-but to yourself, you are telling yourself that you do not have the power to get what you want. You admit that you want something. You admit that you very well may have the potential for achieving it. But . . .

But then you deny yourself what you want before anyone else gets a chance to do it for you. That avoids a direct power confrontation with somebody else. It doesn't give an outsider a chance to reject you. It's always easier to accept rejection at your own hands than at the hands of another.

Joe says: "Yes, I would like to go out with Denise, but she probably already has a boyfriend. She probably wouldn't be interested in anyone who doesn't have a Ph.D." Obviously, if Joe never asks Denise out, he isn't going to go out with Denise— unless, for some reason, she decides to ask *him.*

Yes-but people tend to be procrastinators. "Yes, I know it is important that I do that and I am going to do it, but not now . . . later . . . never." Yes-but people are geniuses at coming up with excuses. Creative excuses. Clever excuses. Complex excuses. But the fact remains that excuses are not action. Fifty excuses will get you a cup of coffee—as long as you pay cash for the coffee.

When You Feel You Can't Say No

Many people have trouble saying no. It may arise from a feeling of guilt. A father feels he must treat all of his four children equally, and so, if he agrees to do something for one, he must agree to any demands the other three make at the same time—even if the total proves an impossible burden. A problem in saying no may also arise from an ardent desire to be accepted. A newcomer to the community is asked to help out on a dozen committees—and agrees to serve on every one. Such responses may arise from a deep feeling that you just don't have the resources to fight when the opposition has more power than you do. Often people with a yes-but habit developed it as children. Usually they had to deal with a parent who was *never* willing to take no for an answer.

Ralph's father explodes in rage if Ralph does not follow orders without a murmur. Every parent needs to draw a line sometimes, but Ralph's father engraves his lines in concrete. Ralph learns to say yes to everything. No matter what the command: yes. But often this response merely postpones his father's wrath. If, later, his father is not satisfied, Ralph resorts to yes-but. He never directly says: "No, you are wrong. No, what you wanted is impossible." He instead says: "Yes, but I tried. Yes, but this happened. Yes, but that happened."

The problem with what might be called the yes-but defense is that it is not a reliable technique for defusing anger. Indeed, it often has just the opposite effect. Renee, for example, works for three partners in a business and is anxious to please each of them. They are equally powerful and have equal power to fire her, and Renee doesn't feel she has the power to refuse their assignments.

Partner A: "Renee, I need four copies of this fifty-page document by 4 P.M."

Renee: "Yes."

Partner B: "Renee, I want the entire contents of the Smithers file faxed to Jones in Atlanta by 4 P.M."

Renee: "Yes."

Partner C: "Renee, type this report and get it back to me by 4 P.M."

Renee: "Yes."

Unfortunately, the overworked Renee cannot possibly have the assignments completed by 4 P.M. Now instead of making one partner angry, she has riled all three.

"You said you could do it. We counted on you," says one.

"Yes, but I tried to finish it all."

"What good is that doing us now?" says number two.

"If you couldn't handle it all, why didn't you say so in the first place?" yells the third.

"Yes, but . . ."

Other Uses of Yes-But

Yes-but is frequently used to shift responsibility. Sid says: "Yes, I agree I should discuss this with my wife . . . but you don't know my wife." Translation: "The problem is my wife, not the fact that I don't know how to deal with her."

Yes-but is used to assert a measure of control that is less than the control you would really like. Ralph's father feels powerless at work and so brings the hostility he feels there home with him. He may not have power in the workplace, but he has power over his children, so he makes that power felt. He has told Ralph to clean his room. He then comes to inspect it. Yes, he has to admit, it looks clean. It looks neat. But, aha! The handkerchiefs in this drawer have not been folded properly. He dumps the contents of the drawer onto the bed. Ralph bites his lip and dreams of running away from home.

Margie, like Alan's mother, is afraid to state what is really bothering her. Margie would like to tell her too-domineering husband to back off. But she's afraid. So instead of confronting him, she simply annoys him. "Yes, the laundry is done, but I haven't folded it yet. Yes, I know you wanted steak tonight, but I didn't have a chance to shop." This is the domestic version of guerrilla warfare.

Stephen fears he can never earn the respect of others for his achievements, so he resorts to building himself up (at least in his own eyes) by knocking others down. Stephen can always find a flaw in anything anybody else does:

- "Yes, it's nice, but I don't think it's necessary."
- "Yes, your way is easier, cheaper, and more efficient, but I like things done *my way.*"
- "Yes, you have done an exhaustive job of research, but I think you should make one more telephone call."
- "Yes, that's a great-looking shirt, but do you really think red is a good color for you?"

A Self-Defeating Defense

As the previous discussion indicates, there are many ways to use yes-but. But whether your yes-buting comes about in order to defend yourself against greater power, or to avoid a confrontation that would prove you lack power, or to excuse a lack of power, or to substitute a petty form of power for real authority, one fact is unchanged: Yes-but is a bust as a power tool. It doesn't just short-circuit your objectives, it may set fire to them. That is, yes-but defeats you when you use it against yourself. And it alienates others when you use it against them.

A Mixture of Menacing Mistakes

Earlier chapters have noted that dumb thinking mistakes come in batches as often as they operate alone. Yes-but mistakes are prime examples of that. Very often yes-but thinking derives from or combines with other mistakes.

Here's an example: Todd's wife, Melissa, wants a divorce. A shaken Todd asks her what he can do to save their marriage. Melissa has prepared a list of seven things she most dislikes about him. He talks to a marriage counselor about them.

"What's the first complaint on the list?" asks the therapist.

"She says I wasn't affectionate, that I never gave her a hug or called her honey. She says I touched her only when we were having sex."

"How many times a day have you expressed affection for your wife since receiving this list?"

"None," replies Todd frankly.

"Why not?"

"Because that's not really what's bothering her. There's something else going on."

"What?"

"I don't know what."

"She *says* this is important to her. Why not do it and see what happens?"

"That's what she says, but it's not the real problem. And

besides, even if I called her honey, she'd still have these six other complaints."

"If you made an effort, do you think you could express affection—offer a hug or call your wife honey—a couple of times a day?"

"Yes, but . . ."

This is a portrait of a man who is going to yes-but his way to the divorce court. Yes, that's what she says, but it is not the real problem. Todd is engaging in the mistake of mind reading. He may be right that Melissa is hiding her true anger, but he cannot know that unless he tests the evidence. If he becomes more affectionate and it has no effect at all, he may have a point. By saying yes-but, Todd makes sure he never finds out.

Todd has pointed out: "Besides, even if I called her honey, she'd still have these six other complaints."

Yes, he could do one thing, but other problems will remain.

Here Todd makes the mistake of perfectionism. If he can't solve all the problems at once, he will not attempt to solve any of them. And thus, of course, no problems get solved.

Yes, Todd wants to save his marriage, *but* he won't do anything to solve his problems.

Here's another example:

Sarah had been a widow for twenty years when she met Timothy, who made it clear he was interested. They got along, their respective children were pleased and expected the two to get married. But Sarah said: "Yes, he's a wonderful man. Yes, I care for him. Yes, he cares for me. Yes, he owns his own business and he's well-to-do . . . but . . . he repairs shoes."

Perhaps Sarah is a perfectionist who demands that the man of her dreams must meet every criterion, or perhaps Sarah is a victim of the what-if error. Perhaps she is making excuses for fear that the marriage won't work out. Perhaps she fears that after twenty years of living by herself, she won't be able to adjust to living with another. Instead of facing those fears and dealing with them, she shields herself with yes-but.

Yes-but combines with all manner of mistakes. It could be that the yes-but person who rejects twenty positive opinions about the shirt he is wearing to focus on a single negative opinion too easily believes all critics. That single no vote may be the tone required to set off an internal tuning fork that exists because this person feels inadequate about his taste in clothing. In any combination, yes-but is dangerous. It takes away pleasure. It limits possibilities. And it discourages meaningful solutions.

Moving Toward Yes

Modifying a tendency to yes-but requires first making yourself aware of how often—and when—you think or say it. Try to count the times you say yes-but.

Listen to yourself. Make yourself aware of what you are thinking.

- "Am I demeaning what I am doing? Am I protecting myself from trying to get what I would really like to have?"
- "What effect does it have on me when I disqualify myself before anyone else has a chance to do it? Does it motivate me? Does it allow me to be more successful? Or do my feelings of dissatisfaction disable me and leave me feeling empty?"
- "Am I demeaning what someone else is doing? Am I alienating others, stirring up arguments? Is making people angry what I really want?" Ask those close to you—spouse, children, colleagues, subordinates—"Do I do this? What effect does it have on you?"

If you decide you want to move away from yes-but, that doesn't mean you will banish those words from your vocabulary entirely because sometimes, as mentioned before, they are necessary and proper. What you want to do is to modify your use of them—or, more exactly, your overuse of them. You want to rein in your yes-buts before they cause any more harm.

Changing Yes-But to Yes-And

You can dispose of some yes-buts by changing them to yes-ands.

Don't say: "Yes, I would like to do it, but here are the reasons I can't."

Say: "Yes, I would like to do it, and here are the challenges I must overcome in order to manage it."

This is the assertiveness equivalent of the difference between seeing a glass as half full rather than half empty. It is a mindset that adds rather than subtracts. Yes-but only gives you excuses. Yes-and is an agenda for action.

In previous chapters, we talked about brainstorming action ideas and breaking down the ultimate goal into small, manageable steps. That technique is also useful here. When you are feeling low, you may know a million things to do, but you can't seem to find a single place to start. "Yes, I know what would help, but there's no way to do it." That quickly becomes: "There is nothing I can do."

To get out of the nothing-can-be-done mode requires focusing on one single piece of the project—a starting point, a thread that leads to other threads.

Suppose this is your original thought:

"Yes, I believe I have the ability to do the job—*but* they wouldn't consider someone my age, *but* they probably have a full staff now, *but* you probably have to 'know somebody' to get a break."

Stop. Write down your goal: "I want that particular job."

Now list the steps that you would have to take to apply for it. List the information you need to help you reach your goal. List the necessary steps to get that information. Follow those steps one by one.

Mao Tse-tung is quoted as saying: "The journey of a thousand miles begins with a single step." He may not have been right about other things, but about this he made no mistake.

If you have written, make a telephone call to the company. You could break that down into:

Get the telephone book.
Look up the number.
Write the number down.
Take the number to the telephone.
Dial the number.

You might say: "That's silly. I don't have to write down 'Look up the number, write the number down.' I would do that automatically."

If you say that, fine. Write it down anyway. The whole point of this exercise is to convince yourself that what you want to do is not as hard as your yes-but thinking has made it seem.

You may have to write downs steps involving determining exactly which office or which person at that company to phone:

Call the personnel office.
Call the head of the department.
Ask questions.

You may want to write a script of what you want to say. Think about what information you need:

Is there an opening?
Who is doing the hiring?
What sort of background information would this person want to see?
A resumé? Prepare a resumé. (Additional steps may be involved in doing this.)
Write a cover letter.
Mail it.

If that telephone call doesn't work out, you begin to list the next steps to be taken, breaking down those steps into separate steps.

This is yes-and. "Yes, I have done the first ten tasks on my list and I'm going to keep on doing these until I reach my goal." With every step you cross off, you can feel yourself getting closer to your goal.

Yes-and stops you from procrastinating. Instead of: "Yes, I'll do it, but later," you think: "Yes, I'm going to do it—and I might as well get it over with. Yes, and when I'm finished, I'm going to reward myself by going out to dinner."

When you hear yourself saying, yes-but—stop. Find a way to change that to yes-and.

Role Playing

A technique that may be helpful in getting you started is role playing. If you have been telling yourself that you can't get anywhere because others don't find you attractive or because employers have a bias against your group—whatever—pretend to be someone else who doesn't have that problem. Be an actor. Play a role. You are not you. You are someone who doesn't face any of the drawbacks you face—someone who doesn't add *but* after saying yes. What would that person say? How would that person act?

You have probably already played many different roles in your life, although you may not have thought that you were acting at the time. Perhaps there were times when you were very nervous about something but acted brave so the children wouldn't get upset. Perhaps you went to a funeral and put on a sad face and told the widow how deeply you shared her loss—even though when the deceased was alive, you didn't like him at all.

You can play a role that will help you to test out that *but* that cancels out your yes. Suppose, for example, you think that a group of people with whom you work don't like you. Yes, it's true they haven't actually said that, but you think you can tell.

You can test that theory by playing the role of someone who takes being liked for granted. Be friendly. Be outgoing. Say hello to each of those people when you meet them. If the opportunity arises to get into a conversation, ask them for their opinion about something. Most people like to talk and to have someone listen to what they say. You can play the listener role. You will soon discover whether they say hello back.

Thought Reversal

Another useful technique in dealing with some forms of yes-but is a reversal of thought that deliberately seeks out a positive rather than a negative.

Instead of yes, twenty people admired your shirt, *but one hated it,* you can reverse that sentence to: "One person hated my shirt *but twenty admired it.*"

This is something the yes-but person will have to make a conscious effort to do. Because seeking the negative is something you are doing automatically, it registers in your brain automatically and you feel terrible automatically. Thus, you must first surface what you are thinking. Then try your thought again in reverse order, excluding the negative instead of excluding the positive. You may literally change your mind:

- "Yes, she's beautiful. Yes, she's an interesting conversationalist. Yes, she shares many of my interests. But she has a very annoying voice."
- "Yes, she has a voice that I find annoying, but she's beautiful. She's an interesting conversationalist, and she shares many of my interests."

Saying Yes to Others

If you sense that saying yes-but to others is creating a wall of animosity between you and them—and this is not something you want—you will want to find a more positive way of relating to them. Here again you must pay attention to exactly what you are doing.

Are you taking out your anger at others on people you don't want to hurt? Are you impossible to please? Do you find you always have to add something? "Yes, that's nice, but the margins could be wider." Are you bringing up a negative when it isn't really important? Are there times when you could just say: "This is good"? And stop?

- "This is terrific lasagna. It's a shame your veal parmesan isn't as good."
- "This is terrific lasagna." (Stop.)

This does not mean that you cannot voice a legitimate objection or make a correction when one is required. The key words here are: bringing up a negative *when it isn't important*. As with all thinking mistakes, yes-but becomes a problem when it is used to an excessive degree.

Saying No to Others—The Power of Positive Assertion

The advice "Just say no" (to drugs, to people, etc.) makes it sound easy, but saying no is, in many cases, very difficult. It calls for asserting yourself, and just the thought of doing that can bring on an attack of what-if thinking combined with the Chicken Little Syndrome. Renee, the secretary with three bosses, may say to herself: "What if I say no? What if one of them gets mad? I'll be fired. I'll never find another job. I'll lose my apartment."

It's true that assertiveness implies some risk. If Renee says she cannot finish all the work, the bosses may well say: "If you can't do the work we want done, we'll get somebody else. Goodbye." On the other hand, saying yes when she knows that, somewhere down the road, she is going to have to say *but* is only a short-term solution to the problem. The same boss who isn't made angry now may only get more angry later.

It helps to remember that being more assertive does not necessarily mean you have to get into a fight. Renee does not have to blow up and toss all the papers at her bosses.

Some problem solving can help. Renee knows there is a problem. What suggestions can she make to solve that problem?

Perhaps someone in the office—an office manager—could screen and prioritize the assignments so that Renee does not have to make those decisions.

Is one boss more senior than the others? Would it be feasible to establish a system that that boss's projects always come first and the others are done as time allows?

Would it make sense for the bosses to think in terms of work priorities, noting on each assignment how important it is that it be done by 4 P.M.?

Would it make sense for Renee to inform each boss in turn of the work already assigned her by the others and ask them to work out the order in which the assignments could be completed?

At that point, Renee could *ask* her bosses whether they would consider some suggestions that would enable her to better meet their needs. It's just possible they might be reasonable people who would welcome some suggested alternatives. Renee has to ask herself how realistic is her projection that if she says no, or if she suggests a way to prioritize her work, the trio of bosses will be furious. Is she mind reading? What evidence does she have? Do these three get angry at everything? Do they fire people?

Dealing With a Yes-But Person in Your Life

The world is full of yes-but people who seem both able and willing to take the joy and feeling of accomplishment out of anything you do. You get an A in your course in physics and the yes-but critic says: "Yes, but what about your grade in algebra?" You get to be the president of the company and your critic says: "Yes, but it's only a small company."

Becoming aware of the yes-but mistake can help you deal with those who are determined to yes-but you. This is not criticism that you must accept without question. Even if you are not in the position to rebut that person directly, you can question their criticism internally. This is simply another way of questioning your critics. It is important to recognize when you are dealing with a yes-but person so that you can identify the mistake as one that person is making, rather than simply accepting that assessment of your achievement. You can say to yourself: "Yes, that's what she says, *but I know better.*

CHAPTER TWELVE

ACTIVATING YOUR SMARTS

Twenty-five therapeutic techniques for minimizing the damage from thinking mistakes have been discussed in the previous chapters. In this chapter and the next, all those techniques—plus others—are reviewed. This chapter focuses on eighteen cognitive techniques. The next chapter will describe seven behavioral techniques.

You might think of these chapters as an extended menu from which to select techniques you feel will be most helpful to you at any given time. When you select from a restaurant menu, you might pick a dish because it's an old favorite, or you might decide to go for something because you feel you particularly need it—maybe it's low in fat or salt. Or you might select something because it goes better with your main course. In much the same way, you can select a technique from this anti-mistake menu. You might pick one that works best for you most of the time. You might pick one because you need it now. You might pick one because it goes better with the particular problem that's foremost in your thoughts. Sometimes you'll select two or three to use together.

The following is a list of cognitive techniques that will be described in this chapter. These techniques are always available to you, wherever you are. They are simple to use and require no equipment and no prescription.

1. Determining meaning.
2. Questioning evidence.
3. Assigning responsibility.
4. De-catastrophizing.
5. Developing alternatives in thought.
6. Developing alternatives in feeling.
7. Developing alternatives in action.
8. Comparing advantages and disadvantages.
9. Labeling your mistakes.
10. Then what?
11. Superexaggeration.
12. Scaling from 1 to 10.
13. Turning adversity into advantage.
14. Developing replacement images.
15. Rehearsing positive images.
16. Self-instruction.
17. Self-distraction.
18. Playing defense attorney.

Determining Meaning

Is it a technique to simply ask yourself: "What does a particular word or specific event mean to me?" Yes. And it is a vitally important technique too, because the meaning that we give words and actions is really quite personal. To one person the word *cheesecake* would bring a mental picture of a dessert, to another the centerfold of *Playboy*. One person says: "I'm scared" and means he is afraid of dying as the result of high-risk surgery. Another says: "I'm scared" and means only that she is worried about not doing well on a school exam. The words may be the same, but the threats are not.

The problem is that we tend to talk—and think—in a form of verbal shorthand. We use euphemisms that obscure rather than clarify meaning. One person may say: "I'm having a bad week" and mean: "I haven't accomplished as much as I would have liked." Another says: "I'm having a bad week" and means:

"I am so overwhelmed by depression I want to commit suicide." It's hardly surprising that the result is endless confusion.

It causes problems in communicating with others because we so often simply assume that whatever we are thinking, the other person is thinking, too. And that is not necessarily the case. John says: "I care for you." He is trying to tell Mary he does not love her without hurting her feelings too badly. He means he is concerned about her and wants to remain friends. But Mary hears: "I care for you" and translates it to: "I love you" because to her that's what caring is all about. Both John and Mary would be better off if John simply stated exactly what he means.

Shorthand thoughts can be compared to a car horn. Sometimes you hit the horn to tell the driver in front of you that the light has changed and it's time to get moving. Sometimes you hit the horn to get the attention of a friend you see on the sidewalk. Alas, the horn sounds exactly the same each time. So you honk to get your friend's attention and the driver in front opens the window and yells: "What are you honking for, can't you see the light is red?"

On top of all the problems caused by the failure to convey exactly what we mean to others are the problems that are caused by our failure to convey exactly what we mean to *ourselves*.

We use the same jargon, shorthand, and euphemisms in our *own* thoughts that we express to others. These thoughts cause an emotional reaction that usually makes the situation worse.

Mary finally realizes that John does not love her and says to herself: "I'm crushed. My world has ended." The result: She *feels* crushed. She feels as if she has *nothing left*.

But what exactly does she *mean* by those euphemisms? She means John does not love her. She means her love is not returned. Has her world ended? What does she mean by *world*? Is her family part of this world? Does she still have a family? Are her friends part of this world? Does she still have her friends? Is her job part of this world? Does she still have her job? Is her health part of her world? Does she still have her health?

Asking herself exactly what she means by the thoughts that flit through her mind will not make Mary feel better about not having John's love, but will enable her to cope better with the *precise* problem, loss, and crisis that face her. It will enable her to move on to other coping techniques.

But the *first step* in coping with any words or events that provoke an emotional reaction is to stop and say to yourself: "Exactly what am I thinking? What is the meaning of those thoughts? How am I interpreting that event? What do I think this event means to my life?"

People often say: "I'm a loser" when what they mean is: "On three occasions, I have not had success in something I have tried, and this upsets me."

People also say: "I'm angry," "I'm fit to be tied," "It's hopeless," "I'm overwhelmed," and the like, and then stop there, allowing their emotions to build. But just as it is difficult—and sometimes impossible—for two people to know how to behave toward each other when they totally misunderstand each other, it is also difficult—and sometimes impossible—for an individual to know how to cope when unexplained shorthand flies unimpeded through one's thoughts.

So you must communicate clearly *to yourself* what you mean by your thoughts.

Questioning the Evidence

Sometimes you know precisely what you mean. You firmly believe you know something. You firmly believe you have every right to be angry, anxious, guilty, or depressed. The technique you may need then is questioning the evidence.

What evidence? The facts on which you have based your conclusion that you have every right to be angry, anxious, guilty, or depressed. What do you think happened? How do you know that for sure?

"I just know, that's all." Or: "Everybody knows that." Or: "I feel it in my gut, that's how." If you think such things or any other such generalization, what you mean is: "I don't have evidence. I'm reacting to feelings alone." That is not a good idea.

Feelings have a way of being wrong at least as often—probably even more often—than they are right.

Of course, sometimes you think you have evidence. It's just that you haven't spelled out to yourself exactly what that evidence is. Once you do that, you can analyze it. How reliable is this, really? Is there an alternative explanation?

The French writer Guy de Maupassant made the human tendency to jump to a conclusion without bothering to check the evidence the basis for many of his short stories. In "The Diamond Necklace," a woman borrows a necklace from a wealthy friend and then loses it. She buys a diamond necklace to replace the one she lost so that the friend will never know and then works for years to pay off the cost of it. Years later, worn down by this burden, she learns that the original necklace was made of paste.

It's fair to say that jumping to conclusions is just about everybody's favorite exercise. You might say: "I know he was angry because I heard a door slam."

And you might be right. Angry people slam doors. But if that anger matters to you, you might want to check your evidence. Can you be sure who slammed that door? Do you, in fact, know whether it was slammed, or did it just slip? Until you know the facts, you cannot properly draw a conclusion. It may not be a real diamond. It could be fake.

Sometimes the evidence you have is not very good. Philip walks into the therapist's office and informs her: "You will not be able to help me because I'm hopeless." "How do you know?" asks the therapist. "Because I have been to fifteen therapists and not one of them has helped me." "How long did you spend with each one?" asks the sixteenth therapist. "I spent one session and I didn't feel helped." "That evidence is flawed," the therapist explains, "because one session isn't enough to make a difference."

Ed, a bank vice president, becomes anxious when he discovers that his office in the new building to which the bank is moving is much smaller than his old office. This is an organization in which the size of one's office advertises the size of one's job—everybody knows that someone whose office has two windows ranks higher than someone whose office has just one or none.

Ed is sure that this is a way of telling him that he is being demoted or that he isn't as important to the bank as he had been. The size of the office is his evidence. Only later, after much agony, does he check that evidence. He measures everybody else's office—and discovers every office is smaller because the new building is narrower than the old.

As sensible as questioning the evidence is, you may find that you are often discouraged from doing it. You may be discouraged from daring to offer an alternative explanation in the absence of facts. You might say: "Well, maybe he didn't really mean that the way it sounded." Or: "Perhaps he was not feeling well." Someone will say: "Don't be a Pollyanna. You are being an apologist for someone who is a jerk."

And maybe he is a jerk. But on the other hand, if you have *no evidence* to prove that one way or other—if another explanation is also possible—than it's just as reasonable to err on the side of the positive as the negative.

Erring on the side of the positive is more likely to lead to questioning the evidence than erring on the side of the negative. You get into less trouble when you question the evidence.

Assigning Responsibility

Whose fault is it? That question frequently comes up. And because people so often think in all-or-nothing, black-or-white-with-no-gray-in-between ways, it is often answered: "It's all my fault." Or: "It's all their fault."

Rarely is fault all one way or the other. And it is important in sorting out one's thoughts to assign responsibility *carefully*. You may be accepting too little responsibility or too much. Take the commonly discussed matter of the responsibility our parents bear for making us what we are today. For many people, just thinking of their parents generates anger. "When I think of what they did to me, it makes me furious. They ruined my life."

Maybe—but only up to a point.

Your parents may well have made your life difficult. It is fair to blame them for being erratic or irrational or whatever they were or are. But once you are an adult, *you also bear responsibility for your life.* If thinking about your parents makes you furious, don't think about them. If hitting yourself on the head with a hammer makes your head hurt, stop hitting yourself on the head. Instead of thinking about what your parents did to you in the past, think about what you will do to improve your life in the future. Assign them the responsibility for what they did; accept responsibility for what you must do now.

Paula was unhappily married for ten years. When the marriage breaks up, her first feeling is one of relief. But later, alone, she begins to have second thoughts. "It was all my fault," she laments. "I should have been more understanding. He wouldn't have flown into those rages if I'd anticipated his needs better. He wouldn't have been unfaithful if I'd been more accepting." Now Paula not only feels lonely, she feels guilty. But if she were to fairly assign responsibility, she would have to note that this was a man who flew into rages, a man who was unfaithful. She might have done better, but he had to do better, too. And *he did not.* Further, whatever was the case in the past, Paula is responsible for what happens in the future.

When you assign responsibility, you must consider not only what has gone before, but what is going on now that *maintains the pain.*

You may feel that punishment is deserved for something that happened in the past. You may feel someone should be punished. Yet the emotion you feel just thinking about it *punishes you more.* Stop thinking about it. Get on with your life. You may feel you deserve to be punished for something that happened in the past. Your responsibility then is to decide what you can do to make amends. What positive contribution can you make now that will mitigate the negative of the past?

It may help you in assigning responsibility to actually put it down in black and white. Draw a line down the middle of a piece of paper and write down what others are responsible for and what you are responsible for.

The contributions may not be equal. Someone may have inflicted terrible damage on you. But unless you are locked in a cell unable to escape, you bear responsibility for your own situation now. Even if you cannot fix everything in your life, you can fix a piece of it.

People sometimes say: "I can't do anything about my situation." For example: "If I say no to my father, he just escalates his complaints and makes my life a living hell." The fact is, people often allow their lives to be made a living hell. It is possible to say: "I can't believe how crazy my father behaves sometimes. I am just going to ignore it no matter how crazy he gets because there is no point in both of us being crazy."

Others try to get us on a hook just as a fisherman tries to catch a fish. The fisherman is responsible for dangling the bait, but the fish does not have to take the bait and end up on a hook. People who know us well know which bait we tend to swallow—but if you know there is a hook, it's up to you to swim away.

De-Catastrophizing

This is a technique that comes in handy when you find yourself thinking that a disaster has already occurred or is about to. "I'm finished," you think. "It's all over. This is a catastrophe."

To de-catastrophize, you must stop and ask yourself: "What is the worst thing that can happen?"

Really. What is the worst thing that can possibly happen?

- "I could die."
- "I could be humiliated."
- "I could be fired."
- "I could be left penniless."
- "She'll leave me."
- "They'll hate me."

Sometimes, just stopping to identify the worst is enough to bring such thoughts to an end. It will often happen that when you answer: "What is the worst?" you immediately recognize that it won't happen, or if it does, it won't be the end of everything. When you are anxious or excited, your mind tends to race along unchecked. Just by naming the worst very specifically, you can often calm yourself down.

Checking the evidence is also helpful here, although you may be reluctant to do that. Suppose, for example, you were asked to go to a high-rise office building where you are *not* known, get into the elevator there, and call out every floor. "Sixth floor. Seventh floor. Eighth floor . . ." You'd probably say: "Are you kidding? People will think I'm insane."

To check that definitively, you would actually have to get on an elevator and yell. What do you think would happen? They may think you are insane. Will they hit you? Have you arrested? Have you committed to an institution? Probably not. They might look at you strangely. Would that really change your life? Someone might ask you why you are calling out the floors. You could say you are doing it on a dare, that someone offered you a thousand dollars if you were willing to do such a silly thing. You could say you just felt like shaking everybody up, it's been such a dull day. You could say you are thinking of doing a show like "Candid Camera" and want see how others would react to a stranger calling out floors in an elevator.

People who live in fear of making a mistake sometimes find actually making a mistake is the best thing that ever happened to them, because they learn that many people don't notice and many of those who do notice don't care. That is, they discover that what happens is nowhere near as bad as what they thought would happen.

A good test of how the public reacts to a mistake can be had by just returning an item of merchandise to a store. Many people hate to do this (comedienne Carol Burnett for one, who told an interviewer that an audience of thousands doesn't intimidate her, but don't ask her to exchange a package at a department store). What do you expect to happen? The store staff will think you are an idiot. (They are entitled to their opinion.) But will anyone shout: "Hey, look, here is somebody who couldn't pick the right size or color the first time!" Doubtful.

De-catastrophizing involves questioning and testing your premise that the worst will happen. It involves questioning and testing the steps that your mind says will lead up to the worst happening. You will very often recognize that what you are thinking is exaggerated when you force yourself to state your thoughts and ask yourself: "Just how likely is that result?"

Developing Alternatives in Thought, Feeling, and Action

Nothing is more paralyzing that the thought that you can do something or think about something in only one way. If that way is closed or leads to pain, you are in big trouble.

Imagine you are driving down a one-way street and a tree trunk falls in front of you and blocks the way. Now what? If you believe that the only way out of that street is blocked, you're stuck. But if you turn around, you can get out and find another route. You can't turn around, some people will say. It's a *one-way* street. True, but if the street is blocked, you might consider *carefully* driving the wrong way or backing out.

Sometimes it is necessary to generate alternative views or explanations for a given situation. You don't have to accept those views to think of them. But thinking of alternative views sometimes provides a way out that you did not see before.

Suppose, for example, you have to work with somebody who invariably finds some flaw in your performance. You have concluded she is a malicious person who is out to get you. Perhaps. But it may help you to develop other possible explanations. Maybe she is a hopeless perfectionist and can't help herself. Maybe she is insecure, and her way of trying to build herself up is to knock others down. You are going to be annoyed at this behavior no matter what the motivation, but if you think this person is insecure or obsessive rather than malicious, you will have an easier time working with her. And if you have no proof that one explanation is more accurate than another, you don't need to stick with the most negative one.

The point made again and again in this book is that your feelings shift as your thoughts shift. And how you feel affects how you act. You can use your ability to think to change the way you feel and act.

Take a few minutes to fantasize about a situation in which you expect to find yourself. People usually just fantasize around the edges. They'll say: "I'm going to a singles bar tonight, and it will be just awful."

Launch an internal dialogue to determine the meaning of that thought—and then develop alternatives. Like this:

"What will be awful? Spell it out."

"I'll feel awkward."

"Why?"

"No one will speak to me."

"If that happens, is there any alternative action I can take? Can I speak to someone?"

"I wouldn't know what to say."

"Then take the time now to think up some opening lines." Some people are very successful just admitting discomfort: "I am very nervous in places like this. I find I want to talk to someone and don't know what to say." (That usually brings the reply: "Me too.")

"But suppose I say that and the person says: "Get lost, creep.' "

"What do I think of someone who would talk to someone that way?"

"A creep."

"Lucky I discovered what kind of person this is before wasting my time."

In other words, fantasize alternative scenarios so that you are prepared in advance to deal with them. If you think there is only one way, one thought, one mode of action, you limit your possibilities.

Comparing Advantages and Disadvantages

Life presents many choices, and unfortunately many of them are not easy ones. You are not asked whether you would prefer a million dollars or a bucket of mud. The choice is between terrible and possibly worse, between one mixture of good and bad and another mixture of good and bad, or between a big risk and a different big risk. In other words, tough choices.

In such choices, the correct answer is not obvious. The best way to weigh such choices is to do it in writing. Writing down pros and cons forces you to think of them and makes it easier to consider. You need two pieces of paper, each one divided with a line down the middle, so that you can draw up *four* lists.

Why four? Because no matter what choice faces you, whether it involves doing or not doing, changing or staying the same, there are advantages and disadvantages to each alternative.

Thus, suppose you are tying to decide whether to continue to live with your mother or to get an apartment of your own. The first page would be advantages and disadvantages of living with Mother. The second page would be advantages and disadvantages of having an apartment. Some of the advantages and disadvantages will overlap, but some won't—so the more you have written, the greater the perspective you gain on your choice.

Once you have written your lists, go back and assign a number value to each advantage and disadvantage. Zero stands for "no significant effect," 5 stands for "very important to me." Putting those numbers down forces you to think about what is important to you.

When you are finished, the four lists—weighted by numbers—will help you make a decision. And, just as important, they will help you to *live with that decision*. It is easier to live with a decision when you make a conscious choice based on pros and cons rather than feeling that your life has somehow been forced upon you. Psychologists use the term *self-efficacy* to describe this phenomenon. If you believe it is your best course, given the circumstances, you are more likely to make the most of it.

Everything has advantages and disadvantages. Lily spends a great deal of time plotting revenge on her despised ex-husband. She spends her money on lawyers. She spends her time thinking of new modes of attack. What is the advantage? She enjoys harassing him. What is the disadvantage? She has no time or energy left to develop a new life for herself. Other men are not interested in a woman who is fixated on fixing her ex. If Lily is willing to sacrifice the possibility of a new relationship to getting her old one, fine. If she feels her life is slipping past her, she may decide that revenge isn't worth it.

Deciding what is worth it is a very personal decision that you can only make for yourself. Indiana Jones wants the Holy Grail, but on the other hand, he doesn't want to fall into an abyss. All things considered, he allows his father to pull him to safety.

Labeling Your Mistakes

Ten chapters in this book describe very specific thinking mistakes—such as the Chicken Little syndrome, yes-butism, perfectionism, personalizing, and the like. No doubt you have discovered that you favor some of these more than others, and possibly some are no problem for you at all.

It helps to keep the name of those mistakes you feel you make—or are likely to make—in mind. Then when your thoughts start to race, thereby churning up your feelings, which then cause your stomach to get upset, you can say to yourself: "I think I know what's going on here. I'm personalizing." Or: "I'm falling victim to the Chicken Little syndrome." When you can put a name to what is happening, it becomes easier to challenge. When you recognize you are making a mistake, it is easier to stop making it.

Then What?

This is a useful technique for examining those imaginary scenarios that stop you from moving ahead. You say to yourself: "I'd really like to go to that party, but . . ." (You can see pictures in your head of you standing all alone.) Or: "I'd like to get my own apartment, but my mother will probably have a heart attack." (You can see the ambulance pulling up to the curb now.) Or: "This traffic is terrible, which means I'm going to miss my plane, and that will mean missing the meeting, and that's the end of my career." (You see yourself being fired.)

Here again, you tend to leap *directly to the end* of the story, and it's bad news. To use this technique requires you to start at the very beginning of the story—and thereafter unfold it s-l-o-w-l-y by answering the question: "Then what?" This can help check those automatic thoughts that propel you directly to disaster and enable you to recognize how you can handle the challenge more easily than you first feared, or it might lead you to another technique—that of developing alternatives.

"This traffic is terrible, I'm going to be late."

Then what?

"I won't be able to park the car."

Then what?

"I'll have to park at the expensive lot."

Then what?

"I might miss the plane anyway."

Then what?

"I'll have to call and say I'll miss the meeting."

Then what?

"The higher-ups will be furious."

Then what?

"I could lose my job."

Then what?

"I'll have to find another."

This scenario still ends in disaster, yet the effect is not the same as the panic that strikes when the mind compiles the disaster in mere seconds. Why not? Partly because then-what pushes the scenario *past* just losing the job and on to the next step of finding another. Partly because the slower pace enables you to consider the probability of each step. You might not miss the plane. You might be able to catch a late flight. When you call, you may be able to rearrange the meeting. The higher-ups may be furious but not fire you. You may like the next job better.

In short, the situation may not be as bad as you think or you may be able to do more about it than you originally thought.

Superexaggeration

We tend to exaggerate negative consequences, which, of course, makes us feel worse than necessary. A good technique for dealing with this is to exaggerate *even more*. If you find yourself thinking mournfully: "I've never been successful," rephrase that even more negatively: "I've never, ever been successful in anything I have ever tried in my whole, entire life, not even one itsy bitsy thing. I never managed to swallow a mouthful of food. Not once."

"I'll never get anywhere" becomes: "I'll never, ever get anywhere, no matter what, even if I was handed a million dollars, even if I went back to school and earned twelve degrees, even if . . ."

Superexaggeration can help you look at things more realistically because when you put the emphasis on the *never* or the *always* and do not allow for a single deviation, you can usually realize that this is exaggeration, that the situation is not quite that bad or that hopeless. Once you put the problem in the worst possible terms, you can begin to de-catastrophize, to check the evidence.

Scaling From 1 to 10

Where would you place your current problem on a scale of 1 to 10? If you feel stressed, sad, nervous, depressed, or otherwise off stride, you are likely to answer that question automatically with a 10. Whenever you find yourself in a thicket of complications, you tend to think: "What could be worse?"

That feeling occurs because people tend not to establish anchor points for that 1 to 10 scale. That's like trying to measure a room by just dropping a ruler on the floor. You have to have some point of reference. What are you measuring? The width of the room from one wall to the other? The distance between the sofa and the wall? Similarly, you need points of reference when assessing the difficulty you are in. To develop these points of reference, first think about the most upsetting event of your life. What death, disaster, setback, or period of anxiety produced what might fairly be called the low point of your life so far? Now think about events or periods—maybe from childhood—that were pleasing, hopeful, enjoyable, or at least less stressful. Which of these would you pick as the high point of your life?

On a trouble scale then, the pleasant time occupies the low trouble end, or 1; the terrible time occupies the high trouble end, or 10. Now you have a basis for comparing what you are experiencing now. Is it as bad as the worst? Or maybe just a 4?

What you are experiencing now may, in fact, be the worst period of your life. But people often see every single crisis at the same level, when this is not truly the case. It can sometimes be very helpful, then, to put your problems in perspective. If by placing what is happening now on a scale of 1 to 10, you realize that you have survived worse in the past, you will be more confident of your ability to survive now.

Turning Adversity Into Advantage

"If life hands you a lemon, make lemonade," goes the old saying. To which most people reply: "Easier said than done." True enough, particularly if you are expecting that lemonade to be made on the same day the lemon arrives. Yet, viewed from a longer perspective, adversity often turns to advantage. Life experience is rarely wasted. And it can help you to keep this in mind.

In the mid-eighties *Time* magazine described a study by psychologists that found "amazing" resilience in people who had lost jobs three times because of plant closings. It was "amazing," according to this story, because one might think that someone who had lost three jobs would be beaten down and discouraged. But that was not the case.

And most likely it was not the case because repeated adversity had become an advantage. The fact is that someone who has lost a job *and found a new one* at least twice in the past probably has more confidence about finding the next job than someone who has always worked in the same place and then unexpectedly ends up in the unemployment line. Just by surviving adversity, you gain the advantage of knowing it can be done.

Alcoholics who recover and then develop careers helping other alcoholics break their habit have clearly turned adversity to advantage. They move into a career they might not otherwise have considered, and they are accepted by those they counsel to a degree someone who has never known the problem will rarely be.

Many people are motivated by adversity. Being turned down only spurs them on to try harder, determined to prove that the person who turned them down was wrong. And they achieve what they might not ordinarily achieve.

Deliberately thinking about how your particular adversity might be turned to advantage can be a very helpful tool. For example: John has left Mary. The adversity is very clear. Are there any possible advantages to John's departure?

They may seem slim, but they exist. Without John, Mary is

open to a new relationship. And she can start a relationship in a new way, perhaps making new demands of it: "I'll never again accept from any other man what I took from John."

Developing Replacement Images

Research tells us clearly that we can practice behavior in our imagination and translate it into actual performance. Figure skaters run through their routines mentally before taking to the ice. Basketball players imagine themselves making a basket even though the crowd (all fans of the opposing team) is booing. That helps them ignore the booing when the real situation presents itself. Athletes of all kinds work with sports psychologists to improve their game. The specialty of sports psychology has grown enormously ever since Olympic gold medal winner Mark Spitz revealed in 1976 that he believed in mental preparation as much as practice in the pool.

What works for athletes works for all kinds of activities. That is, imagining images of success helps you to become more successful. Yet most people seem to insist on practicing images of failure. They want to diet, so what do they think of? Eating chocolate cake. Downing a huge order of French fries. They would be better off imagining themselves successfully refusing the cake, imagining a menu that increases flavor while decreasing portions.

Images of failure have a way of popping up with no practice at all. "I can see it now. I'm going to fail." "I can see it as if it were happening. I'm going to lose my notes." "I can see it now. The bridge will collapse." "I can see it now. I'll be in bed and unable to perform."

Instead of imagining failure, try imagining success. See yourself succeeding. See yourself finding the notes, finishing the speech. See yourself getting to the other side of the bridge. See yourself enjoying sex.

People say: "That's fantasy." So it is. But so is imagining failure. Anything you are thinking about that is not actually happening is a fantasy. So why not imagine success and coping images rather than failure and disaster images?

Such images have to be reasonable ones, of course. It might be fun for a single man to imagine that he walks into a room and ten gorgeous women surround him, pleading for his attention. But that is not the kind of fantasy image that is particularly helpful in real life. Instead, the single man might try to imagine himself walking into a room, seeing a woman he would like to meet, engaging that woman in conversation, making arrangements to go out with her later.

Rehearsing Positive Images

This technique, sometimes called cognitive rehearsal, is an extension of the replacement of negative images with positive ones. It calls for practicing that image a couple of times a day—not just once before you go out, but over and over and over again. What you are doing is mentally practicing a new mode of behavior. Will this *alone* make you successful? No, that would be asking too much. However, practice clearly *enhances* performance. It is simply easier to build on the foundation of a positive image than to come from behind the image of failure.

Self-Instruction

We usually hear about people who self-destruct, but self-instruction is definitely something different. When you self-instruct, your aim is to help, not harm. Self-instruction involves giving yourself very *specific* directions. It's easy enough to say something like: "I'll do better." But you can't depend on something that vague.

If you planned to rewire your house, you would either get a book that instructed you step by step how to go about it, or you would make mental notes for yourself—what to do first, what to do second, making sure that you match positive wires with positive wires and the like. If you plan to go to the supermarket you probably make a self-instruction list. When you list products like milk, butter, or bread, the word *buy* is understood. You are telling yourself to buy milk, buy butter, buy bread. By drawing up a list, you make sure you don't forget anything important.

That same technique can help you face a difficult situation. Suppose you are scheduled to make a presentation in front of a group, and you are nervous about it. You can help yourself by making a detailed list of instructions. Details mean including even such safety devices as "Stop at the rest room first" so you don't have to worry about your bladder, "Check all zippers and buttons" to make sure you are secure, and "Look at the audience" before launching into your presentation.

Try to break down your instructions into the smallest possible steps, because the smaller the step, the less intimidating it is to take it. You may find it helpful to write a script for an upcoming situation. You will say thus. The other person is likely to reply with such and such. If so, you will say this.

Many of the maxims that people keep in mind are just shorthand self-instructions. People remember those that they find most helpful. The early bird catches the worm. You can't win a contest unless you enter it. Never eat at a place called Mom's.

Specific environments have a way of generating their own sets of instructions. Hal goes to work as a busboy and very shortly is instructed by the more experienced young men how to succeed. Rule one: "Look busy. Don't just stand in one place, the boss gets annoyed." Rule two: "Never go into the kitchen empty-handed. If you are going to pick up a water pitcher, take some dirty plates along with you. There are always some plates that need picking up." Rule three: "Never leave the kitchen empty-handed. There is always something that needs taking into the dining room."

It doesn't matter whether those rules would apply to every situation, they clearly worked in that situation. The trick is to anticipate what instructions are needed for any given situation. Those instructions can be very simple. If, for example, your object is to stop drinking, you may have to instruct yourself as you near a bar: "Walk right by, walk right by, walk right by." You are more likely to follow a specific instruction than any vague resolution to "improve."

If your object is not to get caught by one of those emotional fishermen described in earlier chapters, your self-instruction might be simply: "Don't take the bait."

Self-Distraction

When a particular line of thought is upsetting you, it helps to interrupt that line of thought. And one way to do this is simply to distract yourself by introducing a different thought. When the pictures on your brain's screen are getting you down, switch to another channel.

Here's an example: Paul arrives at the airport with a heavy suitcase and discovers the departure gate for his plane is at the opposite end of a very long corridor. He begins to get angry. He thinks: "My arm is breaking. I should have brought my luggage carrier. I'm a jerk for leaving it at home. This suitcase is so heavy it's killing me. That airport gate must be in the next county." These thoughts make him angry and increasingly tense, and that does not make those steps any easier. What can he do to distract himself? He can invent a game. "My guess is that the distance to the gate is 225 steps." Now he has to count each step to see whether his guess is correct or not. Focusing on counting takes his mind off how heavy the suitcase is and how great the distance is. The suitcase doesn't get lighter, yet *the experience will not be as difficult.*

You can distract yourself by consciously conjuring up a success image to make you feel better when you face a challenge. This is often derided. People will say: "Oh, you are just trying to make yourself feel better." Right. Which makes a lot more sense than trying to make yourself feel worse.

You can distract yourself with a relaxation technique. Suppose you are lying in bed anxiously thinking of all the terrible things that will happen tomorrow. This makes it difficult to get to sleep and unpleasant to stay awake. You might try focusing on your breathing pattern. Relaxing breathing involves breathing deeply, from the stomach rather than from the chest. So you have to concentrate on whether your stomach rather than your chest rises with each breath. You can concentrate even more on your breathing, noting the sensation as the air passes through your nostrils. You may try counting the breaths. It's very difficult to do all of that and think of anything else.

Ralph, a twenty-two-year-old medical student, is mortified because he cannot get an erection when he goes to bed with a woman. He just knows that he will fail—and he can see it happening—and it happens. He knows he has to think of something else besides his own body. But what? He decides to think about his partner's body instead. He thinks about her hair, what it smells like, what it feels like. He thinks about her skin—and pretty soon he cannot believe how well his body does when he stops worrying about it.

Playing Defense Attorney

This technique might also be called arguing with yourself. Sometimes that is necessary because we tend to be harder on ourselves than we are on other people. Behavior you would find a way to forgive in a friend, you don't forgive in yourself. Other people can make a mistake, and you forget it. You make a mistake and remember it for the next eighty years.

What is going on is that you put yourself on trial and play every single role but one. You are the accused. You are the prosecutor. You are the jury. And you are the hanging judge. You haven't a chance. What's missing from this trial is a defense attorney. The defense attorney's role is simply to point out mitigating factors: "Yes, this person is guilty, but you have to understand the circumstances." The defense attorney's role is to explain the evidence in a more favorable light. "Yes, this person seems guilty, but that's because you don't know the whole story." The defense attorney's role is to win some consideration in the sentence. "Yes, this person did it, but doesn't deserve the chair."

Whenever you are being hard on yourself, check to see whether a defense attorney is present in your mind. If not, you have to play that role too. Treat yourself as you would a friend. "A failure? No, he's just going through a bad patch." "A jerk? Well, she did something stupid, but she has some good points." "Nothing that person does will work? Wrong, there is no way to predict that."

CHAPTER THIRTEEN

BEYOND INSIGHT

A young man enters a classy bar and orders a glass of white wine. His appearance is impeccable—three-piece suit, conservative tie, wing-tipped shoes. He speaks in a well-modulated tone. He reaches out for the wine—and then calmly pours it on the bar's highly polished floor.

The bartender and the other patrons of the bar can't believe what they have seen. The man himself is the picture of embarrassment. "I don't know what made me do that," he exclaims. "I'm so ashamed." He then runs out of the bar.

The next night he is back, just as well-tailored as before. He once again orders a glass of wine. The bartender hesitates for a second, but then serves the wine. "The poor guy must have been drunk or sick last night," the bartender says to himself. The young man takes the glass—and pours its contents on the floor.

"I just don't understand this," cries the young man. "I'm so embarrassed. I don't know what to say." "Don't say anything, just leave," the bartender snaps. "You need help, mister. And don't even think of coming back to this bar unless you get it."

Three years pass. The well-dressed young man once again shows up at the bar and once again orders a glass of wine. "I remember you and I'm not sure I want to serve you," says the bartender.

"I understand why you would feel that way," replies the young man. "But I want you to know that I took your advice. I have been seeing a therapist three times a week for three years. And it is only because the therapy has been so successful that I felt I could return here."

"Oh, in that case, here is your wine," says the bartender. The young man smiles, takes the glass . . . and pours the wine on the floor.

"I thought you said the treatment was successful," screams the bartender as he strides from behind the bar to toss the young man out the door. "It was," the young man tells him. "I now understand *why* I feel compelled to pour wine on the floor, so I no longer feel embarrassed when it happens."

The moral of that story is: It's not enough merely to gain insight into your mistakes. It's also important to *stop making them.*

From Knowledge to Action

Insight is very important. The bulk of this book has been devoted to providing insight into just how the mistakes you make in *the way you think about things* influences how you feel about them—and therefore the actions that you take. Your new knowledge about how you can change the way you think—and therefore change the way you feel—can help you to diminish those unwarranted feelings of depression, anxiety, stress, anger, and guilt that only serve to hold you back, make you fail, and generally get in your way. Your new knowledge about these common mistakes in thinking will help you to better understand the reactions of others.

All that said, it must be added that insight is not enough. All your new knowledge will not help you unless you *put it to work.* As any scientist would admit, the true benefits of knowledge do not occur until that knowledge is used in practice.

Suppose, for example, that you have spilled the contents of

your salt and pepper shakers together. You have no more of either seasoning, and you are determined to separate the grains. Picking them apart one by one would take forever. It would help you, in such a situation, to have some knowledge of the properties of sodium chloride (salt) and pepper. For example, sodium chloride dissolves in water, but pepper does not. Sodium chloride is attracted by static electricity—while pepper is not.

That knowledge alone will not separate the salt and pepper. You can think about it all you want, and the salt and pepper will stay mixed. What is required next is an action based on your knowledge. For example, you could dump the mixture into a glass of water. The salt will dissolve, the pepper will rise to the top. You then spoon off the pepper and wait for the water to evaporate, leaving a pile of salt behind. Or you can rub an inflated balloon with a piece of fur to create static electricity and then pass the balloon above the salt and pepper mixture. The salt grains will adhere to the balloon, the pepper will just lie there. Problem solved!

Solving your own problems also requires both knowledge and action. Understanding your thought processes is vitally important, but it is also important to use that understanding—not only to think and feel in a new way, but also to act in a new way. If you now understand why you feel the way you do but do nothing to change your life, you will not have accomplished any more than the young man in the bar. You must move beyond insight to action.

You may say: "I'm willing to take an action—I just don't know what action to take. I think I'm ready to steer in a new direction—I just don't know how to start the motor or which road to travel."

The purpose of this chapter is to spotlight techniques that have proven useful in getting motors started, wheels rolling, and paths mapped. Not every technique suits every problem, but at least one—and probably a few—of these techniques will be valuable to you.

Remember: Just reading about—and knowing about—these

techniques is *not enough*. You must use them. You must act. The previous chapter described eighteen techniques. The seven behavioral techniques reviewed in this chapter are:

1. Scheduling time.
2. Planning experiences for mastery or pleasure.
3. Problem solving.
4. Breaking your goal into small steps.
5. Role playing.
6. Trying out new behavior.
7. Relaxation.

Scheduling Time

A written schedule can help you gain control of your life. That may sound like nonsense, but it is true. If you are going to take an action—any action—you must *make time* to do so. A written schedule can help you incorporate into your life those actions that will benefit you.

Systematic use of schedules has proven a particularly effective tool for people who are victims of the Chicken Little syndrome or the what-if block. If, for example, you know that you jump to an all-is-lost conclusion when you fear that you are going to miss a train, you can schedule your day to ensure that you will leave a half hour earlier for the train station than you have in the past. Writing down what you must do before leaving and scheduling sufficient time to do it can avoid uncomfortable anxiety later.

People who think in terms of what could go wrong tend to put off action. They excuse their procrastination by saying: "I just don't have the time." But if you are putting off taking steps that, even if a little risky, are necessary to get ahead, you will find that you can push yourself into doing them simply by putting them on your schedule—by making time. When you write down how you are now scheduling your activities, you may find that a block of time now devoted to watching TV or cleaning your desk for the fourteenth time this month could be put to more productive and satisfying use.

If you write down how you now spend your time, you may find that you spend a great deal of it worrying. In that case, you can decide to schedule worry time and then plan activities that will absorb your mind in a different way at other times. If you question the decisions you have made every minute of the day ("Did I make the right choice? Will this work out? What if I was wrong?"), you will find you have less energy to put into reaching whatever goal you have set for yourself. But if you schedule a specific time to assess progress—at the end of the day, or the week, or the month—you give yourself a better chance to succeed and gain a clearer perspective at the same time.

Yes-buters can benefit from scheduling experiences that will give them skills and experience they feel they lack. Maybe you say: "Yes, I'd like to do that, but I don't know how." You get out your schedule and find time to learn how. If you feel under pressure because there aren't enough hours in the day to do everything you "should," a schedule may help you relieve that pressure. You may find you are not using your time as efficiently as possible. Or you may find that you are saddling yourself with unrealistic expectations.

In sum, experience has shown that, in many ways, planning more effective use of your time forestalls or minimizes thinking mistakes. This entire book is really about making better use of your time—thinking in terms of positive rather than negative *actions*.

On pages 269–271, you will find a twenty-four-hour schedule that marks off the day in 15-minute segments. You will need a ready supply of such schedules. Start by making at least fourteen copies of this schedule. You can either photocopy the pages as they are, or in an enlarged version to give you more space to write, or draw up a set of schedules by hand, using a lined pad of paper or drawing lines with a ruler. Don't actually use the schedule in the book. It is best to keep that as the model from which you can make copies in the future.

Using the Schedule Retrospectively

On a daily basis, for at least one week, record in as much detail as possible how you spend your time. Don't just write: "I'm home" and draw a line from 9 A.M. to 3 P.M. on Saturday. Record exactly what you do during those hours that you are home on Saturday. Eat? Clean? Take a shower? Watch TV? Read? Work on a hobby? It's fair to write "Asleep" across several hours—as long as you were asleep. If you wake up and stare at the ceiling or read a book or watch TV in the middle of the night, put that down.

The purpose of this schedule is to give you a more exact fix on exactly how you spend your time. We think we know how we spend our time—but we tend to know only generally, not specifically. It's more usual to ask: "Where did the time go? Is it Tuesday already?" Or, conversely, to think: "It's only noon? Time is really dragging today. The minutes seem like hours."

Using the Schedule Prospectively

Now that you have a schedule that tells you precisely how you have been spending your time, you need to use some fresh pages to draw up new schedules for the future.

Most people have some kind of "future schedule." It may just be a note attached to the refrigerator that says: "Pick up car at garage 3 P.M." or a note on a wall calendar that says "January 24—dentist, noon." When people make appointments, they generally keep them. If something comes up to make a particular date impossible, they rearrange the schedule.

You can also make a schedule that forces you to make appointments with yourself. You probably know from experience that whenever you say "I must get around to that sometime," sometime tends to be a long way off. If a friend says: "Let's get together one of these days," who knows when you will get together? But suppose that friend says: "How about lunch next Tuesday at 12:30 P.M. at such-and-such a restaurant?" In that case, it is very likely that you will get together either that Tuesday or on another mutually acceptable date. The point is, when you have a specific date and time for something to happen, it is much more likely to happen.

You can make better use of commuting time or find another mind-absorbing activity for hours that are devoted to fretting (go to the movies, telephone somebody, volunteer at a local charity, enroll in a course). You decide what to do and then write down when you are going to do it. And then you *do it*.

Many people feel they are now making the most effective use of their time. They will say: "Believe me, there isn't a minute to spare in my day." Sometimes that may be true. But usually something can be done more efficiently to make extra time available. This point was made in a psychological study of problem solving in an office environment. Two groups of people were asked to solve the same problem. One group was put to work in a room with a table and comfortable chairs. The other was put to work in a bare room with not even a rough bench to sit on. Which group do you think solved the problem faster? The group that had to stand minimized the social chitchat and fooling around that takes place in most meetings—certainly in most meetings where participants are comfortable.

Scheduling During a Time of Crisis

Schedules are particularly useful in times of crisis and extra stress, because when you are going through a difficult period, like divorce or illness, special responsibilities are added to your normal chores, duties, and activities. This can make you feel overwhelmed to the point where you don't even do the most routine things well.

By writing down what you need to do and when you need to do it and simply following that schedule, you relieve the pressure. You don't have to keep everything in your mind at once. Scheduling allows you to program your day in the most productive manner.

Scheduling is enormously valuable when the crisis in your life is the loss of a job and the need to find another. Outplacement specialists (the new name for employment counselors—they no longer find you a new job, they place you "out" of the job you don't have anymore) usually require clients to report for job hunting just as they would report for a job. Job hunting becomes the new job, to be actively pursued for eight hours a day. It isn't something you do only if and when you think of a place to apply, because you schedule hours to think of places to apply.

Scheduling Preparation Time

Did your retrospective schedule include sufficient *preparation time?* Preparation time is often omitted or thought about only casually. Yet it can be crucially important to your success. For example, Alice is nervous about having to make a presentation at a conference. She feels she has prepared by writing her presentation and developing charts to go with it. But by mentally reviewing what is making her nervous, Alice recognizes that she has to allow even more time for preparation. She can avoid the turmoil of Chicken Little and what-if thinking by arranging to take an earlier plane. That might leave her with time on her hands at her destination. But at least she will be where she needs to be instead of spending that time worrying that traffic, weather conditions, or something else will make her miss the all-important plane.

By scheduling her time so that she will be at the conference center much earlier than necessary, Alice will be able to confirm that the equipment is on hand (or arrange to get it if it is missing). That, too, relieves her stress, and relieving stress is usually a good investment of time.

Scheduling Social Time

Did your retrospective schedule include time for *socializing?* Writer Erma Bombeck once confessed in print that she is afraid to give a party. She promises to invite people over just as soon as the sofa is upholstered, the children graduate, or the tax rebate arrives. Which means never. The problem, explains Bombeck, is that she is sure people expect that any party she would give would be elegant and effortless when, in fact, she gets so harassed she can't manage to say hello and goodbye.

As Erma Bombeck undoubtedly knows, millions share this problem. Obviously, it is a case of paying too much attention to imagined critics—and the first step for Bombeck and others like her is to start by examining this matter of just how elegant a party has to be for friends to get together and enjoy each other's company. Does it have to be perfect? And then the second, equally crucial, step is *scheduling the party.*

Instead of waiting until the sofa is upholstered and the children have grandchildren, you turn to your schedule and pick a date. You commit yourself to that date. You schedule the time to draw up a guest list. You schedule the time for writing or telephoning invitations. And when that time arrives, that is precisely what you do. You keep that appointment with yourself. And before long you will have made an appointment with others. Thereafter, you make a list of what you will need for the party and schedule time to get the items on the list.

Once the party is on your schedule, you'll find a way to have it. And your friends will find a way to be there. Most people know this is true. The trick is getting them to schedule the party in the first place. Thinking about it is not enough.

Of course, some people need to schedule time just to think about socializing. They would like to know more people, but they are too busy, too rushed, too insecure even to think about what they might do to expand their social circle. This calls for scheduling a period of time to try something new or even just to think about and talk with others about what that something new might be. And then setting aside time to do it.

Self-Monitoring

Having something on your schedule doesn't mean you lose all flexibility in your life. Quite often something will unexpectedly come up that requires your attention and upsets your schedule. That's all right. It just means that whatever you didn't get to on your schedule is rescheduled to a later time or date. You will find, however, that you are still more likely to do something—even if at a rescheduled time—than if you had never put it on your schedule at all.

Planning Experiences for Mastery or Pleasure

That brings up another related technique. To move beyond insight to action may involve deliberately planning experiences that will increase your skills or your pleasure.

Planning Pleasure

Many people neglect to plan pleasurable activities because they are bogged down by stress and pain and tend to forget that pleasure can exist. Or they neglect to plan pleasurable activities because they prefer to have them happen spontaneously. But it is precisely during times of stress or times when pleasure is not occurring spontaneously that planning is most needed. If you are like most people, there are probably things you like to do that you do only rarely. Katie says: "I love the theater." But when asked how often she goes the reply is: "Oh, once or twice a year."

If you say that you like to do something but do it only once or twice a year (if that), you are not building enjoyable experiences into your life. If you like the theater, it is very likely you can find more than one or two plays to go to in a year. Even if you live in a small town, you will probably find that the local high school has a play each year. There may be a college or community drama group. The shows may not be of Broadway quality, but they are theater. Attending is a way to expand your experience. It can expand your pleasure.

Planning a structured way to increase your pleasure can be especially beneficial to people who would like others to read their mind. Elise, for example, likes to go to the movies and thinks her husband, Frank, should know that and sometimes please her by suggesting that they take in a film. But since films are not high on Frank's list of priorities, he always lets her down.

Elise first has to understand that in asking her husband to read her mind, she is asking the impossible. But the *action step* she is then able to take is to suggest they make Friday night a regular movie night. Elise asks Frank to build this into his schedule because she enjoys movies so much, and since he doesn't dislike going to the movies and wants to please Elise, he agrees. Now, knowing that he is going to see a film on Friday night, Frank occasionally suggests a film to see. And that, of course, pleases Elise even more.

Building Self-Esteem

Success builds self-esteem, and so investing time in activities in which you know you will have success is worthwhile. Those activities do not have to be major life-changing ones—they could include cooking a particular dish or helping to get a mailing out during a political campaign. Anything that you have handled successfully—no matter how small it is—is worth repeating. Any time you can say to yourself: "I did it and I did it well," you enhance your own feeling of well-being, you build the confidence that enables you to reach for the new and unknown.

Planning Practice

When there is something you would like to be good at, but you do not feel you have mastered, plan activities that provide practice. Suppose you have put off giving a party because you feel any party you give would not be, to use Erma Bombeck's words, "elegant and effortless." Most likely, you feel that way because you haven't had a lot of experience in party giving. Those whose parties tend to be described as elegant and seemingly effortless have had lots of practice.

As the old saying goes: "Practice makes perfect." No one expects someone who has not spent a great deal of time practicing hitting a golf ball to win the Masters tournament. No one expects a team to compete successfully unless they have spent time together practicing their moves over and over and over.

It's common for people who face a computer for the first time to feel intimidated by it. "What if it blows up?" (It won't.) "What if I lose data?" (Join the crowd.) Yet, invariably, practice brings ease—and enjoyment. Still, many people feel that one is either born an expert or doomed forever when it comes to some activities—social conversation, sex, party giving, speaking to a group. Wrong. Wrong. Wrong. The most gifted athlete does not achieve without practice. The most talented actor needs rehearsal. Nobel Prize–winning scientists try first this and then that until they find the formula that matters. And so it is with every human endeavor. Even the gift of gab is found most often in those who have practiced talking to others. Thus, if you want to be good at anything, you must build practice into your schedule. If you tend to ask what if, the answers will come with practice. What if the recipe doesn't turn out well? The answer is: "I'll learn from that—and modify the recipe next time."

What if you have a job interview and are rejected? That will probably happen many times as you practice job interviews. Each time, analyze what went well, what did not. And the more interviews you do, the more comfortable you will be in handling them. You'll know what's coming. You'll become familiar with the kinds of questions that are asked. You'll become more adept at answering them.

The would-be party giver may say: "I don't know what to practice because I don't know how to give a party." The answer to that is to start small. Practice inviting a few close friends to your home. See how that goes. When you feel comfortable at that level, begin practicing at a new level—add other people. You can slowly improve on your party formula. Vary the menu. See what works, what doesn't.

The perfectionist may say: "The problem is that even if I practice, I won't be able to achieve my heart's desire. Even if I play football every day—at age fifty—I doubt that I can become the Rams' quarterback." Obviously, the first step is a mental one. If you can't have what you want most, what is your second choice? The next step is the action one: practicing to get that second choice.

Problem Solving

When you are feeling stressed, problems have a way of appearing insoluble.

One of the most useful strategies in dealing with real problems is to ask: "What will it take to solve this problem?" instead of: "Can this problem be solved?" By simply putting the question in the active voice, you increase the likelihood that you will uncover a solution.

Seeking Solutions

When you are feeling stressed, you often reject a solution that occurs to you simply because it has occurred to *you* ("If I thought of it, it can't be any good"). If that's the case, you may be able to help yourself by seeking solutions. You ask: "Has anyone, anywhere, ever succeeded in solving this problem?"

Now you concentrate on determining who you can ask, what you can read, where you can find information about the particular problem you wish to solve. You can then pick from among the solutions others have tried—practicing some trial and error, if necessary—to determine which solution is best for you. For example, Janice, the mother of two, is recently separated from her husband. She feels overwhelmed by her responsibilities. She wants to work part-time to earn extra money, but without money she can't afford day care for the kids.

Janice seeks out people who are in that same situation. She goes to a meeting of a group for single parents and meets a woman who tells Janice she earns extra money by baby-sitting for others, while watching her own child at the same time. That gives Janice two ideas: She distributes fliers around the neighborhood offering baby-sitting services and scans the want ads for part-time baby-sitters who might be able to take care of her kids if she gets a part-time job as a waitress.

Breaking Your Goal Into Small Steps

Possibly the greatest single barrier to reaching any goal is the feeling that the action required is too big, too difficult, too costly, or too threatening. When you start out with the premise that reaching your goal will take too much of whatever it is you don't have, the usual reaction is to give up. Why start, you might ask, if all your efforts are only destined for failure?

A technique for dealing with this is to think about a first step rather than the final goal. If you were standing on the sidewalk in front of a three-story building that had no elevator and your object was to reach an office on the third floor, what would you look for?

Did you say steps?

Right.

The most direct route might be to levitate to the third floor and go in through a window, but, as a practical matter, it's more sensible to find the stairs and walk up one step at a time.

That is also true about reaching goals. Maybe when you ask the question: "What would it take to solve this problem?" you answer: "Too much."

Perhaps you are seeing the solution in terms of bites that are too big to swallow. Before giving up or giving in, back away and ask: "What specific steps would be required to get closer to the solution to this problem?"

Make a list of the steps. Then look at them and break them down into smaller steps—the smaller the better, even if the step seems so small it is silly. (Get phone book. Look up number. Write number down. Dial number.) Steps that are so small that they seem silly become steps that are easy to take.

Role Playing

"All the world's a stage, And all the men and women merely players" wrote William Shakespeare in *As You Like It*, and how right he was.

We often play roles. Haven't you sometimes smiled even though you didn't feel like it? Haven't you sometimes gone through your normal work routine—serving customers, talking on the telephone, whatever—even though you felt sick and would have preferred to have been in bed? Haven't you sometimes acted normal because you didn't want others to know that anything was wrong?

Most people play more roles than they are aware of. They act stern with a child to enforce needed discipline even though they are inwardly amused. They act concerned about a customer's complaint even though they really think this customer is a crank and a nuisance. They act more deferentially on a first date than they do later when they get to know each other.

Yet people often hesitate to play roles when doing so would be *most beneficial*.

For example, Howard feels awkward when he goes to a party. It stops him from approaching others to start a conversation. But what if Howard decides to play the role of a confident party goer? He walks in with a confident air, smiles as if he feels he belongs. Says: "Hi, my name is Howard"—the way someone would who really is a confident party goer.

You might think: "I can't do that." Why not? It's just another act among the many acts you are already called on to perform. Role playing is a very powerful action technique. If you want to behave differently, you can play a different role. Pretend to be someone other than yourself. Pretend to be the person you would like to be.

If you want to be a friendly person, you can start by acting friendly. Smile and say hello. Not everyone will smile back. Not everyone will say hello. But some will. Evaluate the effect that your greeting has on people.

Therapists call this technique *in vivo* exposure. One therapist who was trying to help a client become confident offered to accompany him to a singles bar. The therapist suggested that the client watch him first and then follow his example. The therapist then walked up to a young woman and began talking to her. The client imitated the therapist's manner and was soon involved in a conversation of his own. The next day the therapist confided to a colleague that he'd never had such success in a singles bar before. By playing the role of "confident therapist" (which he felt was a responsibility to his patient), he enabled himself to accomplish what he had always felt too insecure to attempt when he was just "being himself."

You can play any role you want. You can try out a role and see how it works for you. You can practice a role that shows promise.

Writing a Script

It can be helpful to write a script in advance for the role you intend to play. Obviously, unlike a play performed on a stage, you can't depend on the other characters saying the lines that you write for them. But to the extent that your script prepares you for what you might say, you increase your confidence about dealing with the situation. Playwrights typically set the scene and describe what the characters will wear. When you write your script, you can also plan in advance what you will wear. The more prepared you are, the better.

Role playing works in all kinds of situations. If you are going to make a telephone call to sell something, you might pretend to be a salesperson who loves to make telephone calls, who is not at all bothered by fifty rejections because the fifty-first call might be successful. You write a script of what you believe this enthusiastic salesperson would say to someone on the other end of the line. You write some alternatives: "If this is said, I'll say that." Or if you don't feel you have anything to say at a party, read a newspaper before you go. Pick out a couple of stories that interest you. Write down some things you might say about them. "I was reading today that the president thinks our economic situation is improving. What do you think?" Asking for an opinion is usually a helpful bit of dialogue. People are usually interested in themselves and find others who are also interested in them interesting.

In one of his movies, comedian Danny Kaye played an ordinary person who looked like a missing high government official. He was asked to impersonate this official so that people wouldn't realize he was gone. Obviously, Kaye's character couldn't possibly know everything this high government official knows. How could he possibly pass himself off as this other person? He does it by never really answering a question. He puts his palms together so that his fingers just touch his chin, puts on a thoughtful expression, and merely says "Hmmm." Or: "You might be right." Admittedly, this is only a movie. Yet it is true that having even a basic script for handling a difficult situation can carry you a long way.

Writing out a script for a delicate confrontation can help you keep your cool during that confrontation. Sandy needs to talk to her estranged husband, Al, about how his visits with their children will be arranged. Sandy knows that conversations with Al tend to end in yelling matches. "I don't want you telling me what to do!" "Yeah, you never want to listen to anybody, that's your trouble!" She doesn't want that to happen this time, so she carefully plans an assertive but low-key approach.

SANDY: "I'd like to talk to you about the way we're going to handle seeing the kids." If Al says fine, they can begin the conversation. But Al might say: "Not now, I'm busy."

SANDY: "Okay, that's fine. When would be a good time to talk?"

AL (possibly): "I don't know. I've got a lot on my mind now. Why don't we just wing it and see how things go?"

SANDY: "I know you've got a lot going on right now, but this is something we have been putting off discussing for a long time, and I really would like to get it resolved. I'd like to meet one day this weekend when things are less hectic for you to discuss this. It is very important. Would you rather do it Saturday or Sunday?"

AL (probably): "Okay. Maybe Sunday would be all right. How about noon?"

SANDY: "Great. We'll let it rest until then."

Trying Out New Behavior

A related technique to role playing is trying out new behavior. That just means practicing a role. Teenagers commonly do this in front of the mirror. Teenage boys practice looking cool. Teenage girls practice looking glamorous. They try out expressions in the mirror. And what is helpful to teenagers can be helpful to just about anybody. You can practice your script: "Hi, my name is Howard." "Hello, I'm Howard, can I buy you a drink?" You can practice looking calm. You can practice a smile. You can practice just saying hello. You can practice a job interview with a friend.

Relaxation

You might not think that relaxation belongs in a list of action techniques. But consciously making yourself relax can be a very helpful action. When you are all keyed up, any action becomes more difficult. Thus, when you are feeling particularly stressed, anxious, or fearful, doing something that will make you feel relaxed can be an all-important action that will enable you to move forward to other action.

When you are truly relaxed, you know it. Your body tells you. Your muscles feel comfortable rather than tight. You feel pleasantly warm and peaceful.

There are many relaxation techniques. Some people find that something as simple as soaking in a warm tub or listening to beautiful music is enough to lower their tension. Others find it helpful to sit quietly, with eyes closed, and imagine being somewhere peaceful and calm. You could, for example, imagine yourself in a boat, floating on a lake bathed in sunlight. Or walking on a beach while the surf gently rolls toward your toes. Anyplace you have found relaxing is a good place to imagine yourself when you get that tight-as-a-drum feeling. Usually, just picturing the place is not enough. You have to think about it awhile. And that means picturing details. For example, what colors do you see? What color is the beach? What color is the water? How bright is the sun?

Your aim is to take your mind away from whatever is causing tension and fixing it on something that will bring about relaxation. So the more deeply you think about, visualize, and describe to yourself that calming place, the calmer you will be.

Some people find meditation helpful. This is simply another means of focusing your mind on something other than a topic that winds you up. Meditators sit comfortably and breathe deeply while repeating a single word. That word can be anything you choose, any word you find easy to say. Many people simply make the sound *om*. They breathe in, and with the outward breath, they repeat *ommmmmm*. This continues for about twenty minutes. That means twenty minutes of focus on relaxing . . . on calm . . . on breathing . . .

Another helpful relaxation technique is to relax each part of your body in sequence, focusing your thoughts on that part of the body. You might fall asleep at night by saying good night to each toe, to your lower legs, to your upper legs, to your buttocks, to your stomach, and so on. It's even more effective than counting sheep.

Finally, you may want to buy a relaxation tape or make your own. When you want to relax, you simply play the tape and focus your mind on the words and instructions coming from the tape.

What follows is a sample script for such a tape. Read the script into a tape recorder at a slow, measured pace. Then, when you want to relax, sit in a comfortable chair or stretch out on your bed and play it back.

Because many people find it most relaxing to first tense each body part before relaxing it, allowing the brain to register the difference between tension and comfort, this sample script has been written that way. You can, if you prefer, alter the script to leave out the instructions to tense your muscles.

A Relaxation Script

Take a deep breath. Hold it briefly . . . and then let it out. Let it all the way out. Close your eyes.

That begins the relaxation process.

Continue breathing deeply. More deeply than normal. Breathe from your stomach rather than from your chest. You can feel your stomach moving up as you inhale.

Breathe in. Deeply.

Let the breath out. All the way out.

Breathe in again. Deeply.

Let the breath out.

This is the beginning of the process that will allow your body to go limp, to allow your muscles to relax, to allow you to fall into a nice, warm, relaxed state.

Continue to breathe deeply—from your stomach rather than from your chest.

Now think about your toes. Curl your toes up. Squeeze your toes together. Feel how tight they are. Hold them just a little more. Now let your toes go. Wiggle them a little. Notice the difference between how your toes felt when they were curled tightly together and how they feel now that you have relaxed them.

Your whole body will feel different once you have uncurled it. Once you let go of all the tightness and tension and allow your body to be relaxed.

Relax your whole left foot. Let your whole foot feel as relaxed as your toes. Now your right foot. Let it just go limp.

Now, if you are lying down, stretch your legs out as far as you can, straining them to reach farther. If you are sitting, you can press your legs against the floor. Whichever you do, the object is to feel the tension in them. Continue to feel that tension. That's the tension that is in your whole body.

Now let your legs relax.

Relax your calves. Try to picture them relaxing . . . resting . . . becoming more comfortable. Relax the upper part of your legs. Let the tension flow out of your knees, your thighs. . . .

Some people feel warmer when they relax. Perhaps your legs feel a little warmer now. Warm and cozy and relaxed.

Your legs may also feel heavier. So heavy that it would take a great effort to move them. If you feel that now—or later—that's fine. That's a sign that your body is settling in, allowing comfort to take over.

Now tense your buttocks. Tighter and tighter. Feel the tension there. Keep it there just for a few moments . . . just a little more. You want to be able to compare this feeling of tightness and tension with the feeling that you sense after you have relaxed.

Relax. Continue to breathe deeply. Breathing in softness, warmth, comfort. Breathing out tension, chill, and tightness.

Breathe in softness, warmth, comfort.

Breathe out tension, chill, tightness.

Now ball your hands into fists. Squeeze your fingers tightly together. So tightly that it hurts. Hold that tension in your fists. Just a little more.

Now relax your hands. Wiggle your fingers. Let your hands fall limp . . . relaxed . . . and warm . . . and comfortable. Maybe they tingle a little. That's fine. Just let your fingers relax.

Still breathing in.

Deeply.

Breathing out . . . all the way out.

Bring your arms next to your body, with your elbows digging into your waist. Tense your arms. Hold that tension in your arms. Hold it a little more.

Relax.

Relax your left lower arm.

Now your right lower arm.

Your left upper arm.

Your right upper arm.

Continue breathing deeply. You are feeling more and more comfortable. Your arms may feel heavy. Just allow them to go limp. Allow them to drop at your side. Allow them to feel warm . . . and heavy.

Now tense your shoulders. Hunch your shoulders toward your neck. You feel the tightness there. Hold it.

Now relax. Let your shoulders slump. Let the muscles loosen.

Let the muscles of your back loosen as well. Let your lower back relax. Let your upper back relax. Let your shoulder blades relax.

Let your neck relax.

You may feel warm. You might feel a tingle. Anything that makes you feel more comfortable is okay.

Now tense your jaw. Pull your mouth back into a grimace. Tighten your lips across your teeth. Hold the tightness there. Tight. Tight. Tight.

Now relax.

Let your jaw drop . . . let your lips relax . . . when you are tense, your teeth clench . . . now you can feel that your jaws are apart. Let your tongue fall to the floor of your mouth. You can feel the tension leave your jaw . . .

You are almost totally relaxed now . . . feeling warmer . . . feeling cozy.

Relax the muscles in your cheeks. . . .

Relax the muscles in your forehead.

Relax your scalp.

Allow yourself to simply sink into your chair or bed . . . sinking lower and lower into that feeling of peaceful comfort that is relaxation. Lower and lower and lower.

Continue to breathe in . . . deeply . . . and breathe out . . . letting tension go with every breath . . . Just continue breathing in and out to continue this period of total calm in your life.

When you are ready to wake up, count to five slowly . . . allow yourself to emerge . . . You will find that you can become completely alert and feel just fine.

CHAPTER FOURTEEN

LIVING BETTER

You knew before you began reading this book that merely being smart doesn't protect you from making dumb mistakes. But now you know exactly *why and how* so many dumb mistakes are made, even by the best and brightest.

You knew before you began reading this book that few among us (if any) can expect, like those heroes and heroines of children's fairy tales, to live happily ever after with no problems, no worries, just continual bliss. Rather, real life hands us a mixture of pain and pleasure, stress and satisfaction, sorrow and joy. The best we can hope for is to increase our allotment of the latter while minimizing the former. It's fair to say that some people—and perhaps you are one of these—have more than their fair share of bad luck. It's fair to acknowledge that many people are hurt by circumstances they cannot possibly control. But now you know that a great deal of pain, stress, and sorrow arises simply from the way we *think* about life events. Now you understand how easy it is to read difficulty where no problem actually exists, to manufacture misery that is unnecessary, and to make truly bad situations a great deal worse.

"One kind of happiness is to know exactly at what point to be miserable," wrote seventeenth-century epigrammatist François, duc de La Rochefoucauld. How true that is. So many of us seem determined to be miserable well in excess of need and well in advance of need. And that, of course, diminishes happiness. But now you know that *you can fight back*—and now you know *how to fight back.*

A Better Idea

Here's a simple, easy way to remind yourself of the therapy described in this book: Think of the word IDEA as an acronym for:

I— *Identify* the thinking mistake you are making. (Review those automatic thoughts flitting through your brain.)

D— *Define* the mistake. (What does it mean to you? How is it affecting your life? What evidence do you have that it exists?)

E— *Evaluate* your course of action. (Think of alternatives, Consider advantages and disadvantages.)

A— *Act.* Remember insight is only the first step. Now you must take action.

Does it matter if you cannot *precisely* identify the thinking mistake you are making? No, not really. After all, as was mentioned earlier, these thinking mistakes have a way of overlapping rather than popping up one at a time. It's not uncommon for the Chicken Little syndrome and what-if thinking to occur together, or for the problems of personalizing and believing your critics to combine, to cite just two of dozens of possible combinations and permutations. What matters is that you recognize that you may be making *at least one* of these thinking mistakes. What matters is that you stop and force yourself to analyze your thoughts. If you can find a thinking mistake there, that's a start. If you simply recognize that you are probably making a thinking mistake— even if you aren't sure which one—*that's* a start.

Is it vital to match a specific technique to a specific thinking mistake? No. The chart on page 267 is designed to give you an idea of which techniques are most helpful in dealing with which mistakes. But you will find, as you try these techniques out, which are most effective for you most of the time. Like the mistakes they are designed to correct, these techniques also over-lap and combine. Starting with one will lead you to another.

Lifetime Tools

Think of the therapeutic techniques you have learned in this book as *lifetime tools* to be used over and over again. It would be nice if, once you have licked a problem, it never dared to pop up again. It would be nice if, once you have successfully resisted the temptation to dwell on negative thoughts, that temptation would never have to be faced again. But that's not real life. Life is like dust—constantly having to be cleaned up and cleaned off. How-ever, the task is easier when you have power tools at hand.

You will find it helpful to read this book over and over again as you deal with the myriad problems that come your way. Reviewing the cognitive and behavioral techniques with some frequency will keep them polished and ready for use.

Remember that all the tools in the world are useless unless you *use them*. No hammer or saw left sitting in a drawer or hanging in a toolshed ever built a house. Somebody had to first take that hammer and saw in hand and do some hammering and sawing with them. The same is true with the tools contained in this book. Knowing about them will merely be an interesting diversion if you do not incorporate them into your life. You must make an effort. It doesn't take a huge effort. But it also isn't going to happen while you sleep.

The World Is Not All Negative

Sometimes it may seem as if you are lodged chest-deep in a vat of muddy misinformation, indifference, and irrationality. And, no doubt, that's discouraging. But, happily, even with so much misinformation around, there is also good information. There is also positive reinforcement. There are also reasonable people. The world is not all negative. You don't have to remain imprisoned in that mud—you can get out, even if the effort must be made just one step at a time.

Many people give up. The effort of looking for a first step and of taking that first step seems harder than simply accepting the short-term comfort of blaming others for landing you in the vat in the first place. You have to think instead of long-term gains—of how much more comfortable you will be when you get out of that mud.

Taking Responsibility for Yourself

When you decide to use the tools of cognitive therapy to improve the quality of your life, you are essentially deciding that you are responsible for the quality of your life. And that is a major decision indeed.

It means you are saying:

- "I am not going to let my past destroy my future."
- "I am not going to let the hurt inflicted by others crush me."
- "I am not going to allow the barriers that people or circumstances have placed in my path to stop me. I'm going to search for a way over or around those barriers."
- "I may not be able to change others, but one person I'm sure I can influence and change is me."
- And maybe, to quote a famous line from the movie *Network*: "I'm mad as hell and I'm not going to take it anymore."

You can spend a lot of time blaming those feelings that hold you back on a parent who abused or disappointed you, or on unfair criticism, or on a major, undeserved setback of some kind, or on sheer bad luck. And you may be perfectly right that the blows you have been forced to endure are of a life-altering nature. But only you can decide whether those blows will lay you low.

And remember that the word *blame* includes the word *me*. Remember that blaming others—or special circumstances—for your problems will not solve them. They may have *caused* them, but when it comes to a solution, you have to say: "It's up to *me*."

Admittedly, that will strike many people as unfair. Why should "they" get away with what they have done? It may well *be* unfair. But the fact is that they may be dead now. Or they may not care. They might be unaware of the damage they have caused. Or they might be hostile. For a million reasons, they may have no interest in changing your life for the better. So it's up to you. They may have caused the pain in the first place—but what are *you* doing to maintain that pain?

Often, even when we seem to blame ourselves for our problems, we are really blaming others. "Yes, I'm an addict. Yes, I'm depressed. Yes, I'm scared all the time. But what do you expect after what I've been through?" Or: "I'm not really entitled to enjoy life, given my past."

Look at that word *blame* again. *Blame* also includes *lame*. Another interesting coincidence. Because blaming others—no matter how valid your complaint—has a way of hobbling you if blaming others is all you do.

Remember: Your outlook on life is what counts. What you think is what counts. What you do is what counts.

Identify.

Define.

Evaluate.

Act.

"Take charge of your thoughts," Plato said. "You can do what you will with them."

THE TECHNIQUES GRID

The following chart indicates which of the techniques described in Chapters 12 and 13 work best with each of the ten thinking mistakes. In some cases, the technique is helpful with every mistake—and you will see an X in every box. But in other cases, the X marks those mistakes for which the technique is particularly useful.

	THE CHICKEN LITTLE SYNDROME	MIND READING	PERSONALIZING	BELIEVING YOUR PRESS AGENT	BELIEVING YOUR CRITICS	PERFECTIONISM	COMPARISONITIS	WHAT-IF THINKING	THE IMPERATIVE *SHOULD*	YES-BUTISM
1. Determine meaning	x	x	x	x	x	x	x	x	x	x
2. Question evidence	x	x	x	x	x	x	x	x	x	x
3. Assign responsibility						x		x		x
4. De-catastrophize	x				x				x	
5. Alternative thought	x	x	x		x	x			x	
6. Alternative feeling	x	x	x		x	x			x	
7. Alternative action	x	x	x		x	x			x	

	THE CHICKEN LITTLE SYNDROME	MIND READING	PERSONALIZING	BELIEVING YOUR PRESS AGENT	BELIEVING YOUR CRITICS	PERFECTIONISM	COMPARISONITIS	WHAT-IF THINKING	THE IMPERATIVE *SHOULD*	YES-BUTISM
8. Compare advantages and disadvantages		x		x		x				
9. Label mistakes	x	x	x	x	x	x	x	x	x	x
10. Then what?	x		x						x	
11. Superexaggeration								x		x
12. Scale from 1 to 10	x			x			x		x	
13. Turn adversity into advantage							x			
14. Develop replacement images		x								
15. Rehearse positive images		x								
16. Self-instruction			x				x			x
17. Self-distraction	x								x	
18. Play defense attorney			x		x					
19. Schedule time	x	x	x	x	x	x	x	x	x	x
20. Plan mastery/ pleasure experiences	x	x	x	x	x	x	x	x	x	x
21. Problem solve	x		x	x	x			x	x	
22. Break goal into small steps							x	x		
23. Role playing			x	x		x			x	x
24. Try out new behavior	x	x	x	x	x	x	x	x	x	x
25. Relaxation	x							x		

APPENDIX B

DAILY ACTIVITY SCHEDULE

Note: Grade activities M (Mastery)
and P (Pleasure) from 1–10

Day of Week _____

Morning

6:00 A.M.	9:00 A.M.
6:15 A.M.	9:15 A.M.
6:30 A.M.	9:30 A.M.
6:45 A.M.	9:45 A.M.
7:00 A.M.	10:00 A.M.
7:15 A.M.	10:15 A.M.
7:30 A.M.	10:30 A.M.
7:45 A.M.	10:45 A.M.
8:00 A.M.	11:00 A.M.
8:15 A.M.	11:15 A.M.
8:30 A.M.	11:30 A.M.
8:45 A.M.	11:45 A.M.

Afternoon

Noon	3:00 P.M.
12:15 P.M.	3:15 P.M.
12:30 P.M.	3:30 P.M.
12:45 P.M.	3:45 P.M.
1:00 P.M.	4:00 P.M.
1:15 P.M.	4:15 P.M.
1:30 P.M.	4:30 P.M.
1:45 P.M.	4:45 P.M.
2:00 P.M.	5:00 P.M.
2:15 P.M.	5:15 P.M.
2:30 P.M.	5:30 P.M.
2:45 P.M.	5:45 P.M.

Evening

6:00 P.M.	9:00 P.M.
6:15 P.M.	9:15 P.M.
6:30 P.M.	9:30 P.M.
6:45 P.M.	9:45 P.M.
7:00 P.M.	10:00 P.M.
7:15 P.M.	10:15 P.M.
7:30 P.M.	10:30 P.M.
7:45 P.M.	10:45 P.M.
8:00 P.M.	11:00 P.M.
8:15 P.M.	11:15 P.M.
8:30 P.M.	11:30 P.M.
8:45 P.M.	11:45 P.M.

Late Night

Midnight	3:00 A.M.
12:15 A.M.	3:15 A.M.
12:30 A.M.	3:30 A.M.
12:45 A.M.	3:45 A.M.
1:00 A.M.	4:00 A.M.
1:15 A.M.	4:15 A.M.
1:30 A.M.	4:30 A.M.
1:45 A.M.	4:45 A.M.
2:00 A.M.	5:00 A.M.
2:15 A.M.	5:15 A.M.
2:30 A.M.	5:30 A.M.
2:45 A.M.	5:45 A.M.

INDEX